SHADOWPLAY

SHADOWPLAY

BEHIND THE LINES & UNDER FIRE

THE INSIDE STORY OF
EUROPE'S LAST WAR

TIM MARSHALL

Elliott&Thompson

First published in Serbo-Croat in 2002 by Samizdat B92, Belgrade

First published in English in 2002 by BookBaby

This revised and updated edition first published 2019 by
Elliott and Thompson Limited
27 John Street
London WC1N 2BX
www.eandtbooks.com

ISBN: 978-1-78396-445-1

9 8 7 6 5 4 3 2 1

A catalogue record for this book is available from the British Library.

Typesetting by Marie Doherty
Maps by JP Map Graphics Ltd
Printed by CPI Group (UK) Ltd, Croydon, CR0 4YY

Dedicated to Jakša Šćekić,
a Yugoslav who had his country taken away

CONTENTS

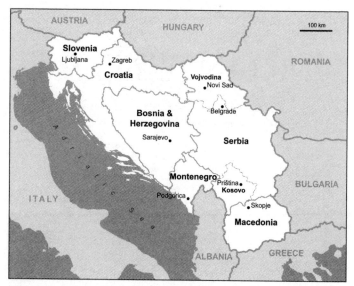

Above: The regions of former Yugoslavia, before it started to break up in 1991.

Below: Serbian population centres in Kosovo and Albanian population in Serbia. Some of these areas may form part of a land swap between Serbia and Kosovo (see pages 287–89).

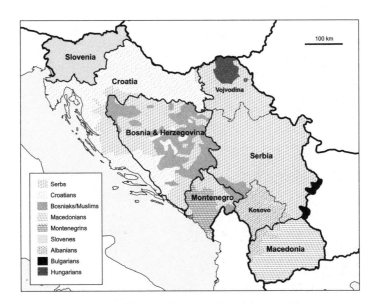

Ethinic make-up of the regions that formed Yugoslavia
in 1990 (above) and 2015 (below).

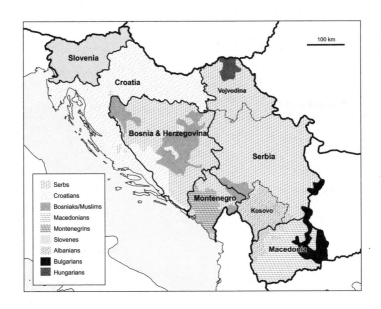

PREFACE

THERE HAVE BEEN OTHER WARS, OTHER STORIES, BUT for this writer none like the shattering of Yugoslavia. The end of something political was, for me, the beginning of something personal. It was the first time I really started to understand the nature of war and conflict. It was also the beginning of a physical journey, as my role as reporter at Sky News took me initially through the former Republic of Yugoslavia – from Bosnia to Croatia, Serbia, Kosovo, Macedonia – and then subsequently on to Afghanistan, Iraq, Sudan, Libya, Syria and other places struggling to hold together.

The shattering of Yugoslavia shattered my naive belief that war in Europe was over. During my later journeys, the events and realities I confronted led me to develop a hard realist view of the world. That was tempered only by the finding that wherever there was pain there was also comfort: on all the roads from Bosnia, even in the most difficult of circumstances, I saw the kindness of strangers to those in need.

But still . . . Bosnia was the first conflict to show me that it does not take much for those of ill intent to pour poison into people's ears and watch them divide from 'the other'. In Serbia and Kosovo, I learned that ethnic and religious identity will often trump political ideas; that emotion can beat logic. Just as a

Serb who would not have contemplated living in Kosovo would still fight to the death to keep the province as his or her own, so an Irish or Italian American, for example, might automatically side with a cause they know little about. In Macedonia, I saw that a quick, sharp and well thought-out foreign intervention can work to pull two sides back from the abyss.

Later, Iraq provided a different instruction: that a long, poorly planned intervention could open the way to that abyss. And yet through all of those subsequent conflicts, my mind would always return to Yugoslavia – the place where I learnt that the phrase 'mindless violence' was rarely correct. There was so often a cold, evil logic behind some of the worst behaviour.

Yugoslavia was also a place I learnt to love for its natural beauty, its music, the tough, often deadpan humour of its people, and their astonishing levels of education and knowledge of the outside world. As the man to whom this book is dedicated said: 'Ah, Yugoslavia – it was a good idea.'

I first wrote this account of the Kosovo War in its immediate aftermath, and it was originally published in translation in Serbo-Croat in 2002. Twenty years on from that conflict, I realized that the story was not yet finished. So here it is, in English, with new opening and closing chapters and new maps. The original text is almost untouched – just tidied up in parts where it was apparent it had been written under the influence of exhaustion, alcohol and a rebalancing of reality after returning home from almost two months in Afghanistan.

The political story remains more important than the personal, though this book is a mix of the two. I hope that, through the less important one, the other is well told.

INTRODUCTION

'Life can only be understood backwards;
but it must be lived forwards.'

Søren Kierkegaard

THAT WAS THEN. THIS IS NOW.

Then, we had bombs and bullets, followed by despair and demonstrations and, finally, revolution. From the burnt ashes of the parliament building in Belgrade, a modern state was supposed to rise and take its place among the community of European nations. The past would stay in the past, not become a barrier to a bright future. Now, two decades on, this remains a work in progress. The past is in danger of once again becoming the present.

Back in 1991, it became clear that Yugoslavia was breaking up as the country accelerated towards disaster. After losing Slovenia, Serbia's President Slobodan Milošević unleashed the might of the Serb-dominated military onto first Croatia and then Bosnia and Herzegovina to prevent them from following suit.

As the situation escalated, the Europeans told the Americans, 'It's OK – we've got this.' Luxembourg's Prime Minister Jacques

Poos said, 'This is the hour of Europe'; Italian Foreign Minister Gianni De Michelis claimed there was a European political 'rapid reaction force'; the EU Commission president Jacques Delors said, 'We do not interfere in American affairs. We hope that they will have enough respect not to interfere in ours.' The US seemed happy to sit this one out, as Secretary of State James Baker responded, 'We do not have a dog in this fight.'

After four years of complete failure by the EU to halt the mass bloodshed, the Americans found their dog and stepped in. They bombed the Serbs in Bosnia, forced Milošević to the table and constructed the 1995 Dayton Agreement which bandaged the open wounds the wars had caused. But the US and the EU then took their eyes off the Balkans ball again as the Serbian province of Kosovo slid towards conflict, which finally erupted in 1998.

Milošević, clinging desperately to what remained of Yugoslavia, was never going to allow the Serbian province of Kosovo to leave. It may have been overwhelmingly dominated by ethnic Albanians, but it was also the cradle of Serb civilization. Clashes between the Kosovo Liberation Army (KLA) and the police intensified, with civilians on both sides being killed. Milošević again sent in the military, and the following year NATO came in on the Kosovars' side. For three months Serbian targets were bombed from the air across the length and breadth of the country. By the time Belgrade's military was forced out of the province, more than a million Kosovar Albanians had been displaced and up to 14,000 killed. Hundreds of Serb civilians were killed in the NATO airstrikes and up to 200,000 were displaced.

Today, the Balkans continues to simmer. Serbia and Kosovo in particular remain hostile to one another and war between them is not unthinkable. In 2018 when Kosovo announced plans for an army, Belgrade responded with the threat of war. In the same year Serbia blocked Kosovo's entry to Interpol. In response Kosovo imposed a 100 per cent tax on imports of Serbian goods and accused Belgrade of 'numerous acts of provocation'. One example was when a train decorated with the Serbian flag and signs reading 'Kosovo is Serbia' attempted to enter Kosovo; it was turned back at the border.

In this atmosphere both sides are considering a land swap to resolve some of the tensions between them, but this massively emotional and complex situation will require huge compromises. It is of course possible this would lead to a real peace, but there is also a danger that it would spark a wider war, opening up the wounds of the past.

Twenty years on, territorial disputes are also rife throughout the region, so, what if trying to solve the Kosovo problem via land swaps creates others elsewhere? The Serbs in Bosnia might step up efforts to join their territory, Republika Srpska, into Serbia proper, a move which would be supported by those in Belgrade who still believe in a 'Greater Serbia'. The Albanians of Macedonia, kindred spirits of the Kosovars, might reignite their 2001 military effort to create a separate state. In turn, both Kosovans and Macedonian Albanians might wish to merge into a 'Greater Albania'. It follows that if the above scenarios came to pass, then what was left of Macedonia would fall prey to division as Serbia, Greece and Bulgaria scrambled to protect their interests. These are indeed 'ifs' and 'mights', but given the history of the region over the past 120 years, they are more than plausible.

And there are other tensions in the area that could escalate the problem. Progress towards EU membership for Bosnia,

Serbia and Kosovo has stalled. Organized crime plagues all three areas. Bosnia and Kosovo have small networks of extremist Islamists that have grown as jihadists have returned from the Middle East, and there are many extreme nationalists in Macedonia, Kosovo, Republika Srpska and Serbia who would seek to pour fuel onto any small fire which broke out in hope of a bigger conflagration. In the 1990s it took years before the EU and NATO intervened to quench the flames, and that was when international armed forces had a much stronger presence. But as the Balkan conflict zones became relatively stable, foreign powers drew down their military power. At one point, there were 80,000 troops involved in Bosnia, now the EU Force has just 7,000. In the current climate, with so few troops in place, and after the disasters of intervention in Iraq and Libya, the USA and the EU might hesitate even longer to escalate.

On the positive side, relations between Croatia and Serbia are cordial, cross-border trade is increasing and, even if the populations still cannot be described as friendly towards one another, Serbs once again sun themselves on the beaches along the Dalmatian coast. There is also a free trade agreement (CEFTA) signed as long ago as 2006 which has helped bind the wider region together incorporating as it does Croatia, Macedonia, Montenegro, Serbia and others. This has boosted economies and doubled exports to the EU. Two of the former Yugoslav republics, Croatia and Slovenia, are now integrated members of the EU, and Serbia became a candidate country in 2012, although without resolution of the Kosovo question that is what it will remain.

As for becoming a modern liberal state in the cultural sense, Serbia still has some way to go. According to Human Rights Watch, attacks on minority groups such as Roma, Hungarians and ethnic Albanians are commonplace and there seems to be a reluctance at both state and societal level to deal with discrimination. Same-sex marriage was legally prohibited in 2006 when Article 62 of a rewritten constitution explicitly defined marriage as being between a man and a woman. Gay Pride marches have repeatedly been attacked by ultra-nationalists to the extent that cars and buildings have been set on fire, and thousands of riot police are required to protect participants in what is a routine event in many European countries. A gay woman, Ana Brnabić, was appointed as prime minister in 2017. However, critics argue that this was simply an empty gesture by the nationalist government to show other EU countries that it was falling in line with their values, rather than a sign of actual progress.

Serbia is indeed a multi-party parliamentary democracy with competitive elections and a vibrant intellectual and cultural society. But it remains deeply socially conservative and in recent years the government has been eroding political rights, as well as trying to restrict media and legal freedoms.

This partially explains why anti-government demonstrations broke out in late 2018 and continued into 2019. Other European countries took little notice of this, or the increasing cross-border tensions, preoccupied as they were with Brexit, the Gilets Jaunes and Catalonia, among other things, but down in the Balkans things were once again stirring.

The demonstrations in Belgrade were visibly similar to those against Milošević in another time. Tens of thousands of people, marching, blowing whistles, week after week, month after month, often in the freezing cold, hoping for a change for the better, but fearing the worst.

Twenty years ago, the slogan on the streets was '*Gotov je!*' ('It's over!'). Echoes of those heady days and nights are now heard in the chant of this new generation of Serbs: '*Pocelo je!*' ('It has begun!'). In March 2019 demonstrators broke into the state-run Radio Television of Serbia building, demanding to address the population live. The last time this happened was in 2000 during the final assault on the Milošević regime.

This is now – what follows was then . . .

PART ONE

BEFORE

CHAPTER 1

*'I know of no safe depository of the ultimate
powers of the society but the people themselves,
and if we think them not enlightened enough
to exercise that control with a wholesome
discretion, the remedy is not to take it from
them, but to inform their discretion.'*

Thomas Jefferson

'YOU CAN'T COME ALONG,' I SAID.

'I'm coming,' was the reply.

'You can't come,' I repeated.

'I have to come,' said Jakša, glaring at me across the table
on the terrace of the Grand Hotel in Priština. It was an autumn
evening in 1998, the weather was warm, the beer was cold
and the conversation was almost as heated as the war between
Serbia and the KLA which had exploded that summer. Both
sides were committing atrocities, both sides were sure of the
justness of their cause, both peoples would eventually lose, but
not before a lot of them had their lives, and some their bodies,
torn apart.

'You're not coming,' I repeated. Sky News producer Jakša
Šćekić was insisting that if I was going to go out and play, then
so was he.

'I have to come.'

We had arranged to go on night patrol with the Serb police out in the badlands where the KLA lived. It hadn't been done by the foreign media and was a chance to really show what it was like out there once the lights went out and things got scary. I didn't want Jakša along, as we all knew it might be a little sticky. I had to go to do the report, cameraman Fedja had to come for obvious reasons, but what was Jakša going to do if we came under fire? Brief me on the Battle of Kosovo Polje in 1389? Take notes?

We had been working together for five years, Jakša and I, and had become good friends. I admired his knowledge, wisdom and honour. He admired my naivety, foolishness and lack of ability to pronounce even simple words in what he called 'Serbo-Whatnot'.

Saying 'Serbo-Croat' had become politically unacceptable about seven years previously when the Croatian War of Independence broke out and Yugoslavs really began to divorce. Some partners argue over children and houses. The Yugoslavs argued over lives, and paid with them. They killed children and burned houses for good measure. All sides committed war crimes by any definition. Tragically, for so many of the people left behind, the most important question remains 'who killed the most?' Then they begin to argue about it and so the circle continues. You can have the same conversation in Bosnia, Croatia, Serbia and Kosovo, and hardly anyone will ask what is really important, the question the Germans asked themselves after the Holocaust: 'How can we stop this from happening again?'

On that balmy late-October afternoon I had a more mundane question and I kept on asking it.

'Why do you have to come?' I demanded.

'You're not allowed to ask stupid questions until it's dark,' replied Jakša. It was a rule we'd agreed on years before when I'd first launched into a torrent of questions about Chetniks, Ustaše and Bosniaks before we'd even finished our breakfast coffee. I thought I knew my history, but actually coming to a region where everyone seemed to have a grievance and an 'itch' at the end of their name was confusing. Milošević. Panić, Ilić?

'Jakša!' I shouted. 'Why do you have to come?'

He looked at me for a few seconds and then with a completely straight face replied, 'Because I have to record your final words.'

At dusk we loaded up the white armoured Land Rover with the TV kit, cigarettes and beer for the police unit, and our flak jackets. None of us usually wore them as they slowed us down, but we always carried them in the vehicle. I was in the back, Fedja and Jakša sat up front.

Mid evening found us under a beautiful starlit sky, on a deserted country road, and in a panic. We'd taken a wrong turn and by doing so reminded ourselves of why most people hadn't bothered to do the night story. It was too easy to stray into KLA territory. Fedja and Jakša were muttering to each other in Serbo-Whatnot. The only thing I understood was UCK, Serb for KLA. With two Serb journalists murdered by the KLA and four kidnapped, Fedja and Jakša were now where they didn't want to be, behind KLA lines. Fedja stopped the engine and killed the lights. The windows on armoured cars don't come down so he opened the door and we listened for a few minutes. At night you can hear for miles across the plain, which leads from Priština to the Prokletije – or 'Damned Mountains' – that divide the Serbian province from Albania. A dog's bark carries across the villages and hamlets. Gunfire can make you jump at more than a mile away.

There was silence, but we knew that within a couple of miles were several KLA units and their Serb counterparts. Both would have heard our engine and neither would have known who we were. I began by thinking, 'Well, I've read about Western journalists being with their local counterparts when the locals get shot, but it wouldn't happen to Jakša and Fedja because they're friends of mine.' Then, a second later thinking, 'Idiot. To the KLA, many of whom have seen their families killed by Serbs, it is entirely irrelevant that the two Serbs they've just got their hands on are friends with some British bloke they've never heard of.' Five minutes after my friends understood the situation I also realized that driving around with Serbs, in the dark, behind enemy lines, with gangs of raging madmen with guns all over the place might not actually be such a good idea. I suddenly agreed with Jakša's opinion of me. Maybe I was just another *glupi international novinar* ('stupid foreign journalist') who he had to explain everything to. There was a private opinion among the domestic Belgrade media corps that too many of the foreign journalists thought the most important thing about the story was that they were covering it. The TV journalists were the worst – on one famous occasion a well-known British reporter shouldered an army medic out of the way so that she could be filmed 'caring' for a wounded civilian.

Along with the rest of Europe I had watched on TV in utter horror at what was happening in our continent. To my generation it just didn't seem possible. War was what happened far away, in places with different cultures. War did not happen in our continent because we'd left all that behind. War certainly didn't happen in Dubrovnik. Surely that wasn't allowed in places where we had been on holiday? But by 1991, people in Germany, France, Italy, Sweden and the UK were watching the evening news and saying, 'Oh look, that wall that's just been blown up in the harbour is near the hotel we stayed in.' Nor did wars break out in cities where you could stage the Winter Olympics, such as Sarajevo. Then it happened. As different regions began declaring independence, the Yugoslav government tried to prevent the break-up of the country; the tanks rolled into Slovenia, Croatia went up in flames, followed by Bosnia. The images from the siege of Vukovar in Croatia looked like a Second World War battle on the Eastern Front.

You either ignored it, became confused or did a crash course in South East European history. Finally the pictures, which for us were only familiar from Pathé Newsreel, reached their mad but logical conclusion with the expulsion of an entire people based on their ethnicity. The echoes of the Holocaust came through the screens – they were faint, but this was the closest Europe had come in the half-century since the Second World War.

'Let's go,' said Fedja. Without turning the lights back on he did a nine-point turn in the dark, crashing the gears, revving the engine and at one point even managing to briefly hoot the horn. He made so much noise the KLA must have wondered why the Serbs were taking their driving lessons so late at night. It wasn't Fedja's fault; he actually knew how to drive these things. The armoured cars the media drive tend not to have power steering. Instead, whoever kits them out with steel plates also appears to fit some sort of sticking device which prevents the wheel being turned in any direction more than about one inch at a time.

This is a shame because it's not what you want in the situation we were in. What you want is a tank.

As none of the major media companies had yet hit upon the idea of buying a fleet of T-92s as company cars, we were stuck with the armoured variety. Fedja beat the gear stick to within an inch of its life and we trundled back along the road in the darkness and turned off into a lane. If it had been mined we would have been in trouble, as we wouldn't even see the ones which were sometimes left on top of the tarmac ahead of a roadblock.

After another turn, we were back on what passed for a decent road. We crawled along at about 5 miles per hour for a few minutes, then pulled into what I could just make out was a petrol station. Fedja turned the engine off and lit each of us a cigarette. We sat and smoked in silence for a minute.

'What's going on?' I said. It was after dark so I was allowed to ask stupid questions.

'Just wait,' said Jakša. We sat for a couple more minutes in total silence. Then I noticed moving out of the shadows a tall man dressed in black from head to foot. He carried a Kalashnikov and had the air of an experienced front-line soldier. Jakša and Fedja obviously knew he was there, and I quickly assumed he was a Serb, which on this occasion was a good thing, as I didn't fancy the alternative. Without saying anything, he simply pointed at us, and then at the ground. We slid out and followed the man back into the shadows by what was left of the walls of the petrol station. I noticed they were shot and shelled to pieces, there was no glass in the windows and there were bullet casings on the floor. 'Incoming and outgoing,' I thought. No wonder the soldier's colleagues were all smoking.

I joined them in a Marlboro Light and affected an air of nonchalance as if I spent most of my evenings like this. They were not just a very tough bunch of guys, they were also not stupid. One took the cigarette out of my mouth, cupped it in his hand and said, 'Hold it like this so the glow doesn't show, that way they'll take longer to zero in on you.' I remembered the only First World War story my grandfather ever told me despite his having spent four years on the Western Front: 'They used to notice the first cigarette being lit, they took aim with the second and they killed the man getting the third light.'

Snipers. Everyone was talking in whispers so I whispered to Jakša, 'How far away are they?'

'About 400 yards,' he replied.

'Mmm,' I thought, 'that's quite a long way away in the dark.'

As if he was reading my mind Jakša then added, 'And they've got night sights.'

The officer in charge explained that a large unit of about thirty KLA men was in a copse, 400 yards away, up a slight incline. The previous night his unit had been involved in a fire-fight in which three of his men had been killed. Therefore, he said politely, it was too dangerous for us to stay. Jakša argued with him for about three seconds before the guy's patience ran out and he ordered us *glupi novinar* to get back into our *glupi novinar glupi vehicle* and 'fuck off' as we had already attracted enough attention.

They were a 'special police unit', not necessarily the type of Serb MUP (Ministry of Internal Affairs) Specials which had carried out so many of the murders that year but 'special' in that they were soldiers. They were a Yugoslav army unit in a forward position which was supposed to be guarded by the police. It was the only way the Yugoslavs could compete militarily with the

KLA under the terms of the ceasefire just negotiated by Richard Holbrooke, and naturally they took it.

Holbrooke was a US special envoy, and the man who three years earlier had put the 'Dayton' deal together which brought a form of peace to Bosnia. His forceful character had led the American press corps to dub him 'The Big Swinging Dick'. With the number of atrocities growing in Kosovo the United Nations had passed Resolution 1203, demanding that Serbia comply with previous resolutions and cooperate with NATO and OSCE (the Organization of Security and Co-operation in Europe) ceasefire-monitoring officials. The resolution was passed under Chapter Seven of the UN charter, meaning it could potentially be enforced with military action.

NATO was now threatening to bomb, unless the Yugoslav Third Army based in Kosovo remained in barracks and the MUP Specials left the province. With things on a knife-edge, Belgrade had already begun to comply and was scaling back.

The ordinary police units would not be able to carry heavy weapons such as machine guns or mortars. The trouble was that the KLA weren't part of the agreement, although they had agreed a ceasefire. The ceasefire was a fiction. It didn't matter how much the diplomats said it was holding; everyone, including them, knew there were shooting, bombing and mortar incidents every night and, occasionally, during the day. It was difficult to tell who had done what, or fired first, amid the welter of propaganda from both sides. Whoever was to blame, each side tried to ensure it had the best weaponry it could get away with.

The outside world had an idea of what was going on. The Americans were using their spy satellites to monitor movement on the ground, while the British did more of the human intelligence. An MI6 officer was living in Priština at the time, backed up by a Foreign Office diplomat. The diplomat wasn't a spy, but we all knew that his reports ended up on more than just one desk in London. Up in Belgrade another team was used to gather the political information. According to an MI6 source, 'we had one man in the embassy who never left it. His job was to sit in a room with a pair of headphones and listen to Belgrade. Mostly it was hard-wired telephone lines, that had been going on since before mobiles came in, so the monitoring of mobiles was left to GCHQ in England and Fort Mead in the States.'

An MI6 communications specialist told me later that GCHQ listened to just about everyone, including people on their own side: 'They used to get exasperated with Robin Cook [British Foreign Secretary at the time]. They sometimes listened in to his mobile conversations and he didn't appear to understand that he was saying things he really shouldn't. Mobile phones? They're like microphones so if you don't want it broadcasting don't say it.'

Naturally Serb intelligence was also playing the game. They had taken an apartment opposite the British embassy. It was useful to photograph whoever went in, and for attempting to listen to the conversations inside. The really sensitive conversations were held in a secure room, swept for bugs and protected from the type of equipment that can hear through walls. Even so, for the Serbs it was worth picking up snippets of the sort of talk that goes on in embassies even outside of what they called 'The Deaf Room'.

The British ambassador between 1994 and 1997, Sir Ivor Roberts, was aware the Serbs were listening: 'Sometimes you can play that to your advantage by getting your message across, and sometimes you can use it for misinformation.'

After Dayton the British had gone down to just two intelligence officers in Belgrade and at times just to the 'Head of Station'. The crisis in Kosovo had led to an urgent review, and a planning team had been put together which liaised with the Foreign Office and army intelligence. Members of both teams would end up in Kosovo a few weeks later disguised as civilian monitors to ensure that the sort of unit we found at the petrol station could no longer operate, but they would also have many other tasks.

We left the 'specials' at the station and found the main road back towards Priština. We could see the lights of the town a few miles away as we pulled up to what was supposed to be the furthest checkpoint the Serbs were allowed to operate outside of the capital. Of course they had units further forward but this was the last official one, and we had permission to film there.

If we had reported the make-up of the unit on the hill it would have led to the Serbs arresting Jakša and expelling me on the grounds of giving away military secrets. Six years of covering conflicts in various parts of the world had taught me which lines to step near but not across. Eventually Serbian newspapers would describe me as a '*Balkanski Ekspert*', but that was some way off, and even then it wasn't true. I was also called an MI6 agent and 'more than just a friend' of paramilitary leader Arkan. That wasn't true either, but the inevitable connections between intelligence officers, journalists and politicians meant you were often operating in a hall of mirrors. Journalists invariably bump into spies because they work in the same areas. The spies pretend to be diplomats, business people or a range of other things. Sometimes each party knows that the other knows all about them, but it's only polite not to mention it. Meanwhile, the politicians are having similar conversations. A combination of 'spooks', 'journos' and 'politicos', added to 'the people', would eventually lead to the overthrow of the president of Yugoslavia, Slobodan Milošević. At this stage he still had a way out. The coming months would box him in, but in the end he virtually gift-wrapped and posted himself first class to a small prison cell at The Hague. MI6 and the CIA helped, but so did Milošević and his own people. It took some time to work out how, but with 'Slobo' gone, the secrets began to emerge.

The checkpoint was situated at a crossroads. There were two bunkers made from sandbags and a couple of shot-up buildings, with fields on all sides and a solitary street lamp. They were ordinary cops, in fact very ordinary. Not at all like the army men facing the KLA on the hill, who were front-line soldiers with experience in Croatia and Bosnia. I was now with men who knew just a little bit more about warfare than I did, which is to say not very much. This thought made me feel a little exposed. There were just six of them. Two were patrolling the area, or rather patrolling about fifty yards in any direction because after that it was too dangerous. This was not why these young men and the others all over Kosovo had joined the police force. Until a few months ago they'd been quite happy back in their Serbian home towns catching burglars, issuing speeding tickets and taking the occasional bribe.

Now they were over here, underpaid and overstretched. Every night some 'crazy *Shiptar*' [derogatory term for Albanian] was shooting at them and they were shooting back. They were not about to go looking for trouble. I got the impression that they were rather hoping trouble would pass them by. They were nervous about cars, because in the past KLA men in civilian clothes had pulled up and thrown hand grenades into the bunkers. They were nervous because they didn't have machine guns, bulletproof vests or night-sights to see in the dark. Ask police officers in Manchester or Milan to take on a guerilla army and they might do it, but only if you give them the necessary weapons. These six didn't even have much experience. Their position was less a checkpoint and more a target. It seemed crazy that they were being left out there to be shot at. They were paying the price for the terrible crimes committed by various units of the Serb state.

I was lying in the middle of the road, staring at the night sky and looking like an idiot. I had put my back out two days earlier when the armoured car went over a pothole. My head had connected with the roof of the Land Rover and a second later the bottom of my spine had connected with the wooden bench I was sitting on. The only way to relieve the discomfort was on my back with my knees up. The twanging nerves were worse than the thought of my hurt pride so I lay down in the middle of the road, with everyone else crouched behind the sandbags. Meanwhile unbeknownst to all of us, a KLA unit was approaching stealthily through the fields.

The police, not knowing who was a few hundred yards away, thought the sight of this '*glupi Engliski novinar*' lying on the road so amusing that they forgot they thought all foreign journalists were lying scumbags who lied for breakfast, lunch and tea – and who were part of the international conspiracy against Serbia. We got on fine, and I was spared the finger-in-the-chest routine.

In the top left-hand side of my chest I have a slight indentation. This has got progressively deeper as the years have gone by. Many outsiders who have worked in the Balkans also bear the mark. It was caused by officials who worked for the Belgrade regime. They, or their supporters, would poke you in the chest while saying 'You (prod) people (prod) don't (prod) understand (prod prod).'

There wasn't much you could say to that, especially as the person saying it usually had some sort of weapon to use against you. It was either a gun, a permit to go somewhere, or a visa stamp. Whenever it happened you had a choice. You could remind the person with the weapon about the atrocities carried out by Serb forces. The response would be greater anger, followed by a list of all the atrocities carried out against Serbs. You would then be in physical danger if they had a gun. You would be in danger of not getting your story if they controlled a checkpoint, and in danger of not even getting into the country if they were in charge of visas.

Or you could simply take the finger and allow it to make the indentation a little deeper. I had a simple rule. If they had a gun, agree with them. If they can let you past so you can do your real job, take the finger in the chest. If it's a senior official in the embassy or the government and it means you'll get a visa then take the finger but tell them, 'I understand what you are saying, but I am not on your side.' It was a good rule and it helped me the following year when, during the NATO bombing, members of the Yugoslav government tried to flatter me into sympathetic coverage of their side of the story.

Taking pity on the foreigner with the bad back, our new friends at the checkpoint allowed us to go with them to patrol the fifty yards in any direction of Kosovo they controlled at that point. Before we'd set off that evening I'd had images of walking through woods and across fields on patrol. These guys were reluctant to leave their bunker.

Fedja and I crept around a wheat field following an unenthusiastic policeman as he rustled through the stalks. The only person who could see anything was Fedja. He had the night vision lens on his camera and so while our world was black, his was green. The night-sight works by picking up any source of light and magnifying it. The stars were out so he could see several hundred yards ahead. The police, on the other hand, were stuck in the middle of nowhere, under-equipped, possibly surrounded by the KLA and even the bloody journalists had better kit than they did.

We returned to the bunker, I lay down on the road again and looked up at the stars. The Balkan night sky in the countryside, in all its majesty, can rival the best. The air is clean, untainted by neon, and is so overwhelming you can quite forget about such stupid things as bunkers and bullets. I breathed in the cool night air and listened to the silence.

Suddenly, something went bang in the night. The sounds of heavy bursts of sustained gunfire made me leap up and into the bunker. Fedja, Jakša and the policemen were all quite relaxed as the firing was coming from up the hill at the petrol station. Fedja was already filming with the night sight which could pick out the contours of the hill and the trees on it, but even with the naked eye we could see what was going on.

From the tree line, the KLA were pouring fire into the disused petrol station, and the soldiers were returning fire at the same rate. The tracers flew across the gap between them. Tracer bullets are often used at the rate of one in every twelve. It looked like constant streams of light in a dotted line flowing between them. What made it even more frighteningly impressive was that in between each dot were another eleven bullets. The tracers were orange because that is one of the easiest colours to see in the colour spectrum. The lines swayed a little as they spat across the gap. When a soldier fires a Kalashnikov set to automatic, or a machine gun, even a fast-beating heart can cause the aim to waver slightly. The heavier thudding sounds were a machine gun, while the Kalashnikov assault rifles made a higher cracking sound.

On the police radio we could hear the officer we'd met asking for assistance. 'We are taking fire and are outnumbered,' he said calmly. His request for an armoured personnel carrier to be sent was denied by some chief, somewhere, on the grounds that it was too dangerous to go up that road until dawn.

After a few minutes the firing subsided. There was the occasional crackle of a short burst, then just a few single shots now and then. The men at the station were a far better fighting unit than their opponents but there was no way at the moment they could take the fight to the KLA.

Fedja had turned back to the fields around us and was looking through the night scope, when he began to hurriedly refocus. He thought he had seen movement. The moment he told the policemen, they asked if they could borrow the night scope to take a look. Strictly speaking we were not supposed to aid combatants in a conflict, but whoever wrote the journalists' ethical code for conflict zones had never been in a bunker at night, with a hostile unit approaching whose members were not about to say, 'There's some journalists up there, so let's call the mission off and attack tomorrow night.' They were going to simply blast away at anything they saw. Of course the absurdity of the situation was that we had gone out looking for trouble, and when it looked like arriving, we wanted it to go away. Well, I did anyway.

The police took the night sight and located the unit. The man looking through the lens muttered something to a colleague; his response was to cross himself and take up a firing position behind the sandbags. There were a few tense minutes as we sat in silence, and the policeman watched the KLA. They were a good 200 yards away and he had difficulty making them out, but he could see that they weren't getting any closer.

Eventually, he told Fedja they were heading in another direction. We sort of relaxed, and about thirty minutes later heard a couple of rifle shots from at least a mile away – something else was on the receiving end.

After another twenty minutes we cracked open a few beers and began to talk. The policemen first demanded to know if I knew Serbian history.

There is no correct answer to this question. If you say yes, you risk being asked a series of questions in which the years 1389, 1878, 1914, 1941 and 1946 will come up. Unless you know the answers you are found to have been firstly lying, and secondly guilty of not knowing the basics of the glorious sweep that is Serbian history.

If, on the other hand, you answer, 'No, I don't know Serbian history', you will firstly be found guilty of not knowing the glorious sweep that is Serbian history, and secondly subjected to a lengthy lecture which will include the dates 1389, 1878, 1914, 1941 and 1946. It will also include several arcane facts that not even Cambridge dons with PhDs in Slavonic Studies know. Serbs are so fascinated by their history that if you ask them 'What time is it?', you risk getting the answer: 'Well, in 1389, it was the time of the great battle against the Turks at Kosovo Polje which resulted in our defeat and subjugation by them for the next five hundred years until finally in 1878 we got our revenge and again became a sovereign nation. A nation able to fight like lions in the First World War against the Germans, a war in which our country suffered greater proportional losses than any other. Alas in 1941 it was the time in which the Germans got their revenge by occupying us. But we fought them again, plucky little Serb nation that we are, even though the Croatians joined the Nazis and killed 700,000 of us in the Jasenovac concentration camp. But they lost in 1945 and so a year later, as the Yugoslavs, it was time to crush the Kosovar Albanian uprising. And now it's ten past three.'

I had learned that the response to the question about knowing history was to mumble something placatory such as 'I know you have suffered many times in the past.' That this failed to address the current situation, in which some Serb units were committing terrible atrocities against civilians, did not make it factually wrong. It usually had the effect of satisfying them enough to talk to me as an equal, as opposed to poking me in the chest. Potentially it meant we could have a conversation in which mention of atrocities by both sides could be discussed.

First though, they talked about the deal about to be signed by President Milošević. Richard Holbrooke had walked into his office in Belgrade accompanied by US air force Lieutenant General Michael Short.

Milošević had stuck his chin out. 'So, you are the one who will bomb us.'

General Short gave him a right hook: 'I have my U-2 spy planes in one hand and B-52 bombers in the other. It's up to you which one I use.'

The police hated the deal. Not so much because it was imposed by the threat of NATO bombing, more because the KLA weren't required to be a party to it and, as we had just seen, there was no ceasefire. Under the terms, 4,000 Special Police (PJP) were on the way back to Serbia proper, taking their weapons with them. This left the ordinary police and the few special units remaining overstretched and outgunned.

Every time they pulled out of a Kosovar village, the KLA moved forward, took it over and began patrolling the roads around it. They quickly controlled large areas of the province. The Serbs were furious as they'd been winning the war, albeit with brutality, and had crushed a KLA offensive.

These young Serbs were trapped. Trapped in their bunker, in their uniforms, in their nationality and in their history. Nothing could convince them that even if the *Shiptars* hated them, and even if the KLA were killing their civilians, it didn't justify what the Serb forces had been doing that summer. If I pointed out that, perhaps, the Serbs had been oppressing the Kosovars since 1989, it was denied. The police would then say 'anyway, before then they had been oppressing us' as if that made driving 200,000 people into camps in the hills an acceptable method of anti-guerilla warfare.

We agreed to disagree. I didn't know if they, personally, had taken part in any of the outrages that had dominated the front pages and TV screens of Europe that summer. Therefore I had no reason to dislike them. They were just young guys who'd rather have been somewhere else. Maybe one of them had taken a fourteen-year-old boy from his mother, bound his hands with barbed wire and shot him in the back of the head as his mother screamed for mercy. Things like that happened. But what do people who do that look like when you take away the dark theatre of uniforms, guns and a scorched-earth operation and they go back to real life? I have met the hardcore, drug-filled, evil, crazy paramilitaries who do some of that stuff, and they are almost reassuringly nasty. Their bandannas, Rambo sunglasses, three-day growths and bandoliers entirely fit the identikit picture. When they got back home they looked pretty much the same, even in trainers, jeans and leather jackets. But we knew that among ordinary units and among the disciplined PJP Specials there were elements who hadn't so much been 'behaving badly' (as one Serb politician squirmingly described it to me) as behaving on an individual basis like a *Sonderkommando* in Hitler's murderous *Einsatzgruppen* in Russia.

These same guys can then have a beer with you, talk football and seem entirely reasonable people. I took the position in Croatia, Bosnia and Serbia that unless I had reason to believe otherwise, the person I was talking to hadn't committed any crime more heinous than double parking. Otherwise you fell into the trap of demonizing all of them.

As midnight approached our conversation somehow got on to the more pressing situation of my back. It was pressing in the sense that, as I later learned, one of my discs was poking through some torn tissue and rubbing against my spinal nerve. Everyone in the world has a bad-back story and the policemen were no different. Like the rest of us, each of them had either had a bad back themselves, or knew hair-raising stories about how their dad had lived for the last fifteen years with severe lower back pain. We exchanged recipes for bad backs. The TV people offered carrying tripods, battery belts and flak jackets as a sure-fire way of getting a hernia. The police guaranteed a bad back from sitting in old Yugo cars for years on end, and then bouncing round terrible roads. Then various cures were offered. These ranged from 'miracle wonder back specialist doctors in Niš whom I should really drop in and see should I ever happen to be in the city', to strange 'healing hands, channelers of energy' in Belgrade.

The Serbs were surprisingly prone to vague beliefs about the paranormal. Forty years of aggressively atheist but softish Communism had failed to eradicate what is true of most cultures, an abiding interest in the unprovable. A glance at any newsagents in Serbia revealed a wide range of magazines devoted to astrology, faith healing and lurid stories of the occult.

During the 1990s the regime's television channel, Radio Television of Serbia (RTS), took advantage of this tendency by devoting hours of programming to Mystic Megović type characters. Their role was to read the future and assure Serbs that it was bright, that the country was going in the right direction. It was obviously a political decision by people who had worked out all the levers of power, and how to use them. One guy, Ljubiša Trgovčević, would come on, and viewers would call in. He would gaze at the studio lights then, turning a ring on his finger, would say, 'Yes, I see now, I see.' This was prime-time TV and was taken seriously. In Britain about eight people took Mystic Meg seriously, the rest knew she only got the five-minute slot on the Lottery Show as a bit of light entertainment before the numbers were drawn. Her Serbian equivalents appeared to be working to a prearranged script designed to persuade the population that everything was rosy in the Serbian garden. This was at a time when wars were raging around the borders, inflation was rampant, unemployment rising, pensions were not being paid and gangsters were becoming celebrities. 'Ah I see now,' said whichever charlatan was on at the time, 'Yes, I see that dark forces are against us, but we will triumph.' Other charlatans would come on to tell Serbs that they were 'The Heavenly People'.

Then another would come on to read the news. This was usually as far from the truth as what had come before. More strange people would be introduced, including the Wicked Witch of the East who would repeat the message that the country's leaders were doing the right thing, and that Serbia would triumph over its enemies. She was called Mira Marković and was President Milošević's wife.

Despite being the leader of the hard-line communist political party Yugoslav Left, Mira Marković looked weirder than all the Mystic Megović characters put together. She had a 1960s bouffant dyed blacker than black from which a variety of foliage would bloom. Her high-pitched voice resembled that of a Balkan Minnie Mouse, and she made the most extraordinary pronouncements about life – both in a weekly magazine column and in her book *Night and Day: A Diary*. A diary entry describing her social calendar is typically underwhelming: 'Today, lunching with friends I asked if they happened to have a cigarette. They had a pack of Winston and a lighter, which I received as a present.'

Another column ended with Mira about to go on holiday: 'I shall have to ask my editor at *Duga* to release me from my obligations to the magazine. If they agree then I would like to take my vacation.'

What she failed to add was that if they didn't agree then they probably wouldn't be editors for much longer.

The police we were with didn't care much for Serbia's First Lady but were more sympathetic to Slobo, despite criticizing him for allowing their hands to be tied behind their backs. I suggested this might be a bad analogy seeing as the threat to bomb Serbia was partially due to the fact that too many Kosovar hands had been tied behind backs with barbed wire that year.

It was a good time to go. We had got on fine but I realized I'd crossed a line with this last remark. I was talking to men who had seen their colleagues shot. They may not have carried out atrocities, but they weren't happy about an outsider criticizing Serb forces. We decided we had enough for our story and exchanged an amicable farewell.

We bid them a safe night, bundled into the armoured car and set off back to Priština and the Grand Hotel.

Ah, the Grand. Brown rooms, brown tap water, lumpy beds, terrible food, suspicious staff and tracksuited gangsters in the lobby. All that for just fifty dollars a night. Still, it was better than what we were leaving behind and much better than the conditions in the makeshift camps in the hills where many Kosovar Albanians had taken refuge.

That was to be our destination the following night.

CHAPTER 2

'When a man is abandoned by
the sun of his homeland,
Who will illuminate the path of his return?'

Ghisari Chelebi Khan (Turkish warrior)

IN THE DARKNESS A TINY HAND REACHED OUT AND clutched mine. The hand, which was warm despite the cold outside the tent, squeezed and held on, as if letting go would plunge its owner back into the maelstrom.

I flicked my lighter. A two-year-old boy smiled at the fire and then at me. Perhaps I was seeing things but he looked right into me. A two-year-old boy looking right into you is a rare thing, especially if he is not your own. My own boy was back home, sleeping peacefully in a warm bed. As far as he knew, the world outside was a nice place, as indeed it mostly was, but this two-year-old had written into his eyes what he had witnessed.

I never knew his name, because I failed to ask. His mother and father were with him, along with about six other children, aged three to ten. They were all living in a makeshift tent, placed on a cold hillside, along with three hundred people from the same village.

A stream ran diagonally down the hill. This was why they had all stopped running. It was far enough away for the Serbs to have stopped chasing them. It was clean, and big enough for their immediate needs.

A month on from their flight, and this two-year-old boy was hanging onto my hand as we smiled at each other. I lit one of the candles I'd brought, and then brushed the boy's hair with my hand a few times. Maybe the gesture was a little overfamiliar, but his smile had so much anxiety in it that there seemed nothing else to do.

The boy's village had been shelled by Serb forces who then entered the perimeter. Everyone picked up the bags they always kept ready and ran. A two-year-old doesn't know much, but it knows when its world has just been turned upside down.

The people in the camp insisted that the KLA had not been in the village. This may or may not have been true. The KLA frequently sheltered in villages. In most they had support, in others they were merely tolerated. Just as the Serbs were not above shelling a village, nor was the KLA above murdering what it saw as Kosovan 'collaborators'. Not allowing the KLA to use the village to shelter in was, to them, proof of collaboration, so they sheltered pretty much anywhere they wanted. Either way it didn't make much difference to the two-year-old in the tent.

Reuters TV cameraman Mark Chisholm and I had travelled up to the camp in the late afternoon. With us was Reuters photographer Yannis Behrakis and print journalist Kurt Schork. Kurt went everywhere, on every story. He was brave, meticulous and passionate. Two years later, in May 2000, he went to Sierra Leone, where on a dirt road, in a jungle, he was shot dead by a militia gang. Associated Press cameraman Miguel Gil Moreno de Mora, who we'd left in Priština, was also killed. They'd been travelling in an army lorry. Mark was with them but survived with just a bullet in his hand, Yannis was also in a vehicle and escaped unhurt. Kurt was braver than many and he broke a rule which is often broken: don't travel with the military in a combat zone.

In 2001 when I was in Afghanistan, four colleagues did just that and did it in the dark. They didn't just accompany a military vehicle; they rode on top of one to a fluid front line, which had just changed hands, again, twelve hours earlier. They paid the same price as Kurt. It's obvious that just setting foot in a country at war is reducing the chances of nothing happening to you that day. Each time you venture further the odds fall again. Travelling with the military at night to a front line is almost as far as you can push it.

Being in the camp at night was pushing it for me, but for Kurt this was almost routine. Few of the media ventured out at night, and certainly not to cross the front line which was why we had set off in the afternoon.

There was no way Jakša or Fedja could have come, as we were going to KLA-controlled territory. Jakša had Kosovar Albanian friends in Priština – it's not a big city and so it only took a couple of phone calls to let the KLA know we were coming. They had men in town, in plain clothes, and as long as it was done discreetly, contact could be made. What you didn't do in this Serb-controlled town was shout it around that you wanted to meet the same people that the Yugoslav army wanted to meet. Most of the media corps knew how to do it, but there was the occasional reporter who came down and failed to realize what country they were in. The subtleties of conflict entirely escaped them – this was often simply because they hadn't done their homework.

Once, in the then ethnic-Serb-controlled enclave of Krajina in Croatia, a journalist from South Korea showed up. He was a perfectly nice man, but he didn't know what country he was in. After getting all the way from Seoul, he presented himself to the UN in Zagreb and got his credentials. With these he negotiated the last Croatian checkpoint before the Serb-controlled area, and then arrived at the Serb version. He was escorted to the Serb militia headquarters whereupon he was welcomed to the '*Republika Srpska Krajina*', given a permit, a lecture, a poke in the chest and a stamp on his passport. In return he thanked his hosts effusively and then wished them good luck in their brave fight against the nasty aggressor Serbs who were trying to destroy Croatia.

He was expelled from the self-styled 'Republika' a minute later. Three minutes after that he was in a car, which drove straight back to Zagreb.

Jakša and the others knew what country they were in. There was no way they were coming up that hill. At the worst the KLA would have shot them, or if they were in a good mood they would simply have taken them hostage. At best, if they liked me, Jakša and the others would be tolerated. But even if that happened, what we saw would be restricted. The KLA would have just one opinion about my two friends: that they were Serbian spies.

So this was a strictly non-Serbian affair. We made it through a Serb checkpoint where, being policemen, the guards wished us to know that they could 'no longer guarantee' our safety if we went any further. This was a face-saving way of explaining that there were areas of Serbia where the Serbian police couldn't go.

The sun was still shining as we rolled off the tarmac and on to a rutted track. No-man's-land was just under 2 miles in depth. For the first half-mile or so there were no people, no animals and no undamaged houses. Then we saw a civilian, an old man bending over some crop in a field. He straightened up and stared as we drove past. He probably only saw a couple of cars a day. Gradually there were more people and fewer damaged houses about, and so we approached the KLA checkpoint.

They were as much fun as the last lot. They hadn't been told we were coming and they didn't care when we told them that certain people in Priština were supposed to have called them. Nor, when for a joke I showed them my British passport, did one particular KLA man find it at all amusing. Not even when I pointed out that it clearly stated inside the front cover that Her Majesty the Queen herself required that 'the bearer', which as I reminded him was me, be allowed 'to pass freely without let or hindrance, and to afford the bearer' (that's me again, I told him) 'such assistance and protection as may be necessary'. Maybe our Kosovar translator didn't quite explain it properly, but instead of smiling the KLA man simply shouldered his Kalashnikov and stared at me without saying anything.

I was just passing time. The moment we heard they weren't expecting us, we knew we were in for a long wait. During the hour we sat there before being allowed through, there must have been several mobile phone calls made. The checkpoint guards would be chasing down whomever had given permission because they'd been told not to allow journalists through at night.

Once we were on our way, it was relatively simple. We drove up a steep dirt track full of potholes and stones. Each side of the track was heavily wooded. After about five minutes and with the sun beginning to go down, we passed into the clearing where the villagers had pitched their tents.

The sun goes down fast in the Kosovan hills, especially as winter approaches. People were already lighting fires, cooking food and preparing their children for bed. A month earlier they'd had houses with satellite TV and possibly even phones with which to call their relatives working over in Germany, Italy or the UK.

This was a small camp. Our 'guide' explained that further up were more people and in total there were about 1,200 people on the hill. It was quite believable. At the time the UN Refugee Agency estimated there were 200,000 people living outdoors. The smoke from the fires drifted through the dusk. With the sounds of children laughing and the stream running down the centre it was almost a pleasant sight, until you thought for more than a second about what it really meant.

There were at least three armed KLA men in the camp. One claimed that the Serbs occasionally fired into the tented area at night. He suggested I should not report their presence as it might cause the Serbs to attack the refugees.

This was military information, and just as I hadn't reported on the make-up of the Yugoslav army at the petrol station, nor would I report on their location, even if, technically, they weren't supposed to be there. They would have argued that they were there to protect the civilians. It was an example of how clear-cut guidelines on conduct in war, written in the calm stately halls of the UN in Geneva, can blur during the real thing. And this was the real thing.

Many Serbs still hold to a conspiracy theory that the KLA had ordered the people up into the hills, and kept them there because they'd cottoned on to the power of the Western media. The more coverage of the Kosovars' 'alleged plight', argued the Serbs, the more the West would be fooled into intervening.

The KLA did do their best to bring in the outside world, but to believe that particular conspiracy theory is to believe that thousands of Kosovar mothers and fathers had willingly taken their own children out of their homes, put a few basic necessities in a bag and taken to living on a cold hillside with winter approaching. It didn't add up. On a few occasions I put that reply to a Serb and each time received the following response: 'Ah, but you don't know the Kosovars, they are not like us, they would do it.' The person really believed that Kosovar mothers didn't care for their children the way Serb mothers did. At that point you may as well have ended the conversation. It wasn't always their fault – most Serbs at that time had never been to Kosovo and weren't likely to any time soon. The only thing they knew about Kosovars was what the state-controlled TV station RTS told them. It said the KLA smuggled drugs, ran prostitution rackets and murdered civilians. The organization did do that, but that didn't mean ordinary Kosovar mothers loved their children any less than any mother, anywhere.

The villagers had organized a school at the camp. The premises were a relatively flat piece of ground. No floor, no walls and no roof. The equipment was a teacher. Still, given their circumstances, it was a heroic effort at staying in touch with the real world, while living in a nightmare.

Once night had completely fallen, the fires were extinguished, the lanterns turned out, silence and darkness fell upon the place. Silence, broken only by the noise made by two blundering idiots from a foreign television crew.

Mark and I tottered about, bumping into each other and tripping over rocks. Laurel and Hardy would have been proud.

'Tim!' hissed Mark. 'Where's the spare battery?'

'I thought you had it.'

'No, you had it in the last tent we were in.'

This meant that, having already barged into someone's tent and their nightmare, I was now going to go back and ask our translator to translate that I was terribly sorry 'but I appear to have left the spare battery for the TV camera in here, so would you mind if I rummaged around in the dark for a few minutes and wake up your sleeping children while I find it?'

A few minutes later both the spare battery and myself were back with Mark. I couldn't see his face, but I suspect the sunny smile that was usually spread over his open South African face might not have been there. I had a lot of time for Mark. Like most of the best camera operators he mixed a healthy respect for the idiot journalists with a healthy disrespect for them. 'Reporters? Wouldn't feed the bastards' is almost a mantra in the camera departments of the major news broadcasters. Behind the scenes the 'star' reporters seen in far-flung places are being mercilessly teased about their obsession with hair, double chins and 'face time'. Face time is the ten seconds during which you talk to camera.

Almost losing an expensive camera battery pitched me into the 'idiot journalist' category for a while. It wasn't the expense, it was that without the battery you couldn't do more filming, and filming in these camps after dark hadn't been done before. We had the night scope with us again, and its ghostly green images befitted the feel of this strange place. A few quiet conversations could be heard drifting from tents, usually from adults. Most pitiful were the coughing sounds from small children. They were beginning to fall ill and each night it got colder. This was high ground; the snow would fall within a month.

Almost everyone had bedded down for the night. There was little else to do. The rhythms of their lives had been altered in so many ways. Everything that was normal was in their houses, in the valley below us, but they weren't about to return without assurances of safety.

And so it was that we ended up in the tent with the young boy with the strong grip and the sad smile. While he snuggled down under a quilt with his brothers and sisters, and we groped our way back to the Land Rover, lights were burning in offices far away across Europe and the Atlantic. The Americans and British had decided 'Something must be done' and they were about to do it.

John Raven (name changed to protect identity) was working late at his office at the Ministry of Defence in London. He was thinking. That was work to him, because he was paid to think. Some people in his department, Military Intelligence, were paid to find out what the problems were. He did a bit of that as well, but he earned his money, and respect, by thinking of solutions to those problems. 'The Problem' was Slobodan Milošević and it was a fairly new problem.

During the Croatian War of Independence and the Bosnian War, Milošević had been regarded as 'The Solution'. In 1995 the Western powers were inching towards a peace deal and the then president of Serbia was a man with whom they had to do business – able as he was to stand up for the interests of both Croatian and Bosnian Serbs. No 'Slobo', no peace deal – but first he had to be persuaded to play ball.

In August 1995 the Croatian army and militias launched a lightning offensive – Operation Storm – against the ethnic Serb enclave in Krajina. They were partially trained, armed and financed by the United States. In a murderous campaign they swept all before them, burning, shooting and looting as they went. (One of the men involved in 'Storm' was Agim Çeku, whose name would surface again in 1998 when he became the KLA's chief of staff and eventually prime minister of Kosovo in 2006.) Two hundred thousand ethnic Serbs were 'cleansed' from the region their families had lived in for 400 years. They fled Croatia and made their way across Bosnia and into Serbia.

Slobo never lifted a finger to help them, the 'International Community' hardly said a word in complaint, and the international media hardly lifted a pen to report it.

The week after 'Storm', I met a US special forces colonel in Dubrovnik. He had been involved in the operation and was working to support a push that the Bosnian army was about to make against the Bosnian Serbs. He told me that the Americans were conducting clandestine arms drops to the Bosnians in Tuzla, using NATO equipment but without telling NATO about it. In the end it was Operation Storm, and the subsequent advance in Bosnia, that persuaded Milošević to agree peace terms at the Dayton Conference.

Milošević loved being the centre of attention at these affairs; he regarded himself as an equal even if no one else around the table had any illusions about the character of his regime. As an MI6 agent put it: 'We knew we were dealing with gangsters, but we were pragmatists on both sides of the river.' ('The river' is a reference to the Thames which separates the MI6 headquarters in Vauxhall and the Foreign Office in Whitehall.)

'The British operation in the Balkans,' he continued, 'was always more joined up than the Americans', there were no dust-ups between Main Building and Vauxhall.'

So for years no one came to John Raven for a solution about Milošević, because although he was considered an unsavoury character, he was more of an irritant than a problem. After he had been forced to the table at Dayton in 1995 the attention of the great powers turned elsewhere. Even when his regime was rocked by three-month-long anti-Milošević street demonstrations in Belgrade in 1996, the British and Americans did little to support the Serbian opposition. This was partially the opposition's own fault. A more depressing set of bickering, preening, theatrical egomaniacs would be hard to put together.

Sonja Licht, then working at the George Soros-funded Open Society organization in Belgrade, summed them up: 'They were weak. Dissident politics was the politics of amateurs and they were fighting the experts. Some of them are my friends, but I tell you, they didn't know how to handle politics, they were too vain.'

So, when the call went out to the Foreign Office for real help, the response was: 'Come back to us when you grow up.' There was help with broadcast equipment and computers, but it was low-level stuff.

As a result Milošević became convinced the West wouldn't really move against him when he sought to smash the separatist KLA. The population might have trouble getting visas to leave the country, there were sanctions, times were hard, but he was OK. In fact he felt emboldened when US Special Envoy Robert Gelbard called the KLA a 'terrorist group' in February 1998. This was understood by Belgrade to translate as 'This is your affair'.

A major Belgrade industrialist and friend of Milošević later told me the following story: 'In 1997 I had lunch with Sir Ivor Roberts, the British ambassador. My job was to discuss what was an important financial deal for us concerning a bank. But Ivor only wanted to talk about BOOM 93, this little opposition radio station in Požarevac, which we didn't really care about, but had closed down. I said, "Your Excellency, we can talk about the radio but can we deal with the financial matters first?" He wanted to talk about the radio, so we gave in to him, agreed it could go back on air. In return he didn't put up any arguments against the financial deal. It was clear the Foreign Office was pressuring him to raise what were for us insignificant questions. When I got back to Milošević and told him he said, "The message is that they don't care about this place anymore."'

Sir Ivor saw things differently. He had more than forty meetings with Milošević; some of them quite heated affairs. On one occasion the Yugoslav president had given him what he calls the 'maximum volume treatment', saying, 'If you are here to represent your government then you are welcome. If you are here to interfere with our country, then you are not!'

It was another five months before their next meeting.

The ambassador was indeed interested in the independent media which, given the sorry state of the opposition politicians, was considered likely to make better use of any support. The British embassy had already used its diplomatic bags to help the most important independent broadcaster, B92 Radio. In the early 1990s B92 began publishing music CDs. They were printed in London, and then flown into Serbia, inside the British diplomatic bags. If you look closely at some of the CDs, you can see the names of certain British diplomats, stamped on the inner circle.

Sir Ivor got involved in something much more serious. B92 distributed its radio signal to seventeen other independent stations around the country. Belgrade kept cutting or jamming the signal. To get round this, Sir Ivor Roberts organized decoding equipment to be brought into Belgrade through the diplomatic bags. B92 staff would collect the equipment from the embassy, and then get it to the radio stations. This allowed B92 to send their signal to London on a phone line, the BBC World Service would scramble it, beam it back into Serbia, and the radio stations would decode and rebroadcast it. The regime was furious.

'They made enquiries,' said Sir Ivor, 'and realized what was going on. I received an early morning summons to the Foreign Ministry. They said I was illegally importing equipment. I said, "No, I'm not. The equipment may be in the hands of the radio stations, but it remains our property and as such we are entitled to bring it into the country." We argued for a while, then I said, "Come on, don't give me any of that breach of Vienna Convention stuff when you know you are trying naked censorship." I said if they wanted to make something out of it, then I would do my utmost to reverse the recent slackening of trade sanctions at an EU level.'

The embassy was also used to 'ease B92's cash flow problem'.

Sir Ivor was doing his best, and sending recommendations to London for a Dayton Mark 2 conference on Kosovo, but London took its eye off the ball. Most people did. The phrase in the newsrooms at the time was 'Bugger the Balkans'. The Foreign Office types were saying it too, but in a little-understood language called 'diplospeak'. It's what diplomats from most countries use when they write memos which might one day be made public, or if they are speaking to the media. They write or say things like 'The Foreign Office does not, at this time, feel that Her Majesty's Government needs to commit more resources to the region.'

This translates as 'Bugger the Balkans' but is careful to suggest that more resources may be needed in the future as of course this is a volatile region. At high levels in the British government this type of memo was flying about. Whoever wrote them turned out to be very wrong and it's difficult to understand why they ignored what people down the food chain were telling them in plain English.

If you listened to what the Foreign Office field workers and MI6 agents were saying to their bosses, it was obvious the region would eventually explode. Somehow, at a certain level, that information was disregarded. Most of the top foreign journalists who worked in the region warned it would happen. More significantly, the plugged-in Serbian journalists were saying the same thing. And yet the British, and to a greater extent the Americans, took their eyes off the ball for two years.

Sonja Licht described how she, in her own words, was 'almost screaming' at a group of very senior US State Department officials in Washington DC in 1997, '"Hey, people! Why won't you help civil society in Kosovo, women's institutions, youth, media? It's a big, black hole that's going to explode, do you want a big black hole in Europe?" The answer was: "We cannot help civil society in Kosovo because it will help secessionists." Nobody was ready to do a damn thing for Kosovo then.'

When you think of the money spent during the subsequent NATO bombing campaign, the cost of early intervention via what the diplomats and intelligence people call 'political warfare' pales into insignificance.

Political warfare takes many forms. It can be 'black arts' placing of newspaper articles to undermine someone, or simply supporting grass-roots organizations. But as Sonja said, 'Nobody was ready to do a damn thing'.

Most of the Europeans and Americans seemed to stop concentrating in the years 1996, 1997 and even as late as February 1998. A Foreign Office field operative who worked in the region at the time explained the problem: 'We had hundreds and hundreds of people involved in the planning and targeting once it looked as if we might bomb, but we didn't have them before that for political warfare; not even on making sure sanctions worked. I suppose it is to our discredit. In retrospect we should have used other weapons at our disposal. The sort of thing we did later, we should have done earlier.'

By the time the little boy was clutching my hand in autumn 1998, and about a thousand people had died, the ticking on the time bomb had got loud enough for everyone to sit up and take notice.

They had a problem. They needed a solution.

John Raven wasn't the only person sitting and thinking. His colleagues at the MOD were joined by people at MI6, the Foreign Office and Downing Street.

The thinking is usually pooled once it gets to a certain level. It's one of many reasons why Britain remains such a player on the world stage. The British are usually very good at it and now that the alarm bells had gone off, the Whitehall machine swung into action. A similar process was going on at the State Department and the Pentagon. The problem there was that competition between them meant they often failed to pool information. It wasn't, as the MI6 man said, 'a joined-up operation' but it was getting there.

One of the Americans who straddled the gaps in Washington was a US navy intelligence officer called Mark Kirk. He was also on the staff of the US House International Relations Committee and had conducted congressional missions to forty-two countries including Bosnia and Kosovo. He was in the position to know a lot of things and one of the things he knew was that: 'Through the 1990s everyone felt we could work with Milošević. His mastery of the English language stood him in good stead. But eventually we opened up a huge operation against him, both secret and open. We felt that if we don't get rid of him he's going to start a war in Montenegro and Macedonia, and this not only risked a humanitarian crisis, it also risked our NATO allies Greece and Turkey being dragged in.'

British thinking at the time had not yet come down on the decision to topple Milošević but they knew it was time to step up a gear.

John Raven's job was just on the UK military side. The MOD's solution was fairly obvious, but only once you thought of it. Thinking about solutions is more difficult than answering questions on *Who Wants to Be a Millionaire?*, which is to say, if you know the answer, the question is easy.

Theoretical solutions aren't right or wrong until they are proved so. Which means it is not an exact science. So those who come up with them are under quite a lot of pressure. If, in Raven's case, he were to come up with a solution that got an unacceptable number of British soldiers killed, or resulted in a very embarrassing diplomatic incident, then that would probably be deemed a failure. So he knew he had better get it right. There's a joke in diplomatic and journalist circles that the title 'military intelligence' is a contradiction in terms. It isn't. The British military 'Intel' people, at senior levels, are highly skilled tacticians who blend military acumen with an awareness of politics and diplomacy. In purely professional terms the British military is held in high regard the world over. This is not just because of the men and women on the ground, it's because of the planning and thinking that goes on before they are committed to action. Mistakes are made, cock-ups happen, but by and large the Intel operation is a crucial part of the success of the military. British soldiers are no longer 'lions led by donkeys', even if sometimes the politicians controlling the top brass tend to bray a bit.

Of course the men and women at MOD Intel don't decide policy. Suggestions of action are kicked 'upstairs' for approval and then, depending on their sensitivity, higher still. A recommendation or request to deploy special forces abroad, even as 'advisers', will be seen by the 'Director Special Forces', a regional chief at the Foreign Office, and representatives of MI6 and MI5. The Secretary of State for Defence would sign off on it, but this would just be a tick on a paper to say he or she was aware of the course of action.

If troops might be involved in action then the ministers of the above departments would be informed and asked if they agree. That means the Defence Secretary plus the Secretary of State for Foreign Affairs, the Home Secretary and possibly the Secretary of State for Development.

If the expected action were likely to be intense, or extremely politically sensitive, then the prime minister would want to be informed. If not, then he or she would demand to know why they had been left out of the loop, and, therefore, the decision-making process. The maxim 'information is power' is no less true for being also a cliché.

One of the MOD 'mandarins' at the time when Tony Blair was prime minister believed that the structure of information in the British government was one of the strengths of the British system. He said that Blair got 'expert analysis, possibly the best. Look at the stuff he came out with after the September 11 attacks in America. The Whitehall machine swung into action. Compare what Blair was saying with Bush and his 'folks' and his almost banal pronouncements, they bore almost no comparison.

Blair's words were from analysis from the MOD, the FCO and the Cabinet Office. Downing Street put it together and helped put the brakes on Washington. Later on, the analysis helped Blair row back a bit on sending thousands of troops to Afghanistan because we were advising strongly against it.'

In the run-up to the Kosovo War in 1999, Tony Blair made sure that, if necessary, he would be involved in decision-making at an early stage, in effect bypassing some of his cabinet ministers. This later became especially true in all foreign policy. Sending the Special Air Service (SAS) to another country is a projection of British foreign policy, so Mr Blair wanted 'in' on this type of information at an early stage. By the year 2000 most of the people engaged in the process were reporting directly to the Cabinet Office. The Cabinet Office equals 10 Downing Street, and 10 Downing Street equals the prime minister.

In the case of the solution proposed by John Raven to the problem of Slobodan Milošević, once it was approved, all over Britain men and women from the armed forces were telephoned to be on standby to go to Kosovo. Britain wasn't at war, there were no declarations in parliament, and the MOD issued a press release which simply declared that a few serving military officers were going to advise the Kosovo Verification Mission (KVM) – the group set up to monitor whether both sides were abiding by the terms of the October UN Resolution.

What the press release didn't say was that at least a hundred elite British military personnel were already on their way to Kosovo, wearing civilian clothes and carrying diplomatic passports.

CHAPTER 3

*'Secrets have a way of making themselves
felt, even before you know there's a secret.'*

Jean Ferris

A T HEREFORD BARRACKS THE PHONES WERE RINGING.
The solution devised by the MOD was simple. If Milošević
had agreed that 2,000 foreign civilians could ensure that the
Serbs were behaving in Kosovo, then the UK was not about to
pass up a rare opportunity to do a spot of forward planning –
even if it meant being a bit 'sneaky'.

In some circles, military operations that are on the 'interesting' side are known as 'secret squirrels' or 'sneaky beaky'. While
this might sound a little juvenile, it does serve as shorthand for
what the MOD was about to do – carry out a sneaky beaky *par
excellence*.

Both the MOD and the Foreign Office had contingency
plans in case of war against Yugoslavia. It was now enough of a
priority to mean that soldiers should be inserted into the territory of the potential enemy to take a look around. This wasn't
just planning in case of eventual war; it was also planning to
protect British soldiers' lives in the short term.

The MOD wasn't about to send dozens of unarmed soldiers to Kosovo without some sort of back-up. In 1995, the

Bosnian Serbs had humiliated the United Nations by holding UN observers hostage to prevent NATO bombing their positions. The situation had been desperate but almost comical. The sight of the 'Blue Berets' shackled to lamp posts and trees had underlined the impotence of the whole UN operation in Bosnia. The men representing the organization designed to stabilize the world were shown on television, standing in the heat of a Bosnian summer, while handcuffed to a lamp post. No wonder the Bosnian Serb leadership, and their puppetmasters in Belgrade, didn't take the UN seriously.

The MOD had watched that farce play out and were determined its people would not get caught the same way now. The back-up for the troops inserted into Kosovo came in the form of the King's Own Border Regiment. Their phone was also ringing. A few dozen members of other units might be going to Kosovo, but hundreds of the King's Own were about to load up and move lock, stock and large gun barrels to Macedonia. If their colleagues in neighbouring Kosovo had to get out under fire, they were to act as the cavalry and charge to the rescue.

The SAS took the call in Hereford. Within minutes backpacks were being readied, pallets of equipment moved and troops from the SAS requested to return to base and be ready to mobilize. Several sources active in the region suggested that an SAS team was part of the KVM mission, and that while the British government was working for a diplomatic solution and ceasefire, there was more going on behind the scenes. Officially there were a handful of unarmed military personnel, commanded by Major General John Drewienkiewicz – or DZ as he is known – but unofficially there were also members of 14th Intelligence and the Royal Signals.

This deployment of different units is simply a modern version of what the British army has been doing for hundreds of years. It's called 'IPB' or 'Intelligence Preparation of Battlefield'. The concept goes back at least to the Duke of Wellington, who used to ride around the battlefields ahead of the fighting in order to spot all the potential problems. The situation was now so bad that Britain was prepared to do IPB on Kosovo.

Each team had a different task. '14 Intelligence' is an elite army unit of men and women who are trained by the SAS to provide what is known as 'deep surveillance'. The information they provide often then forms the basis for many of the actions planned by the SAS. As the defence analyst put it: 'These are the people who perfect Irish accents, wear civilian clothes, and hang around in pubs and cafes in Belfast.'

When the 14th Intel soldiers arrived at a Serb or KLA checkpoint or barracks that autumn, they didn't just shake hands and agree that 'No you're not shooting anyone right now', they were also making mental and sometimes physical notes. They noted the cap badges of the officers to check the units. They asked friendly questions such as, where did the officer go to school?

Everything they saw told them something. By the time this information was pooled, interpreted, typed up and sent to a desk at the MOD it had been translated from seemingly minor facts into potentially vital information: 'Captain Serb commands an elite force which our records suggest has experience in Bosnia and Croatia. His force appear highly motivated and well equipped.'

That may or may not appear interesting, but to the MOD intelligence planners it was potentially life-saving information. If in a future scenario a British unit needed to advance, the decision on which way to go would be easier if the commanding officer knew that Captain Serb and his top-notch fighters were to his left, while Sergeant Serb and his bunch of frightened conscripts were to his right.

The Signals were there for what they do best: secret squirrel communications. They know there is not much point in collecting lots of useful information if you then shout it into a megaphone. The 'Siggies' were experts at short-burst, one-time-pad communications. This basically means that reams of material can be compressed into a few seconds of encrypted information and then transmitted. Finding, catching and decrypting the transmission is extremely difficult.

The SAS had a different role. Once the shooting starts the SAS can be used as forward air controllers to help guide missiles to their targets. They can also locate those targets in the run-up to a conflict, but in this case they had a different job: they were looking for the way out if the KVM had to leave, or if some monitors were taken hostage by a renegade group of Serbs or the KLA.

The SAS interpreted the layout of the countryside and looked for cover in case a fighting withdrawal was required. They found sites to land helicopters, and places to bury equipment they might need later.

According to Duncan Bullivant, an ex-army officer who was spokesman for the KVM, special forces were also sent to Macedonia: 'Among the British Contingent of the NATO Extraction Force was a squadron of SAS and another from the SBS, more than a hundred men in all.'

The plan was that if things fell apart, then the mechanized troops of the King's Own would move to the border to back up the special forces. The special forces would liaise with their counterparts in the KVM, go into Kosovo, secure a helicopter-landing base and rescue the monitors. The King's Own would only enter the province if there was a 'permissive environment'. In other words, if the Yugoslav army wasn't shooting at them. The NATO extraction force was too small to fight its way in without serious casualties, but it was useful as a way of sending a message to the Serbs, as cover for the special forces and, in a worst-case scenario, to actually conduct a quick in-and-out operation.

Not all of the officers were overjoyed at the latter prospect. They called it 'Operation Certain Death'. It would have involved moving armoured vehicles up a narrow valley, which offered excellent cover to defenders over 3 miles. They consoled themselves with the knowledge that London planned to withdraw its KVM contingent long before things got as bad as requiring an armoured push into a sovereign country.

On one unreported occasion, the regiment was actually ordered up to the border in a show of strength during a particular tense episode in Kosovo. They stared down the Yugoslav border troops, but there was never any intention to go across. The British could have sent a strongly worded telegram to Belgrade, but moving several hundred troops to the border said a lot more and was easier to understand, as it wasn't written in diplospeak.

By mid December a large proportion of the 160 British KVM were in Kosovo and the King's Own had arrived in Macedonia. I travelled over to the former Yugoslav Republic to report on their preparations along with a couple of colleagues.

The troops were in a freezing muddy field in the Krivolak Training Area south of the capital. This is a dismal place to spend a winter and the military phrase 'if you can't take a joke then you shouldn't have joined up' must have been deployed along with the troops. It was minus two degrees Celsius during the day, and it went down to minus eighteen at night. There were no barracks, no TV, no phones, no beer and no newspapers. Instead, there were lots of tents, lots of snow, lots of cold lashing rain, as much mud as you could possibly want, plus dozens of tracked vehicles churning around. The nearest paved road was 6 miles away. I spent one night with them and then ran away to the capital, Skopje, and a hotel I never imagined I would be glad to see, the Continental with its interesting brown wallpaper theme.

They spent week after week, month after month there. To prevent morale falling they must have needed reminding that they were on a potentially crucial mission, and that this was no longer an exercise to keep in shape – this was an exercise in the possible near future.

As honoured guests of the King's Own, we were given a roof over our heads. This was luxury, but only relatively speaking. It may have been minus twelve in the shed we were in, but relative to outside it was six degrees warmer. Bathing in this luxurious warmth, I made the mistake of cracking open the beers and whisky we'd brought along for our hosts. Beer equals full bladder, equals going to the toilet, equals going outside in the middle of the freezing night and locating a pre-dug, foul-smelling hole in the ground.

We had a very civilized if chilly evening with some of the officers and men. They fell upon the British newspapers we'd saved and devoured them, but took it easy on the alcohol. Our presence was just a small diversion for them. They were taking the mission very seriously.

For most of the night I shivered in my sleeping bag, placed conveniently on a concrete floor. The rest of the time I was shivering in a T-shirt, shorts and boots as I picked my way across the snow to the stinking hole in the ground while cursing the whole idea of beer. Everyone else clearly had an enormous bladder, and fifteen out of the sixteen of us snored the night away. I spent the entire night awake. When I wasn't outside, cursing beer, I was curled up inside, and cursing my 'warm up to minus eight' sleeping bag for not putting on weight once it realized it was going to be minus twelve. All the military people I know say that no matter how low the temperature, your sleeping bag keeps you warmer if you only have shorts and a T-shirt on. I tried that. It didn't work. Every hour or so I put on another layer. By the time we got up I was already fully dressed.

The army let us lie in until ten past five in the morning. Then the torches came on and the military men all got up and got on with life, while the three civilian softies played their role perfectly, assumed the foetal position and stayed in their sleeping bags until the last possible moment. Opening one eye, I peered at the soldier next to me as he peered into his boots. He examined them with such interest it appeared the secrets of the universe might lie within.

'What are you doing?' I asked.

'Checking for scorpions,' he said.

'There are no scorpions in Macedonia,' I mumbled.

'I know,' he said, 'it's a reflex action.'

We queued up for breakfast in a tent outside. After I politely refused the sausage and bacon but accepted the scrambled eggs and sloppy tomatoes, the cook spotted my deviant tendencies immediately.

'There're no vegetarians in the army, sir,' he grinned, and slid a sausage onto my plate. A masterly move. He let me know that 'veggies' were 'wusses who should bloody eat what they're given, this is the army, not a holiday camp' while at the same time being polite.

British soldiers are ordered to address male journalists as 'Sir', and female journalists as 'Ma'am'. It's a very strange feeling to be addressed as if you are an army officer by an ordinary soldier. I always want to look behind me to see who they're talking to.

After my vegetarian breakfast with added protein we set off to watch the day's exercise. It was quite an education. The scenario was that the King's Own was entering Kosovo, with agreement from both sides, but with the situation still extremely volatile. It's pretty much what happened to the British army the following year.

The commanding officer, Major Jeff Moss, assembled about a hundred troops on a hillside to watch one particular unit being put through its paces. Twenty-three-year-old Lieutenant Jamie Waterson had been left behind with twelve men and a Warrior armoured fighting tracked vehicle.

He was told to turn up in ten minutes and that his orders were to go from position A to position B and collect a group of pretend KVM monitors. He wasn't briefed on what to expect except trouble.

Three armed infantrymen half-dressed in civilian clothes stood behind a large mound of earth piled up on a dirt track. This served as a checkpoint, and they served as KLA or Serb forces, it didn't matter which – they were the bad guys.

Eventually we heard the growl of the Warrior, which was churning up the track a few hundred yards away. The Warriors carry twelve men and a large gun. I don't know the calibre, as I'm not very good on the technical aspects of warfare. Often, during hostilities when something goes 'Bang!' very loudly a colleague might ask, 'What was that?'

This gives you the opportunity to cock your head on one side, as if listening intently, and then say, 'I think that's an FBG.'

'What's an FBG?'

'A F***ing Big Gun.'

The Warrior slid round the corner, spraying mud in all directions, and then clanked to a halt about 30 yards from the roadblock.

It sat there huffing and puffing for about two minutes while Jamie Waterson assessed the situation. Eventually he climbed out of the back, walked round to the front and hailed the three men.

'Good morning,' he began. 'I'm Lieutenant Waterson of the British army. I need to get past this blockade, please stand aside.'

The infantrymen were clearly delighted that for once they didn't need to say 'Yes, sir' and were determined to play their roles to the hilt. You could almost hear them thinking, 'OK, let's see how good this Rupert [soldier slang for officer, based on the idea that Rupert is a middle class name] is.'

One stepped forward, aggressively brandishing his SA80 rifle, and did a passable imitation of a Checkpoint Charlie, the type that operated all over the Balkans in the 1990s.

'Me no speak English. You go back.'

The lieutenant swallowed hard. I don't know if he had a plan B or was making it up.

'I have permission to drive down this road, now please get out of the way.'

The pretend bad guy, trying hard to keep a straight face, shouted back, 'We control road, you leave now!'

The three Checkpoint Charlies smirked and lit cigarettes. Waterson walked back to the Warrior and had a think. He had only graduated from Sandhurst eight months earlier, and hadn't faced such a realistic scenario before. The easy, short-term option would have been to order his twelve men out, have them shoot the cowboys behind the roadblock, and then drive on. Fortunately there are enough officers in the British army who understand that this sort of thing might lead to their entire team getting butchered at the next checkpoint. Still, Waterson had his orders, and he had to get through.

After a couple of minutes, six infantrymen piled out of the Warrior vehicle and split up. Three raced to one side of the vehicle, three to the other, they took cover in a nearby gully and trained their rifles on the checkpoint. Using a mixture of sign language and Basic English, the Lieutenant indicated they were coming through, right over the roadblock if necessary. Two men checked for landmines, the Warrior crushed the roadblock, everyone got back in and they ploughed on. Round the next bend they ran into another problem. The five 'KVM' monitors had been taken hostage by a 'KLA unit'.

This time Jamie Waterson wasn't given time to reflect. Almost as soon as he dismounted with his men, the KLA began to 'rough up' the KVM, who all shouted for help. The Lieutenant took about four seconds before he personally 'opened fire', killing two of the KLA. As the others ran off, the KVM were bundled into the Warrior.

The commanding officer, Major Moss, then gathered the hundred or so soldiers around him.

'Right, you're in a Court of Law. Is Lieutenant Waterson guilty of murder, or was his action justifiable killing? Who's voting for murder?'

'Ah,' thought the eight men who'd been acting as the bad guys. 'Another chance to stick it to the officer.' They all raised their hands and found him guilty of murder. The others voted for justifiable killing.

Waterson explained his actions.

'They were grappling on the floor, I couldn't see their hands in relation to their weapons. So I stood on them and shot them.'

The Krivolak Training Area showed that the British were involved in a belt-and-braces operation. They were forward-planning in case of fighting, but at the same time attempting through diplomacy, to rein the Serbs in.

On 18 December a high-level meeting took place at the Foreign Office. The Whitehall machine gathered to assess the Kosovo situation. This wasn't at cabinet level, it was more important than that. The inner cabinet makes decisions on issues of national security partially based on information given to it by Whitehall. Therefore what is decided at the meetings such as that on 18 December is crucial. One of those present in the oak-panelled room in King Charles Street described the mood: 'All the agencies were there. The DIS [Defence Intelligence Staff], which had assets on the ground, took the line that the Serbs were showing great restraint. Some of us round the table knew that wasn't the whole truth, but the line was that they were showing restraint, so we would show restraint. At that time we weren't on board for a war against them.'

That was the expert advice, which went up to Tony Blair. It was true that the Serbs were not showing full restraint, but neither was the KLA. On 14 December, a Serb unit killed more than thirty KLA fighters as they crossed the border from Albania. Revenge was swift. That night, six Serb teenagers were playing pool in a bar in Peć. A group of masked men strode in and murdered them. The night before the Foreign Office meeting took place, the Serbian mayor of the village of Kosovo Polje was abducted. As officials left the London meeting, news filtered through that his body had been found. This was a mixed-up, messed-up, situation. Most people understood that the Serbs carried out the majority of atrocities, but anyone who really followed the events knew that the KLA weren't exactly the good guys either.

Blair took the advice. He had spent six months watching the situation and had taken care to help formulate some of the UN policy and resolutions. At both diplomatic and military level the British were still trying to avoid going to war in a faraway country, in a far from clear-cut situation. If it came to it, they wanted war to go through legal channels. All of the major European countries took the same view, but the British were the ones that really mattered, because they were the ones with the influence in Washington.

Several Yugoslav and UK sources suggest that the British did try to avoid bombing at this time but they had a problem. There were elements in Washington who appeared to be working to a very different agenda.

CHAPTER 4

*'As a general rule, the most successful man in
life is the man who has the best information.'*

Benjamin Disraeli

THE AMERICANS WERE AHEAD OF THE GAME. A HUGE
CIA operation was already underway in Kosovo. Earlier
that year President Milošević had allowed in an organization
called the Kosovo Diplomatic Observer Mission (KDOM) to
monitor the situation. The scale of the fighting meant that they
were seriously understaffed. Naturally, all the people working for
it were known as 'Kondoms' by the journalists, NGO workers,
Serbs and Kosovars.

Officially it was run by the Organization for Security and
Cooperation in Europe (OSCE), known alternatively by the
Belgrade media corps as 'Odd Seriously Confused Europeans'.
Unofficially, the CIA ran the 'Kondoms'.

Duncan Bullivant arrived with the British contingent of
the KVM in late October to help oversee the ceasefire and the
restrictions on military movement: 'By the time we came in as
KVM, the United States was already running a well-established
CIA operation. Everyone knew what the KDOM really was. It
was staffed mostly by DynCorp people, but they weren't very
efficient.'

DynCorp is a US company, based in Virginia, near to Washington DC. Many of the people who work for it are former members of US military elite units, or the CIA. They are under contract to the State Department. When the Agency needs to put people into places but also needs to 'not be involved', it turns to DynCorp, or a rival company, MPRI (Military Professional Resources Inc).

Rollie Keith, a former captain in the Canadian 8th Hussars, was in charge of the KVM team in Kosovo Polje near Priština: 'I didn't like what I saw. I didn't want the Americans around me; they were working to a different agenda. Some of them were military attachés from embassies all over Europe. One, in my team, said he was a former major in the Seals. I'd assign him a monitoring job, but he'd task someone else to do it then go off on his own taking his GPS with him.'

It was not just former special operations personnel and military attachés in KDOM. A defence analyst believes 'The Americans even put in a senior defence attaché from the Pentagon's Defense Intelligence Agency. The organization was just packed with them.'

When the KVM was set up in October most countries simply transferred their KDOM diplomats into it, to speed up the process of getting the 2,000 monitors which the Holbrooke agreement stipulated. The United States refused. Instead, it carried on with its own KDOM team which meant that KDOM was pretty much an American operation. Then the US Secretary of State, Madeleine Albright, went a step further. She insisted that the head of the KVM would also be an American. The man she chose had an interesting CV. What it lacked was in-depth experience of Yugoslavia.

William Walker had been the US ambassador to El Salvador

in the late 1980s. It was a challenging time, during which Washington was giving military assistance to the government in its fight against leftist rebels. The government controlled several death squads. On one occasion six Jesuit priests were murdered and eyewitnesses said the perpetrators were wearing army uniforms. A nasty business, but as Walker said at the time: 'Anyone can get hold of uniforms. The fact that they were dressed in military uniforms does not mean they were in the military.'

Walker was later caught up in the Iran/Contra scandal, in which senior US officials in President Reagan's administration facilitated the sale of weapons to Iran, despite the Islamic republic being the subject of a US arms embargo.

So, William Walker knew a bit about death squads and covert operations. What he didn't know, he later insisted, is anything about a CIA operation in Kosovo: 'Overnight we went from having a handful of people to 130 or more. Could the agency have put them in at that point? Sure they could. It's their job. But nobody told me.'

Walker kept interesting company for a man so out of touch with what American intelligence was up to. Duncan Bullivant says that Walker's deputy, Mike Phillips, was a former US air force intelligence officer. Phillips had extensive experience as a military targetter. He was now the KVM's 'Military Adviser' and had known Walker since their days together in Latin America. Another Latin American connection was John Fernandez. One of the European monitors had something of a personality clash with him and felt that Fernandez was not suited to monitoring ceasefires or diplomacy. He went to see Walker and was told: 'Well, you know John and I go back a long way.'

An MI6 man operating independently of the KVM says, 'Walker wasn't working very subtly or very well.'

Officially the Americans were in Kosovo to monitor the situation. One of the KVM Europeans found that they had a wide interpretation of the task: 'They weren't just monitoring. The Americans were doing a bit of low-level training of the KLA and were giving them equipment, satellite phones and suchlike. They were quite good at that, especially at communications.'

In the run-up to NATO's bombing campaign in the spring of the following year, the KDOM and KVM had to evacuate their personnel from Kosovo in a hurry. The Americans handed over their equipment to the KLA. The satellite phones and global positioning systems were useful once the planes went into action. The joke at the time was that NATO was the 'KLA's air force'. Duncan Bullivant believes that, 'The US agenda was clear. When the time was right they were going to use the KLA to provide the solution to the political problem.'

The French were also active. The moment they'd heard about the creation of the KVM they tasked a special forces unit, which immediately painted several vehicles bright orange, flew them into Macedonia and drove to Kosovo accompanied by agents from the Directorate-General for External Security, the rough equivalent of MI6.

The Russians did their best, but their budget only stretched to one car. Unfortunately, it couldn't go 'off-road' which meant the Russian monitors were a little limited in finding out what was going on. The guerrilla war wasn't being fought on Main Street; the front lines were out in the hills. The Russians, ever the pragmatists, did what they could, and then retired to the bar of the Grand Hotel.

As far as is known, the French were just making sure they knew what was happening, but the Americans appeared to be trying to make things happen. At this point it wasn't a 'joined-up operation'; the turf wars in Washington meant that not everyone was on board for supporting the KLA and getting tough with Belgrade, but central to ensuring it became policy was Madeleine Albright.

Albright had not been a great success at the State Department nor as US ambassador to the UN. She had been behind the UN's grand declaration of 'Safe Areas' for Bosnian Muslims. The declaration had about as much use as 'a chocolate fireguard', to use a British military term. The Bosnian policy was announced, but without the military guaranteeing they could make it work. One NATO commander, present in Bosnia at the time, says: 'She may well have been able to say the words "Safe Areas" but she had no idea what that meant militarily, or how to achieve it.'

The Europeans were the ones with troops on the ground and they would have had to achieve it. That could have led to a significant loss of life, but the Americans were not about to put troops in. Albright was an interventionist, but the Clinton policy was not to endanger US soldiers.

There was a good deal of grumbling about this within NATO at the time. The joke in the canteens at Brussels and Mons was that the Americans felt so strongly that 'they were prepared to defend Bosnia to the last European'. The American viewpoint was an exasperated 'do we have to do *everything*?'

The idea of 'Safe Areas' may have been a good one, but only if it had been backed by the genuine threat of force. Without it, it became a murderously sick joke and nowhere was the joke less funny than at Srebrenica. In July 1995, the Bosnian Serbs, supported by Belgrade, murdered 7,000 Bosnians.

The policy should never have been declared without being able to back it up. Srebrenica was made a UN Safe Zone, and

7,000 men and boys were killed, one by one, over a period of three days, more or less in front of the UN. It was the most humiliating, tragic episode in the UN's history of working in Europe, and it has weakened the organization. Everyone involved in the diplomacy of Bosnia at the time was marked by the event.

By 1998, General Jacques Klein was the UN's chief representative in Bosnia and as such he was party to sensitive material regarding Kosovo. A British army officer took him for dinner in Sarajevo that autumn: 'Klein started to talk about how Maddy and the State Department had decided "OK, Slobo is now the problem, and the solution is to get rid of him". Klein and his people appeared to think that what they called "Maddy's Gang" wanted to make their mark on history with an act for human rights.'

After the debacle in Bosnia, Albright was determined that the 'threat of force' be a policy priority in Yugoslavia. She is on record as saying she felt Kosovo was an opportunity to right historical wrongs. According to the *Washington Post* she had told a conference in London in March 1998: 'History is watching over us, and we have an opportunity to make up for the mistakes that had been made four or five years ago.'

Albright wanted action. She was determined to 'lead through rhetoric'. This meant she was willing to go out ahead of official policy, with bold statements, sometimes in public. The intention was to thereby influence opinion, leading to her getting her way, when it came to decision time. It worked, and by October NATO was ready to bomb, unless a compromise could be found. Holbrooke found it, and bombing was averted.

But by then Albright's policy was creating facts on the ground. The CIA was training, and partially supplying, the rebel

KLA fighters. This was at a time when other departments in the US Administration and the Europeans were still trying to get peace agreements to stick.

With the US engaged, Albright pressed on. The idea of getting rid of 'the problem' began to gain credence in Washington. In the four months leading up to 24 March 1999, when the bombing began, there is little evidence to suggest that the US State Department, and eventually the Clinton administration, had any intention other than to get rid of Milošević, or fight him on the way to getting rid of him.

The former Yugoslav president would never have made a professional chess player. Faced with a move by the other side, he usually had a counter move, but he lacked a long-term strategy. This meant eventually he would be on the wrong side of a checkmate. He failed to read the moves correctly and, until late on, did not believe that NATO would go to war with Yugoslavia. He appeared to completely miss the fact that most of the players on both sides of the board were stealthily moving against him.

The Yugoslav intelligence services had failed to penetrate far into US thinking. They knew that the KDOM was a CIA front, but they couldn't pierce the real long-term intentions of Washington. They detested Walker, but couldn't work him out. KVM spokesman Duncan Bullivant had first-hand experience of an incident which sent mixed messages to Belgrade:

'A Serb unit had fired over the heads of a few American KDOM people and they were badly shaken. I interviewed them and believed the incident to be true. William Walker said·to me, "Duncan, I want to go strong on this. Let's get a statement out, condemning this in the strongest possible terms." So I did just that, then left for a meeting in London. Walker, meanwhile, left for a meeting with Milošević in Belgrade. He was kept waiting for eight hours but eventually got in to see him. Slobo opened by denying the incident had ever happened, and demanding to know why this aggressive statement had been issued by the KVM. Walker backed down, then when he came out he gave a verbal statement to the media that "Duncan Bullivant overstepped the mark and has not checked the facts." I was getting phone calls in London saying, "Do you know what this guy is saying about you?" When I got back to Priština I went to see him. He said, "Maybe I owe you an apology." I said, "I don't mind you hiding behind me, but the bigger mistake is that you've sent the wrong message to Slobo. You've backed down.'"

If, as Duncan Bullivant says, Walker backed down, it begs the question: why? Possibly he personally couldn't stand up to Milošević's forceful character, or possibly he sent a false message, which encouraged Milošević in the belief that the Americans wouldn't bomb him.

Shooting in the direction of US officials goes down very badly at the State Department, no matter which party is in power. Why would Walker's bosses tell him to back down? People at his level didn't often get the chance to see Slobodan Milošević. When that chance came, he had had the time to get himself briefed on how far he could push the Yugoslav leader. At least eight hours. When he went in to bat, he didn't even swing at the first ball.

After this incident, Duncan Bullivant began getting calls from friends who had read the situation. They all had the same message: 'He's made sure you can't do your job properly, get out of there.' A few weeks later Bullivant left the KVM and returned to London.

'The job was difficult anyway. Weird stuff was happening.

After the fourth time my interpreter failed to appear, despite being booked and informed of the job, she came to me in tears. She said she'd been ordered by the KVM not to show up. Then, in meeting after meeting I'd show up at, say, ten, having been told ten, and they would be saying, "Hey, Duncan what's up? You're an hour late." I wondered what was going on until friends came to me and said, "Take care."'

Walker's actions had caused a colleague to resign. Duncan Bullivant believes that 'in Kosovo the battle between the Americans and the British was about who would speak to the media'.

The KVM was in a mess. It was being pulled in different directions. To support it, NATO had set up 'Operation Eagle Eye'. This consisted of photographic reconnaissance over Kosovo by unmanned 'drone' aircraft from Germany's 100th Drone Battery. Eagle Eye operated out of Macedonia and was commanded by a British general, David Montgomery, known locally as Monty.

The drones were supposed to over-fly the Serb and KLA positions to check if they were obeying ceasefire rules about movement and weapons. In theory they were valuable assets in the monitoring process. As a British defence analyst later asserted, the reality was different: 'DZ [General Drewienkiewicz] would ask for Eagle Eye facilities, but Monty couldn't get the drones to do what he needed, because the Americans kept using them to photograph bridges, ammunition dumps, buildings, barracks, well, everything they hit the following year actually.'

I went to see the 100th Drone Battery in late 1998. The German officer, who conducted the tour, was straight out of the 'School for German Officer Stereotypes'.

'Ve vill have five minutes in zis room and then ve vill move to ze next.'

I thought he was joking, until, after finding myself in a particularly interesting room full of huge computer-enhanced aerial photographs of Kosovo, I wanted to stay a little longer. He actually checked his watch and said, 'No, ze five minutes is now over and ve vill move to ze next room.'

He was just obeying orders, and the orders appeared to have come down from on high, that the Americans had first call on the drones.

DZ had other problems. He had served very capably in Bosnia, after the Dayton peace deal, but some officers believed he lacked two things that the job in Kosovo required. One was a deep knowledge of the situation; the other was combat experience. He was respected by his peers, but was described by one of them as 'an accidental general'.

'DZ used to go to see a VJ [Yugoslavian armed forces] general, a big tough guy who had sent young men to their deaths, who had experience in Croatia. Now this guy knows what the KLA are having for breakfast, and his intelligence people have told him all about the foreign general he's now meeting. They'll have told him he has little experience in this, that he hasn't even served in Northern Ireland. The VJ man might well think that Slobo's an arsehole, but he also believes, rightly, that Kosovo is Serbia. DZ wasn't the right choice if we wanted to be taken seriously by guys like that.'

The Holbrooke deal had put a plaster on an open wound. The KVM were supposed to try and make it stick. It may not have worked even if it had been given a chance, but without it, the war between the KLA and the Serbs was always going to break out again. Neither side had finished with the other.

The KLA were being trained by the Americans, partially equipped by them, and virtually handed territory. They were sitting in the very trenches the Serbs had been forced to pull back from. From this position they made it clear in late December that they would be launching an offensive in the spring of 1999.

The plaster was already coming off. On 21 December a Serb policeman was shot in Podujevo. Two days later a Serb farmer was murdered. A day after that the KLA announced that the ceasefire was over and that they intended to liberate Kosovo from Serbian rule. Ceasefires were no good to them. They wanted the whole thing: independence. Whether you believe that they had the right to take up arms to achieve that aim depends from where you start.

Both sides made convincing claims for sovereignty based on their history, ethnicity and language. From the KLA's perspective, it was legitimate, and moral, to take up arms against 'the oppressor'. There was no other choice. It followed, in their minds, that taking up arms included not just hit-and-run attacks on the Serb police and army, but also murdering postmen of either ethnic group on the grounds that they were helping 'the oppressor'. All government officials were 'fair game'. And, if it came to it, Serb farmers or other civilians might have to be kidnapped and murdered. This is what happens when nationalism turns into fanaticism. No wonder Robert Gelbard described them as 'terrorists'. The KLA behaved appallingly. So did many Serbian units.

From the Serb perspective of sovereignty, it was legitimate and moral to fight back against the illegal separatists who, even if they were the regional majority, wanted to detach an integral part of Serbia. It followed in many Serb minds that the fight might require shelling villages since, after all, they were 'sheltering the enemy'. Some went even further and would support the lining up of civilian men of fighting age, and boys of fourteen, and shooting them, because, after all, they might be KLA.

This was what war did to the civilian populations on both sides. They began to support these fanatical positions. All these things happened, both sides committed them, and yet few people in either population can actually admit it. Instead they take the 'yes, but' and 'you started it' approach to the argument about whether war crimes are justifiable.

If you were to give an account of a war crime, but not include any names, dates or places, everyone would probably agree that it was a war crime. It's when you add in the names, dates and places that the disagreements and accusations and attempted justifications arise; these details mean so much to people who've been through a war that objectivity becomes impossible. They forget that, as James Rubin (Madeleine Albright's spokesman) once said: 'A war crime, is a war crime. There is no justification for a war crime.'

The Kosovans and Serbs went through a traumatic experience, the likes of which the generations of Western Europe have not known for decades. This may explain why so often I've heard the argument that killing 'is just what they do down there; it's what they're like'. Some people go further. They also believe that in some strange genetic way, 'people in the Balkans are not like us'.

As in Croatia and Bosnia, in Kosovo the people were pushed, and they fell on one another. There was nothing 'genetic' about it.

In order to prevent a repeat of the Second World War, the West and North European countries formed what has become the EU. That's EU as in the 'this way we can't fight each other' pronunciation.

Marshal Tito kept Yugoslavia together after the war, and actually convinced a lot of people that they really were Yugoslav first, Croat/Bosnian/Muslim/Serb second. After his death, too many petty nationalists took the old hatreds out of the freezer, and began to cook. They stirred up too much hatred, too quickly. When the separation came, instead of trying to divorce amicably the then leaders threw plates at each other. The Czechs and Slovaks managed to part without burning each other's houses down, but admittedly they hadn't slaughtered each other during the Second World War.

The 'old hatreds' of the Serbs and Kosovars were unfrozen. Of all the former rivalries in Yugoslavia, this was perhaps the one where memories were longest and resentment simmered throughout the 1990s.

There is a school of thought that says Kosovo should have been dealt with at Dayton in 1995. Those who disagree say that would have ensured Dayton failed and that the Bosnian War would have continued. Dayton was a bandage on a wound. It held, but needed attention. The guerrilla war in Kosovo in 1998, while terrible, was low-level in comparison to Bosnia, where the death rate over a twelve-month period was about 1,000 per cent higher.

Even so, as Kosovo faced 1999, things had gone so far, and positions were so entrenched that everyone knew the coming year could only bring war.

CHAPTER 5

'Everything comes to him who
hustles while he waits.'

Thomas Edison

'HAPPY CHRISTMAS, YOU SEMI-HEATHEN.'

It was 6 January 1999 and I'd called Jakša to wish him the best on the Orthodox Christmas.

'Thank you,' he replied, 'but you know that I was raised a good communist, and if you knew anything about politics you'd know that they are atheists.'

'Shut up or I'll bomb your country.'

It's not often you know someone from another country so well that you can drive a bulldozer through one of its most sensitive spots without being punched. Jakša knew me well enough to understand it was a joke, and to respond: 'If you do, I'll come and burn your village.'

Behind his joke was the idea that for the outside world, Serbs were just village-burning, murdering rapists. They had earned this reputation early on in the 1990s, when some Serbs had been exactly that. But so had groups of men from all sides.

The Bosnian government had the international media on its side, which, given the siege of Sarajevo, was understandable. The Croatian government spent millions of dollars hiring

American and Canadian PR firms to create a more favourable image of what was, under President Franjo Tudjman, a state controlled by extreme right-wingers who operated their own village-burning death squads.

Belgrade, governed by a bunch of stolid, communist, nationalist, out-of-touch, criminal conspiracy theorists, told the outside world to mind its own business, and prodded visiting journalists in the chest. They lost the public relations war along with all the other wars, for two reasons. Firstly, their side committed the majority of the crimes; secondly, they were stupid and didn't even bother with PR.

Serbs who escaped the Belgrade regime early on moved to London, New York, Paris or Munich, and spent the next ten years telling people they were 'from Yugoslavia', or 'from the Balkans'. As one said, 'It wasn't worth the arguments or the cold shoulder if you told them you were a Serb.'

This wasn't a problem for Milošević, as he didn't care what the outside world thought, but it was a problem for anyone who wanted to be part of the modern world. Jakša still says he's a Yugoslav. Not because he's ashamed of being a Serb, but because he was raised to be a Yugoslav, and quite liked living in Yugoslavia. As he says from time to time, with a smile I can never quite make out, 'Ah, it was a nice country, it was a nice idea.' He knows the idea of Yugoslavia exists only in memory and on international documents, but as he says, 'I was born a Yugoslav, what choice do I have?' Choosing to change nationality is different to having your country taken away from you.

Many of the Serbs I have met say that before the wars they were Yugoslavs first, and Serbs second. The only reason they are now Serbs first is that there is no second. As late as the spring of 2002, I heard the Serbs described on national British radio as a 'pariah people'. Many ordinary Serbs were furious that they were tarnished along with the regime. The counter-argument is that not enough of them did enough to get rid of Milošević until after he'd lost four wars. This is harsh on active opponents, who spent ten years battling the Yugoslav president, and on large proportions of the rest of the country which lived under his peculiar form of 'democratic dictatorship'. They voted for him, but he made it very difficult for his political enemies to muster any credible alternative. The Serbia of the 1990s is a worthy study project in how to control a culture.

In the end, the opposition was only strong enough to remove the grip Milošević had on people once the outside world stepped in and helped them. In this unhappy New Year, 1999, that world was about to fall in on Miloševic, and the Serbs.

'We're going to be seeing a lot of each other this year,' said Jakša.

'What now?' I sighed.

In between my occasional visits to Serbia, Jakša and I kept in touch via email and phone. He was the doyen of the Belgrade journalists who now worked for the foreign media. He'd been forced out of his job at state-owned RTS, after the rabid dogs of nationalism were put in charge in 1989 and 1990. He may have been outside the system, but he was still connected. What Jakša didn't know was hardly worth knowing. Sometimes he even told me what was going on.

He outlined events in Kosovo just a few days into the New Year.

Twenty-one people had already been killed, including three Serbian teenagers blown up by a bomb in a cafe. Civilians retaliated with attacks on innocent Kosovars. Three Serb policemen were then killed in an ambush, another died in a separate attack in a nearby village.

Holbrooke's sticking plaster had been peeled away; both sides were gearing up for action once the snows melted and spring came.

On 15 January there was a fierce ice storm in Washington DC. Madeleine Albright huddled against the wind as she stepped from her car and into the White House. Inside, she made her way down to the basement and the 'Situation Room'. The other players in the 'Kosovo Strategy' team were already there, situation reports, or 'sit reps', at the ready. They included the National Security Adviser, Sandy Berger, along with various intelligence, military and political chiefs.

Albright again argued that they must agree to threaten to bomb 'this son of a bitch'. The others, led by Berger, were still cautious. Albright left in a mood as foul as the weather and travelled back to the State Department. What she didn't know, as she stared out at a snow-filled capital, was that far away in Kosovo, fifty-four men, women and children were lying dead on the snowy slopes above a tiny village called Račak.

The village has become one of those unfortunate places forever associated with the calamity that befell them. Their names become shorthand for more than a group of buildings: Columbine is synonymous with school shootings, Omagh with bombings, the Iraqi town of Halabja with chemical warfare against civilians. In Balkan circles you just have to say Račak and it is understood as shorthand not just for the village but also for the terrible incident that occurred there and which ensured that NATO would bomb Yugoslavia.

There are two versions of what happened there and each has vocal supporters. The first begins with Serb forces surrounding the village at 6 a.m. on 15 January. They shelled it, forcing a KLA unit to retreat to a hill overlooking the village, from where it returned fire. Then, heavily armed and wearing ski masks, a Serbian death squad entered. Several people were shot during a house-to-house search before a group of thirty men and boys were discovered hiding in a cellar some time between 1 p.m. and 3 p.m. They were forced out to a ravine on the outskirts of Račak and then shot.

Within a few hours William Walker showed up, and, horrified at the carnage, declared on the spot that the 'Serb police forces and Yugoslav army' had massacred civilians and described it as a 'crime against humanity'. Of the total fifty-four bodies, nine were in KLA uniform, two were women in civilian clothes, and forty-three were men or boys in civilian clothes. Western diplomats and most of the media accept this version.

The second version is that the Serb police invited a crew from Associated Press TV agency to film the assault on what they said was a KLA stronghold. They also told the OSCE, which sent several observers in cars with American diplomatic number plates. That afternoon a police communiqué said the operation had been a success and that fifteen KLA men had been killed. The police withdrew. At 4 p.m. a French journalist drove through the village and met the OSCE observers who were talking with villagers. That evening the KLA issued a press release mentioning seven deaths. The next morning the village had been reoccupied by the KLA, who escorted the OSCE and reporters to the bodies in the ravine. There were more bodies on the ground than spent bullet casings. The suspicion is that the KLA came back during the night, removed the uniforms from their dead comrades and re-dressed them in civilian clothes.

No one except Belgrade accepts this second version as fact, but reporters from *Le Figaro*, *Le Monde*, *Libération* in France, the *Berliner Zeitung* and the Canadian Broadcasting Corporation have leant towards it.

Establishing fact one way or the other now is like trying to nail jelly to the wall, which is to say impossible. It is possible that the KLA set up the situation to bring in NATO. It is also plausible that the first version is what happened.

Belgrade reacted with fury to William Walker, saying he had been judge and jury, and that he had spoken without even a cursory forensic or police examination of the crime scene. He was expelled, but stayed on following intense diplomatic lobbying. Whatever the truth, Račak changed everything. Four days later the NATO commander, General Wesley Clark, flew into Belgrade to see Milošević.

The president received his visitor in the usual fashion, placing Clark on a settee slightly lower than the large armchair he used. There was more between them than the coffee table: there was also bad blood.

Milošević didn't like being threatened, and every now and then Clark threatened him. This time Clark went armed with full colour photographs from Račak, which he laid out on the coffee table. Milošević was furious. He claimed that Račak had been staged, and called Clark a war criminal.

At the same time, Albright was at another meeting in the White House Situation Room – this time her view won the day. Once the US administration was on board, the British reluctantly signed up to it, bringing with them extra leverage inside NATO and the European Union. At the time Britain held the presidency of the EU. The previous October, London had been prepared to bomb Yugoslavia as a last resort.

Now the thinking switched, and bombing began to appear inevitable.

It didn't take much persuading. The most senior civil servants and military officers in London were in the same jobs as they had been under the previous Conservative government. They'd watched Bosnia descend into savagery; many feared that Kosovo was going the same way. The thinking was: 'We're going to get involved eventually, why not now?'

The senior politicians felt the same way. According to a Balkan specialist at the Foreign Office: 'As early as 1996–97 we started to think, "Isn't this guy *ever* going to do something *for* his country?" We still thought, "OK we can keep trying for a diplomatic deal", but that started to fade.'

London still attempted to avoid bombing. Several Yugoslav officials say that some British diplomats even briefed them about the traps the Americans would lay for them; nevertheless, if it came to action, the British would back the Americans.

Račak wiped out the idea of a deal, and brought into sharp focus the alternative. The Ministry of Defence, the Cabinet Office, the Foreign Office, MI6 and Downing Street suddenly got very busy. The staff had just one thought in their heads: 'It looks like war. Start preparing.'

At the same time, residents in Perthshire, Scotland, began noticing an increase in the number of low-level runs the RAF fighter-bombers were making through their valleys. The beginnings of the Scottish Highlands are one of the few places the RAF can train in the UK. They need terrain similar to many other parts of the world, and fewer people to deafen than in, say, Surrey. The people in Dunkeld, Pitlochry, and all the other villages up the A9 didn't know it then, but they were listening to the opening notes of a symphony of war, which would begin within eight weeks.

It is virtually impossible to go to war immediately. Even taking off one morning and bombing your enemy without warning is difficult to achieve. Those who attacked the Twin Towers on 11 September 2001 managed to do it, and that is what is meant by the phrase 'the planes came out of a clear blue sky'. That one sentence resonates with two meanings.

One is a description of the weather that awful day. The second is the fact that US intelligence had absolutely no idea it was about to happen. It was the biggest failure in US intelligence since Pearl Harbor in 1941. They had hints that something was being planned, but they had no idea what.

As far as Yugoslavia was concerned, the signs were there to be read on both sides of the Atlantic. It was clear there was a strong likelihood of action so the RAF thundered over Scotland, the special forces read up on Yugoslavia, and at the MOD, a number of men and women got out large maps and photographs and planned what to drop bombs on.

It wasn't that difficult as most of the targeting work had already been done. As John Raven told me: 'That sort of work is done on a regular basis, even if the country isn't in the news. It's passed upstairs, because remember, just because the country isn't in the news now, doesn't mean it won't be in a few years' time. And we don't want to start from scratch.'

Starting from scratch would be a bit like in 1982, when Argentina invaded the Falkland Islands, and everyone at the MOD, Foreign Office and MI6 said, 'Oops'. Two decades later, in the bars and restaurants around Whitehall, they were still arguing about whose fault it was. They missed it coming.

The situation in Yugoslavia was what the Americans call a 'no-brainer' and they were as busy as the British.

The MOD has computer files of scenarios where Britain goes to war against a variety of countries. Some of them are on the European continent. One of them was Yugoslavia. So, they weren't starting from scratch, and the SAS and 14th Intel men and women hadn't only been monitoring a non-existent ceasefire for three months. Nor had the Serbs been only conducting operations against the KLA. The Serb forces had also been moving troops, equipment and computers since at least October of the previous year in preparation for bombing. Even so, they only just managed it. Milošević required some of the best equipment for the war against the KLA; he only allowed it to be moved a few days before the bombing broke out.

In 2000 Sky News broadcast a report, with video footage, detailing how the Yugoslav forces had hidden their hardware and emerged from the war virtually untouched. We saw how some of the best planes were towed into tunnels, how command and control headquarters were moved into deep underground bunkers, and the plans to build dummy tanks and planes. The same source that led us to the footage told us that they hadn't just scrambled in the spring of 1999, they'd been planning for war since the autumn of 1998. Slobodan Milošević appears to have known that NATO would eventually bomb from about the same time as Madeleine Albright made up her mind.

The media in the West has concentrated on President Clinton's personal dilemma during this crisis, and some commentators argue that the 'Wag the Dog' theory applies to Clinton in this case ('Wag the Dog' being shorthand for 'using a foreign war to avert attention from the trouble I'm in'). A different version, which surfaces sometimes, is that the war against Yugoslavia was 'Maddy's War'.

Less attention has been paid to the woes of Slobodan Milošević. As far as is known, Slobo was not the kind of guy who would give a young girl a cigar in his presidential office. Slobo was disappointingly ordinary. He didn't have interesting habits, such as buying thousands of shoes, or keeping human body parts in the fridge. The strangest thing you could say about him was that his favourite Western song was 'My Way' by Frank Sinatra. He usually preferred old Serbian folk tunes, or Russian songs. He appeared to be utterly in love with his wife.

Nevertheless, back in October 1998, he had his troubles, and it wasn't his taste in music. Nor was it the threat of bombing – as he proved later, he could come through unscathed. It certainly wasn't his marriage. He had a different problem. He was becoming more and more unpopular. It had been happening since 1992 and, as with Mr Clinton's problems, it was a bit embarrassing, and it kept happening. Still, every time he got into trouble, war would break out. This would give him a bit more time to think about the problem. He seems to have worked out that he might lose power one day, and he just couldn't take it.

Political expediency is a hell of a reason to go to war. A Yugoslav insider said: 'In autumn 1998 Slobo made a few moves. Some senior people had come to him with arguments about why he shouldn't go to war. Given this opposition to his authority, Slobodan didn't want to risk taking on NATO then. After the crisis faded, those opposed to war were either retired or demoted. The new appointees, all Milošević men, set about planning for NATO bombing. He just bought some time.'

First to go was the army chief of staff, General Momčilo Perišić. The more compliant General Dragoljub Ojdanić took his place. By January several other changes had been made, and a Milošević confidant, General Nebojša Pavković, was put in charge of the Third Army, which was responsible for Kosovo. This situation was a lot easier to read than the Falklands; the threat of war was about to be made, and almost certainly carried out. For Milošević, over the next eight weeks it was a clear and almost omnipresent danger that must have occupied his every waking moment. First, though, there was the no small matter of a peace conference. It was to be held at a chateau in Rambouillet near Paris.

On 26 January the KLA and the Serbs were invited to attend. To encourage full participation the conference included full French hospitality including fine wines and food. As an added incentive, on 30 January NATO again authorized its 'activation order', allowing the bombing of Yugoslavia.

Rambouillet is now shorthand for either 'the place where the Serbs were given the chance to avoid being bombed, but turned it down', or 'the place where the Americans handed a surrender document to the Serbs, knowing they could never sign it, and so ensured they could bomb'. The Rambouillet talks appear to have been a giant game of poker in which neither side blinked first, because key players on each side went into the game already knowing the result.

CHAPTER 6

'A thing we all pursue; I know besides,
'Tis but a giving over of a game
That must be lost.'

Francis Beaumont, 'Philaster'

ON THE FIRST DAY OF THE RAMBOUILLET CONFERENCE the Milošević team in Belgrade had fun playing games. This meant that the CIA in Kosovo had a problem. They were up in the hills with the KLA delegation to Rambouillet, and were supposed to deliver them safely to Priština Airport for the flight to Paris. They had just heard that Belgrade had announced that instead of negotiating with the KLA delegation in France, the Serb police intended arresting what they called the 'killers and kidnappers' the moment they arrived at the airport.

Two of the CIA men were ahead of the column of vehicles and were training their binoculars on the airport to assess just how serious the Serbs were and if there was an armed unit there capable of arresting the KLA. Another agent was making urgent calls to Washington, Belgrade and Paris. At Rambouillet the diplomats had flown into a panic. They were throwing a party and it looked as if no one was going to come.

After letting them sweat for a few hours, Milošević gave the nod and word came through that the KLA could travel.

The Americans hustled their charges down to the airport, eager to see them off before Belgrade began playing games again. Unfortunately, when the KLA people had set off early that morning, no one remembered to say, 'Now, have you all got your passports?' Several members had either forgotten theirs, or never had one to begin with. The French hurriedly scrawled out a few travel documents, the delegation got on the plane, and a few hours later were whisked into the chateau at Rambouillet. What began as farce more or less continued that way.

The Yugoslav delegation consisted of a Milošević man who knew what was going on, a Milošević man who was used as the fall guy, and a host of colourful characters who had no idea what was happening, but who were useful as decoration. The man who knew what was going on was Nikola Šainović, a Yugoslav deputy premier. His job title is irrelevant. In Belgrade politics, titles were scattered around the way they are in big American corporations. You could be called Deputy Executive Director Vice President, but unless you were part of the boss's inner circle it didn't matter. Šainović didn't have a big job title, but he had a big job. The official leader of the delegation was a constitutional expert, Ratko Marković, but Šainović was the one talking to Milošević every night.

The fall guy turned out to be Milan Milutinović. He had a great title, president of Serbia. He was so important that sometimes President Milošević of Yugoslavia would actually say 'good morning' to him.

The decoration was Milošević's proof that he represented all the peoples of Yugoslavia. He sent along a Yugoslav Turk, a Yugoslav Egyptian, a Yugoslav Gypsy and a tame Yugoslav Kosovar Albanian. No one had ever heard of any of them before Rambouillet, and no one has heard of them since. They quickly proved their expertise in negotiating international treaties by downing large quantities of very good French wine, commandeering a piano in the chateau and singing folk songs until the early hours of the morning. A senior cleric, Bishop Artemije, also showed up at the chateau's gates saying he was part of the delegation. It's not known if he would have joined the carousing because he wasn't allowed in. The KLA delegation had its own problems. Most of them were out of their depth, and most of them hated each other almost as much as they hated the Serbs who disturbed them late at night singing their rowdy songs.

The conference began on Saturday 6 February. The French had the bright idea of locking the delegates inside the chateau until the occupants came up with a deal. Nothing was supposed to leak out.

The media locked themselves in the cafes and bars opposite the chateau and were almost flooded by a deluge of off-the-record briefings. With the French, Russians, British, Italians, Americans, Serbs, Kosovars, EU and OSCE all represented, these were an almost daily occurrence. A lot of it was disinformation, or, to be more generous, wishful thinking, on the side of whichever delegation was briefing. Most of it was useless, and worse, whenever one of the 'advisers' came into a cafe to have a quick word with a journalist from their country, reporters from other countries would realize what was going on and try to muscle in on the conversation.

Aside from a failed peace conference, the only other thing Rambouillet is famous for is a breed of sheep. The media corps, myself included, honoured this tradition by flocking to the tables to try and overhear the conversations. Jakša and I were fortunate enough to have the mobile numbers of two of the

British delegation, and would arrange to meet them at a patisserie further into town which was populated only by grumpy locals, unhappy about the presence of about 600 journalists in the main square. These meetings failed to produce much of significance, but were a good opportunity to have a gossip.

One of the delegates regaled me with a picture of the atmosphere inside the chateau: 'The Serbs and Kosovars won't even be in the same room. Milutinović is the only Serb even making an attempt to negotiate, but he and [EU negotiator Wolfgang] Petritsch are having screaming matches with each other. The French have got every room bugged, including ours, there's lots of teams monitoring mobile phones, and we think the Serbs have got the KLA tapped.'

The Serbian secret service loved mobiles; they used to call them 'devices for spying which can also make phone calls'. A middle-ranking delegate from the Serb team told Jakša that they had another source of information apart from electronic surveillance. One of the Italians was briefing them about what was going on in the other rooms. Eventually the Americans found out and Albright ended up calling the Italian Foreign Minister Lamberto Dini to say: 'You're the Houdini of the Serb delegation. Everything is escaping from your people, please get it to stop.'

As the conference neared its end, Jakša made his mind up what was going to happen.

'They will bomb.'

We were walking in the grounds of a nearby chateau, the Domaine de L'Abbaye des Vaux de Cernay, which was as grand as it sounds. The world's media had descended on the small market town of Rambouillet and the hotels there were booked solid. The price of staying at the chateau was less than many major chains, and unlike them it had a twelfth-century abbey in the back garden and a suit of armour in the breakfast room. It was a beautiful, clear, cold winter morning. A light frost crunched under our feet as we meandered among the ruins of the abbey. We often walked and talked, pooling information to try and pick apart the deals stitched up in private.

'They will bomb because there is no way out for either side.'

A source back in Belgrade had told Jakša that Milošević was saying one thing to Šainović and something different to Milutinović. He had also been told about the military provisions, which had been inserted into the draft of the Accords. As long as they were in the text, it was clear to anyone who knew anything about Yugoslavia that Belgrade would not sign the document. The Accords were supposed to be a way to get the Serbs to agree to an international peacekeeping force for Kosovo and yet Appendix (B) guaranteed the opposite.

Appendix (B) paragraph 7 said 'NATO personnel shall be immune from any form of arrest, investigation or detention by the authorities in FRY [Federal Republic of Yugoslavia].' In other words, Yugoslavia would no longer have complete legal rights over Yugoslavia.

Paragraph 8 said that NATO personnel shall enjoy 'free and unrestricted passage and unhindered access throughout the FRY'. This clause would have allowed NATO the right to position troops and tanks anywhere it wanted in Yugoslavia, in Belgrade for example. NATO sources insist they only wanted the right of through passage in order to get to Kosovo, but it wasn't worded that way.

Paragraph 11 said 'NATO is granted the use of airports, roads, rails and ports without payment' and paragraph 15 gave

NATO 'the right to use all of the electro-magnetic spectrum'. This meant NATO could commandeer Yugoslavia's TV and radio stations, and its telephone system.

Separate to the military provisions was a remarkable clause in Article 2, paragraph 1 which said the parties signing the document agreed to 'Reallocate ownership . . . in the following areas: government-owned assets, (including educational institutions, hospitals, natural resources and production facilities)'. This meant that Yugoslavia could be told to hand over its most valuable natural resource, the billions of dollars' worth of minerals in the mines of northern Kosovo.

The Serbs were given a document asking them to agree to allow foreign troops anywhere in Yugoslavia, who would not be subject to the legal process of that country. In addition the foreign troops would not pay for the use of airports etc, and could, if they wish, take over the electronic media and redistribute the only natural asset the state had.

Seen in that light, the Rambouillet Accords resembled a surrender document of the type handed to a defeated power.

All those concerned knew that the document could not be signed by the Serbs in that form. Belgrade and Milošević weren't now talking about far away Slovenia, or the Krajina region of Croatia, or some tin-pot town like Pale in Bosnia, they were talking about the sacred homeland.

One of the British negotiators at Rambouillet later said: 'We put the military stuff in, expecting them to try and negotiate it out.' Another delegate from the British team agrees: 'The military document was a draft. If the Serbs had come back and said they needed to take things out, we would have agreed on a number of points.' That may, even at this stage, have been the position of the British, but on 18 February the American negotiator, Chris Hill, sent a very different signal to Belgrade during a press conference: 'We consider these military aspects essential to the completion of this settlement.'

Dan Goure, who at the time was deputy director of military studies at the conservative Center for Strategic and International Studies in the USA, believed that 'Albright was basically trying to find a pretext for bombing'.

Robert Hayden, then director of the Center for Russian and East European Studies at the University of Pittsburgh, concurred: 'Members of a Western delegation drew up a proposed partition of Kosovo that would have given most of it to the Albanians. Albright prohibited it from being presented to the Serbs for fear they would accept it. When the military annex was presented at the last minute she said "Take it or leave it" and said it was non-negotiable.' The former British ambassador to NATO, Sir John Goulden, disagreed, telling me that: 'I think all of us, including the Americans, wanted a peace agreement. After all, the Americans knew there would be some difficult times if there was a war, and difficult decisions to be made after it.'

The Serbs' strategy, other than drinking and singing, was to do nothing. Most of the other delegates were puzzled, and worried. After the opening statements on 6 February Milutinović arrived, shouted at people, and the rest of the Serbs behaved as if there wasn't very much to discuss.

The French secret service tapes would throw some light on events but so far nothing has come out. Each evening someone from the Serb delegation would go to the Yugoslav embassy in Paris to talk to Belgrade via what they hoped was a secure communication system. Most medium to large countries have these systems in their embassies, and it is very difficult to intercept their transmissions. However, the Americans were trying. If they caught any signal from the Yugoslavs, whether it was out of Kosovo, Paris or Belgrade, they sent it to Menwith Hill in Britain, and from there bounced it to Fort Mead in Texas for deciphering. How much they got is unknown.

In the absence of the French secret service transcripts, which won't be released for years to come, if ever, many people have suggested their own theories on the tactics of the Serb delegation. A Yugoslav who used to travel with Belgrade nego-tiators in the Middle East says: 'Slobo read Albright's mind as early as October. He knew she wanted to bomb, so he prepared for it throughout the winter, and at some stage decided he could actually provoke the bombing when he was ready and could benefit from it. He knew she would oblige, he was a willing partner as well as an enemy.'

There was only one hurdle to get over. The KLA hadn't worked out what was going on. The Americans were stunned when the Kosovar delegation also refused to sign the agreement. Unless they signed, it would be impossible to bomb Yugoslavia, as Belgrade wouldn't be to blame. The KLA delegates were insisting on a guarantee of a referendum on independence within three years. Everyone knew that an independent Kosovo could reignite the war in Bosnia and destabilize Macedonia and Montenegro, so it was a no-go. Eventually the Americans spelt it out. If the Kosovars signed, the Serbs would be blamed and bombing could commence. Perhaps only then did leaders such as Hashim Thaçi work out that they were small fry in all this, that despite their 'demands' for independence, their high-level meetings in Washington and their interviews on international television, they were still small-time operators. The die was cast.

And so Jakša and I walked, and talked of ethnic cleansing in the 1990s, of the Vietnam War, of the Blitz and the Dunkirk spirit, of Serbia's history, of the sheer bloody-mindedness of people who make up nations, and of a way of thinking the Western generations had almost forgotten.

Rambouillet broke up without an official agreement but with the KLA understanding what was about to happen. The theatre moved to Paris two weeks later for a formal signing by the Kosovars. There were just a couple of loose ends to tie up.

I didn't bother to go to the 'talks' at the International Conference Centre on Avenue Kléber in Paris – referred to unofficially as the Kléber Centre. There were other things to do, like packing for a long trip. The players showed up of course; there had to be a formal ending of Act 1. The shadowplay was there as well. During the week of the Paris meeting, an MI6 man, someone from the EU delegation, contacted a member of the Yugoslav team: 'I wasn't being disloyal by talking to them,' he told me, 'because I was in the business of information gathering. Basically they asked, "Is there anyone sensible in your government that we could talk to?" They wanted to get the message across that they believed there were still some decent, sane people in the Belgrade leadership. The message was, "Look there *is* going to be a war, the Russians are now onside and they are not going to save you." I'm sure the message reached all the way up to Slobo, but he repeatedly said "Fuck them all".'

The MI6 man was an individual we called 'The Man Who Doesn't Exist'. He had been one of the MI6 operatives in Belgrade during the 1990s. He hosted excellent parties, and knew everyone worth knowing. His nickname came about because officially he was a diplomat and so when we wanted to discuss him in certain company, he would simply be 'The Man

Who Doesn't Exist'. By 1999 he had been posted elsewhere, but surprisingly he turned up at the Kléber Centre.

One of the Yugoslav journalists who worked for a foreign news agency spotted him outside the gates. 'I said to a couple of friends, "Look, it's The Man Who Doesn't Exist." Then I went over and asked him what he was doing in Paris. He wasn't happy about me seeing him but I said, "Come on, what are you doing here?" He said, "Well, I'm here dealing with agriculture", and then he asked me if I'd seen the Russian guy who used to work for the TASS news agency in Belgrade. Well, we hadn't. He walked off and then two minutes later the Russian showed up. So, same question, "What are you doing here?" and he says he's here to write a book about France, and by the way, have we seen The Man Who Doesn't Exist? Anyway they found each other and went towards the Arc de Triomphe, I dunno, maybe to discuss a book about French agriculture.

'Then it got even weirder. One of Petritsch's people came out and we said, "We've just seen The Man Who Doesn't Exist." The Petritsch man says, "No you haven't". At dinner that night we brought it up again, this time he said, "You can't have seen The Man Who Doesn't Exist, because The Man Who Doesn't Exist, doesn't exist!" Weeks later he admitted that, "Yes, the guy had been there", but that even the British delegation didn't know what he was there for. Basically he was sent to nail down the agreement that the Russians weren't going to start World War Three over Yugoslavia once the bombing started. They also sorted out that the former Russian Prime Minister Yegor Gaidar could offer his services for the inevitable peace negotiations whenever they would happen. The Russians basically knew the bombing would soon start, and that they couldn't really stop it.'

CHAPTER 7

*'Let your plans be dark and
impenetrable as night, and when you
move, fall like a thunderbolt.'*

Sun Tzu

THE MAPS WERE ON THE TABLE, THE FLIGHT SCHED-
ules checked, the troops mobilized, the chief of operations
briefed – and that was just my boss. Sky's then head of news,
Nick Pollard, had been asking for briefings from various staff
as it became clear there was going to be a war. We spread out
the maps, argued the situation and agreed we needed teams in
Macedonia, Albania, Montenegro and Belgrade. It was going
to be crucial to our coverage to be in position for the flood of
refugees we knew would pour over those borders once the air
strikes began. The missing place, of course, was Kosovo.

Getting a visa had been difficult. It had taken weeks. Having
handed one out, the Ministry of Foreign Affairs wasn't about
to grant us the second one we needed to also cover Priština.
Actually the Foreign Ministry would have given us one. The
problem was that when it came to journalists getting visas the
Foreign Ministry was controlled by the information minister.
Enter Mr Goran Matić, also known as 'Snake Eyes'.

Goran was a tall, lean man of about forty-two. He had the disconcerting habit of staring at you with the eyes of a cobra and beginning each sentence 'Mmm, mmm'. He wasn't just information minister; Goran was part of the inner circle that, almost every day, could whisper into the ear of 'Wicked Witch of the East' Mira Marković. In the Court of King Slobo, access to his wife was treated with the same sort of reverence as access to the man himself. Goran knew the journalists weren't going to be allowed to remain in Kosovo, therefore he decided Sky only needed one reporter in Belgrade, where he could keep an eye on me.

At what were described to me later as 'the very very highest levels', the decision had been made that only two representatives of the foreign media would be in Kosovo once the bombing started. They were Goran Tomašević, a Reuters photographer, and the late Miguel Gil Moreno de Mora from Associated Press Television News. Belgrade clearly didn't want too many foreigners around, and so ordered both men to work under the control of the Priština media centre. They did a good job in reporting as much as they could under very difficult circumstances.

With no back-up, there wasn't much point in my going down to Kosovo and leaving Belgrade uncovered. I'm glad that decision was made. Within a few days the media people were to be ordered out of Kosovo at gunpoint; some were assaulted, some had their cars burnt, others had their armoured vehicles stolen by the Serb forces. When they showed up at the Hyatt Hotel in Belgrade, their journey out of the province was written all over them. Some just took a shower, got back in their cars and carried right on to the Hungarian border. And no one could blame them.

We needed to be in Montenegro for a second reason. Two weeks previously the republic hadn't been on NATO's target list; now it was. The republic was the junior republic in the federation of two, which was all that was left of Yugoslavia. Its president, Milo Djukanović, was the enemy of federal President Milošević, and had the police on his side. He knew that if NATO bombed his republic, Milošević might launch a coup d'état, and install people who would back Belgrade. When NATO did hit Montenegro they took care to only fire at targets connected to the Yugoslav army, which was still loyal to Milošević. A coup d'état could easily have included Djukanović being thrown against a wall and shot in the head. So either he took that risk and agreed that NATO could bomb the republic, or NATO thought they'd risk it even without his say-so.

Either way, Montenegro appeared on NATO target lists very late in the day. When the first missiles struck, our reporter Aernout van Lynden was in position and covered it live.

It wasn't rocket science working out where to be. We were certain there would be war, the US bombers had been moved to Europe, the Kosovo Verification Mission had withdrawn, the embassy staff were almost all out, and the Rambouillet document (the text of which did not appear in the House of Commons until 1 April) was a strange piece of work. We were also sadly confident that there would be refugees. Jakša and I had told Nick Pollard that there would be a minimum of tens of thousands of people moving. The maps showed which routes they would probably take, and a little knowledge of local politics completed the picture.

The question is, did the great powers not know there would be refugees and that their bombing might trigger the movement? Or did they calculate that it might happen, and that they would take the risk? According to a Foreign Office

Balkans specialist: 'There was an internal debate about the effect that bombing would have in Kosovo. We just didn't believe that what happened would happen.'

Despite the evidence from Croatia and Bosnia, some of the experts still couldn't bring themselves to believe just how far things could go. This despite President Milošević himself telling the German Foreign Minister Joschka Fischer: 'I am ready to walk on corpses, and the West is not. That is why I shall win.'

Others, including a British ambassador connected to the region, knew that bombing would lead to a movement of peoples and loss of life, but argued that it was the lesser of two evils: 'At the Kléber conference, in Paris, the Serbs told us to piss off. We could see things were going to get much worse and that the Serbs were going to go for a big scenario. They knew the KLA was going to get better and more organized, everyone knew a lot of people were going to die. The Serbs had turned the corner and escalated the situation.'

The Kosovo 'leaders' appeared to have made the same choice. Several sources agree with a NATO ambassador who was in touch with the KLA: 'Before the bombing, they were telling us that they knew people would flee, then during the war they said to us, "We know you are making mistakes and some of our people are being killed, but keep going."'

There is a former stately home in the Home Counties that is used frequently to host international relations study sessions. These are not secret meetings. Journalists, diplomats, business people, professors and others come together and discuss issues. It is a useful place to think things through. In 1999 a couple of Yugoslavs were invited and went to a session of 'war negotiations', a theoretical version of diplomatic manoeuvres. One of the Yugoslavs present described the following scene: 'One guy threw this scenario in. He left the room and came back in and said he'd just been on the phone to Slobo and the message was: "If you bomb, we're gonna kill all the Albanians." The Brits in the room didn't like this much as it complicated the pretend negotiations. But, you know, I think they knew all along what would happen. They just didn't care that much.'

The following year the British government's Foreign Affairs Select Committee concluded that: 'A very serious misjudgement was made when it was assumed that the bombing would not lead to the dramatic escalation, displacement and expulsion of the Kosovo Albanian population.'

Former US navy intelligence officer Mark Kirk had a good idea of what might happen. He had been in Kosovo shortly before the bombing and, knowing what some units in the province were capable of, spoke to the MUP general, Petar Lukić, in Priština: 'I said to him, "What are you going to do if we bomb?" He got really mad. I said, "Look, it matters how you conduct yourself." He kept getting madder and I said, "No, General. I mean it matters how you personally conduct yourself." Because of the intercepts I knew what he'd been up to, and I was warning him that he too might one day end up in The Hague.'

After the bombing started and the ethnic cleansing accelerated, German intelligence leaked a document via Joschka Fischer saying that the Serbs had long planned their action and codenamed it 'Operation Horseshoe'. There's a debate about whether 'Horseshoe' ever existed. In the document the word 'Horseshoe' was spelt the way the Croatians spell it, not the very similar Serbian way. Either way, an operation of some sort was already going on. Even during the Paris 'talks' villages were being shelled, there was fierce fighting and refugees were fleeing. Things got a lot worse.

Several of the clued-up media organizations moved staff to Macedonia and Albania, but the international aid agencies were in a more difficult position. If they sent large numbers of staff and set up tens of thousands of tents in the expectation of arrivals, they could be accused of encouraging people to move, even before the bombing. If they didn't act, they might not be able to cope, because no one knew just how many refugees there would be. As a result, when the tidal wave poured over the border, the aid agencies were woefully understaffed and ill equipped.

In Serbia, and elsewhere, these arguments are sometimes used to suggest that the greater crime was committed by 'the West', for provoking what happened in Kosovo. Those who believe that seem to forget who actually carried out the crime. For all their meddling and muddling, in the final analysis it wasn't Madeleine Albright, Bill Clinton, Tony Blair, the Western media or any other bogeyman who pulled the triggers in the killing spree that followed. The scale of killing never approached the propaganda claims made during the conflict, but that should not disguise the fact that it was still a murderous event and that the Serbs carried it out.

In early April, British Foreign Minister Robin Cook and US State Department spokesman James Rubin were making farcical claims of tens of thousands of dead and 100,000 missing men. Rubin even said that the sports stadium in Priština contained 20,000 prisoners. His source for this far-fetched idea was the KLA commander Hashim Thaçi. The Serbs quickly allowed a TV camera into the empty stadium. By 19 April the State Department went even further, announcing that 500,000 Albanian Kosovars were missing, feared dead. The reality was hideous enough without inflating figures for NATO's propaganda purposes. Villages were burned and looted, and civilians were killed. The final death toll will never be known, but the estimates of organizations such as Human Rights Watch, Amnesty International and the UN now suggest that the Serb forces murdered between 3,000 and 6,000 people. Some Serbs point to how low that is in comparison to the claims made during the fighting. Few point to how utterly shameful the figure of at least 3,000 is.

On Saturday 20 March I kissed my fiancée and son goodbye at Heathrow Airport. Time was running out and soon the borders would be closed. Something funny was already happening in airspace. Flights were delayed and the Budapest/Belgrade route didn't exist. I found myself routed firstly to Brussels, then to Munich, and then down to Athens. Athens was closed. Not the runway, but the airport. I got in around 1 a.m., with five hours to go until a connection to Macedonia. I made my way through the deserted corridors towards the area for flights to the Balkans. I knew I was going the right way as the decor began to get a little shabby. Still, it wasn't as bad as in a couple of airports in Germany. They have what are little better than cattle sheds, which they use for people travelling to places such as Albania, Bulgaria or Kazakhstan. They are at the far end of the airports, are often crowded and have few facilities. There's no signs up saying 'second-class citizens this way', but you get the message from the general decor of the place, especially when you enter it after having walked through the gleaming temples to airport shopping that are used for everyone else to wait in. The major British and French airports don't use cattle sheds for the people from countries where women still wear headscarves, and it's a wonder why the German ones did.

I dozed on one of those red plastic chairs that are designed to be almost comfortable for about a minute, and after that to be a form of modern design torture until you stand up. I was the only person in the waiting room. The lights were mostly out, the floor was dusty, the air cold and the reporter miserable. Even the vending machine seemed to mock me for not having any Greek coins. I had had no idea I was going to be in Greece and the bureau de change in the main building had unhelpfully closed at midnight. At about 4 a.m., wraith-like shapes began to appear. I cleared my eyes and realized they were cleaners. By 5 a.m., I was shuffling through passport control and at 6 a.m. was in the air heading for Macedonia and a cup of coffee. From there it was a short hop into Belgrade.

Everyone else was making plans to leave. The families of the Western diplomats had already gone, and the remaining staff had their bags packed. Some of the more prescient Serbs had sent their families off to Hungary or out to the countryside. They knew it was war, but no one knew what would happen during it. I checked into the Hyatt Hotel. By coincidence I was put into the same room I'd had on several previous visits. My colleague Aernout van Lynden had also been assigned that room on several of his stays in the early 1990s before he was thrown out of the country. Even stranger were the two occasions I came in from a day's work and found that the telephone receiver smelt strongly of aftershave, which I never use.

On Tuesday 22 March, 'The Big Swinging Dick' Richard Holbrooke swung into town for the last time on a mission with no chance of success. The Serb parliament formally rejected Rambouillet, but did accept the idea of UN troops, including Russians, in Kosovo. No dice. Holbrooke met Milošević and asked him if he understood what would happen if he left Belgrade without Milošević giving in.

'Yes,' replied Milošević, 'you will bomb us.'

He had already told Holbrooke that he felt there was nothing to negotiate, saying, 'If it's Sunday, but you say it's Wednesday, then it's Wednesday. If you say you're going to bomb us, you're going to bomb us.'

Holbrooke waited in his hotel suite until late the following afternoon, Wednesday 23 March. About two hundred media people waited in the foyer next to the sign which said 'Guests, please remove your guns before entering the hotel'. The planes waited to take off. It was just beginning to get dark when the Swinging Dick entourage stormed through the foyer. Holbrooke's face was like a dark cloud, presaging the thunder which was about to roll. He made a brief statement, then swept on and out to the convoy of US embassy vehicles. As the media pack broke up to file their stories, I caught sight of one of the senior men at the British embassy almost running down the marbled steps.

'I'm off,' he said.

'Don't leave me,' I replied, only half jokingly.

My friend hadn't even broken stride – he had a lot of work to do before heading for the border. He threw me a grin over his shoulder and said, 'You're on your own, mate.'

A lot of journalists were leaving too. Many people assumed that as soon as the diplomats crossed to safety, the first missiles would be fired.

The British and Americans went back to their respective embassies to shred papers and light fires. Another source inside the British compound says: 'When we heard that the Americans were smashing their cryptographic equipment we knew it was time.' The Americans resorted to using sledgehammers to get at their hard drive computer disks. The British didn't need to resort to such methods: 'We carried our communication kit out of the secure room and took it with us. We also burnt and shredded a lot of material. One man became so engrossed in some of the secret documents that a colleague had to say to him, "You're supposed to burn them not read them." It was a bit of an anti-climax in some ways because we'd been through this process the previous October and had destroyed most of the stuff then.'

By now the embassy was mostly dark with just a handful of staff inside. Ambassador Brian Donnelly walked through the empty corridors wondering if he would ever return. Then a security officer, formerly with the British military police, locked the front door. Donnelly and the others got into their cars and drove over to the American compound without a backward glance. From there a large convoy of vehicles set off for the Hungarian border.

The Serbs were also busy. As early as 1997 the Yugoslav military intelligence had assessed that one day it might come to this. Since October 1998 analysts at a little-known office in Kneza Miloša Street had been putting into operation a plan worked out during the Cold War in case NATO or the Russians ever attacked Yugoslavia.

The troops in Kosovo were put onto 'Random Movement Orders'. Large formations stayed where they were, but lots of small units were travelling all over the province. Twenty miles above them the US spy satellites picked up a lot of the movement, but the picture interpreters were brought down to earth. None of the movement made sense. A lot of decoys were also put into position. The Yugoslav military knew exactly what to do – they'd been rehearsing it for years.

In the weeks leading up to this moment NATO officials had travelled to Macedonia, Slovenia, Croatia and Bosnia to talk to former Yugoslav army officers who knew the basics of the above plan.

A Yugoslav military intelligence officer who had kept his links with former colleagues after the break-up of Yugoslavia says: 'They asked them to write all the information down. But when they got back to Brussels and analysed it, they realized that only the Bosnians and Croatians had told them anything worth knowing. The Slovenes and Macedonians had told them a load of confusing rubbish.'

A Norwegian military intelligence officer at NATO backs this up: 'It took ages to work out what was what. We lost time doing that, eventually we just went with what the Croats and Bosnians said.'

The war of words was now over. The diplomats from most of the EU and NATO countries made it across the border without incident, the Yugoslav forces went to highest alert, NATO's planes were on the runways. Serbia waited.

PART TWO

DURING

CHAPTER 8

*'If there is ever another war in Europe,
it will come out of some damned
silly thing in the Balkans.'*

Attributed to Otto von Bismarck

THE MOBILE PHONE RANG. A VOICE HISSED IN MY EAR, 'The geese are flying!', and then cackled. It was a friend from the foreign desk at Sky. The B-52s were taking off from RAF Fairford in England and were heading our way. His pretend subterfuge wasn't necessary; all the twenty-four-hour TV news stations were taking live pictures of the beginning of the war. It was mid-afternoon on Wednesday 24 March and spring had arrived in Belgrade.

I was sitting at a pavement cafe in Republic Square enjoying the first really warming rays of sunshine that year. The streets were full, the cafes packed, the atmosphere tense. I glanced up at the air raid siren placed on top of one of the buildings in the square and wondered how long it would be before its chill wail would herald the beginning.

I looked at the people. We all knew it was coming, but I was the only one in the square who knew that even now the giant B-52s were roaring across Europe, on their way to the city. I had the surreal feeling of being frozen in a moment, while all around me ordinary life moved at a quickened pace. I was with cameraman Veljko Djurović who had just agreed to work with us for at least the duration of the war, however long that would be. We were lucky to get him. Two hours later Reuters tried to hire him, and two days later the BBC tried to poach him. Veljko has a highly developed sense of honour that he has carried through El Salvador, Nicaragua, Beirut, the West Bank, Northern Ireland, Cuba, Slovenia, Croatia, Bosnia and Kosovo. He told us he would work with us, and that was his word. He was of course immediately dubbed 'Velcro' for sticking with us.

We went back to the Sky office in New Belgrade, near to the Hyatt Hotel, and sat around talking with Jakša and a group of people from Reuters as the light began to fade. Then it was the turn of Jakša's mobile to ring. It was one of the Western diplomats: 'Jakša, I just wanted you to know that I'm in Budapest. The planes are about to cross into your airspace and release the missiles, good luck.'

'Thank you,' replied Jakša. As he said afterwards, what else was there to say?

Within minutes we heard a low-pitched hum. It grew louder and the pitch went up, then began to fall and rise again. Many of us had heard air raid sirens before in various parts of the world, but they still throw a chill onto your heart. Everyone moved at once. The camera crews filmed the cityscape from the windows of the office, and the journalists reached for the phones to call in the news.

And then, nothing. For a long time, nothing, and then, a deep deep crash like a giant steel door being slammed shut far away, and then a rumble, flowing through the city streets and washing up against the glass on the windows of the office. NATO was bombing Yugoslavia.

Over the next couple of hours I was too busy to think about anything other than getting a report to London. Veljko and Reuters had a few pictures of people running for the air raid shelters, we interviewed someone for reaction and I did a 'report to camera', then took the material to a nearby building to edit and conducted a few phone interviews into Sky's open-ended programming.

An hour later I was back on the street and on the mobile. I had to speak quietly in case I was overheard using what would soon be called the language of the 'NATO fascist aggressor'. Gangs of men were already busy smashing up every McDonald's in town, along with the French Cultural Centre, the British Institute, the Air France Office and anything resembling Americana.

'Jakša, what time can we send the report?'

He replied in a low monotone, 'There isn't going to be a report, don't come to the office.' Then he hung up. I'd never heard him speak like that before.

His conversational skills were limited because he was pressed nose-first to a wall, with his hands in the air and a gun pointing at him. Everyone else in the Reuters office was in a similar position.

A faction of the various units of plain-clothes police were searching for Western reporters, in particular CNN's Christiane Amanpour, who had upset a lot of people with what was perceived as biased reporting.

At about the same time forty or fifty media people, who had gone up to the roof of the Hyatt to film the explosions, were arrested and taken downtown. They were held overnight and had their equipment confiscated.

I didn't know this was going on and so returned to the hotel. It was in uproar. The foyer was full of people I didn't know but recognized. Anyone wearing an expensive black leather jacket, black polo neck sweater, black jeans, a sub-machine gun and a scowl was with the secret police. Fortunately they didn't recognize me. I slipped up to my room and sat on the bed wondering what to do. After a few minutes someone knocked on the door, then hammered on it with something heavy. I crept to the spy hole. A leather jacket and machine gun were on the other side.

I felt very, very silly standing behind the door pretending not to be there. To my surprise the leather jacket left almost immediately. I waited a few minutes then went into the corridor and began walking towards the lifts. Three plain-clothes policemen, all with machine guns slung around their necks, were coming the other way. Summoning up the remains of my almost extinguished confidence, I looked one of them in the eyes and without breaking stride, said in my best gruff Serbian accent, '*Dobro veče*' ('good evening').

He barely glanced at me. Once we had passed each other, I went round to another corridor, ducked into the stairwell, went down a couple of floors, then sat on the concrete stairs and wondered what to do next.

Downstairs, Amanpour was frogmarched out of the manager's office by several armed men. Those who saw it assumed she was being arrested. Actually, a senior government minister had arranged for his own security team to save her from whichever outfit was looking for her. An ambassador from one of the Scandinavian countries was waiting outside; he drove her to his embassy, and from there she was smuggled out of the country a couple of days later.

Things calmed down. The unit searching the hotel was from the Serbian Republic level of authority, not from the Federal government, which had taken a couple of hours to stamp its full control on Yugoslavia.

In the confusion that night, a lot of influential politicians, not all of them Milošević supporters, were trying to throw their weight around. There were many armed units in Belgrade of which almost all were still loyal to Milošević, but there were also armed 'militias' who answered to a Milošević rival, Vojislav Šešelj. At the time his 'Radical' (read fascist) party controlled the Serbian Ministry of Information. They took it upon themselves to declare that all foreign journalists were to be expelled, and they sent out the orders to the plain-clothes specialists to go and get them.

There were a lot of interesting phone calls made round Belgrade that night as officials, politicians, armed units and gangsters checked to see who was in charge of what. The answer was still Slobodan Milošević. As word got round, orders from higher up were sent out, and the plain-clothes men left to be replaced by a couple of uniformed policemen. They sat in the lobby looking as if they wouldn't have a clue what to do if the tough guys came back.

Outside, the city was in darkness. The authorities had cut the power to cause a blackout to try and make NATO's job more difficult. I crept down to the Sky/Reuters office and made my way to the first floor. The stairs presented a challenge. The staircase was darker than a dark thing at night. I felt my way up, clutching the bannister, and at the top headed for the glow coming from several candles in the office. To my relief, there were no police there, and it was full of people who knew what was going on.

My friends explained what they knew of the political situation, and what had been hit by the air strikes. At around 2 a.m.,

Jakša and I walked back up the road. It was still so dark we couldn't see if anyone was around, and so we spoke in whispers.

'How's your family?' I asked.

'Fine, they're all up in the Hyatt for safety.'

Due to the passions running through the city that night, Jakša had moved his wife and two sons into the hotel. Some of their neighbours knew that Jakša worked for a company from a NATO country and most understood, but a few felt very strongly about it. By now my mobile had cooled down. Friends on the foreign desk had asked our colleagues at Sky News Australia, Talk Radio UK and Fox News in the US to stop calling me. They knew this was going to be a marathon and that I needed some sleep. So they gave me three hours' worth.

The following day was punctuated by sirens, explosions and, for the foreign media, was dominated by one question. To go, or not to go?

The expulsion order at the Serbian level still stood, and the implicit threat of violence hung heavy in the oppressive atmosphere. I filed a couple of phone reports and headed to a press conference held by Vuk Drašković, a Federal Minister of State. He said the foreign media would not be expelled, but couldn't give any assurances about safety, nor of the whereabouts of two journalists who had disappeared. It later transpired they had been thrown out of the country, and assaulted before they crossed the border into Croatia. Several people who took that route out were beaten up.

At the same time, then British Foreign Secretary Robin Cook was at Westminster telling a packed Houses of Parliament that the British journalists should leave Belgrade as they were only giving comfort to the Milošević regime. So, for the first and only time in his career, Robin Cook agreed with Vojislav

Šešelj. Sky had patched his comments down the phone and asked me about them. I was furious and crossed the line from journalism into polemic. Live on air I said, 'Mr Cook appears not to understand the basics of journalism. Perhaps the Foreign Secretary would be doing his job a little better if instead of bleating about us leaving, he was defending our right to do our jobs.'

By mid-afternoon some of Arkan's paramilitary force was seen in the Hyatt and Intercontinental hotels, and the Radicals were still issuing threats. The media people from Kosovo began to show up with tales of having their cars burnt, and their equipment stolen at gunpoint. The hotels began to empty.

I was getting jumpy. I'd been in the Serbian part of Bosnia when NATO bombed in 1995 and in Baghdad ahead of US bombing in 1997, but in neither place had we been ordered to leave, and in Iraq the population remained friendly. This was very different. The BBC had left en masse. Some of their staff had literally run out of the Hyatt and thrown their bags into a coach. One of their correspondents, John Simpson, then played a masterstroke. He'd agreed with the rest of the team to leave, he even put his bag in the luggage compartment, and then, with the engine running, said, 'You know, I think perhaps I'll stay after all.' The coach pulled out, heading for Hungary, leaving Simpson as the only BBC reporter on the story. Alas, I was told he'd gone with them, and that Julian Manyon of ITN had also left. The reception staff told me just twelve journalists were left at the Hyatt and they included Greeks and Russians who for historical and cultural reasons stood a better chance of being left alone.

As it grew dark I walked through the deserted reception hall, my footsteps now echoing on the marble floors. The Radicals were waiting for the cover of night as the sirens sounded again. Because of the levels of violence we'd seen throughout the region over the years, and the fact that I had been told I was now the only British reporter still in town, I was scared. We'd also received the first rumours that the militia squads and MUP units operating in Kosovo were wearing ski masks, which usually heralds terrible deeds. On my way outside I noticed my friend Steve Erlanger of the *New York Times* on the phone at the check-out desk. He was talking to a Yugoslav cabinet minister and asking if perchance he could stay at his house.

'Full marks for trying,' I thought, but it was clear from Steve's side of the conversation that there was no room at the inn.

For the tenth time that day I asked Jakša if I should go. Perhaps just to put an end to my stupid questions, or perhaps because he now felt the menace in the air as keenly as I did, he finally said yes. I didn't ask again, but rushed up to my room, picked up my already packed bags, checked out, hugged Jakša and dived into a battered old jeep driven by Chris Bird of the *Guardian* who had just made his way up from Kosovo. The last light of a fiery red sunset was disappearing over the horizon, darkness fell, the sirens sounded again, and we headed for the motorway praying we wouldn't get stopped.

We crossed into Hungary without incident at around midnight, ate a bowl of soup at a dingy roadside cafe and continued up to Budapest. I rang my fiancée to tell her I was safe, then fell into a troubled sleep for about four hours. I began the next day with a stupid question to Jakša.

'Should I come back?'

He argued forcefully that I should. No, he couldn't guarantee my safety, what sort of a stupid question was that, he wondered. Yes, the situation had calmed down, the army were taking control of foreign journalists, he could get me back in, and we'd take it from there.

It was one of the most difficult decisions I'd ever taken. I paced up and down in my hotel room for the hour I'd given myself to decide.

In retrospect, it all seems rather melodramatic, but at the time I had no idea what would happen and so worried about the things you would at a time like that. My thoughts were not just with my family, I was also thinking of myself. I have an instinctive aversion to being arrested, beaten up or killed.

I rang my boss in London, Nick Pollard, who to his credit made no attempt whatsoever to persuade me one way or the other. After receiving his word that my family would be looked after if anything happened, I took a deep breath and made the call to Jakša.

'OK, how are we going to do this?'

He'd been pulling strings. He arranged with a certain Yugoslav ministry to get two cars to the Hungarian border. One was for me; the other was an unmarked police car. I showed up at the border a few hours later and bumped into several other media people, including an ITN cameraman, who had been waiting there for about two hours.

We stood at the Yugoslav side while the border guards rang down to Belgrade to see who would go across. I had a secret weapon called Jakša Šćekić, and so was the only one who was going to get the magic stamp in the passport.

The guards were not best pleased to see us. Given that it was planes and missiles from our countries which had been bombing them I understood why, but couldn't resist asking a cleaning lady, who was making them all coffee, if perhaps we could also have a cup. She spat invective towards me. I didn't really need a translation but one of the more friendly border guards was kind enough to tell me,

'She said "get your own fucking coffee".'

Fair enough, I thought, no worse than what my friends on the foreign desk say to me most days when I'm in London.

After about an hour I was waved through. The others began to complain, but the guards said they didn't have authority from Belgrade to let them enter. The car was an Audi 6 fitted with leather seats and a civil servant. The police car went ahead and we drove south towards Belgrade. As we neared Batjanica I noticed two Yugoslav MiG fighters jets parked in the middle of a ploughed field, covered in camouflage.

We'd already been pulled over a couple of times at checkpoints, but our police car and my civil servant got us through without difficulty. Things changed as we drove past the front gate of Batjanica military airbase which had been hit by a cruise missile the night before. A civilian car had got between our vehicle and the police escort, which meant the driver didn't notice an army unit waving us down. Before the civil servant could say anything a soldier had opened the passenger door, asked me a question, then pulled me out when I couldn't answer. I was pushed against the side of the vehicle but within seconds the civil servant intervened, the police car came back, and we were on our way again.

Jakša greeted me at the hotel, I checked in, went up to the bar on the eighth floor and the first person I saw was all 6 feet 3 inches of Julian Manyon. I'd met him before of course, perhaps seven or eight times. I'd seen him in London, in Baghdad, in Belgrade and the funny thing was, each time we met, he appeared not to have the faintest idea who I was and would say things like 'and what's your name?'

Strangely enough, this time he deigned to speak to me first, or rather to roar.

'You there! What the bloody hell do you mean by leaving my cameraman behind at the border?'

As a way of saying 'hello', this left a lot to be desired.

'Excuse me?' I replied.

He jabbed a finger towards my chest in true Belgrade style and boomed, 'You abandoned my bloody cameraman at the border, he had to make his own way back to Budapest without a bloody car!'

I asked if he was suggesting that I should have not bothered getting back into the country but instead accompanied his cameraman back to his hotel in Budapest?

'That's not what I'm suggesting at all!' he snapped. 'You should have taken him with you.'

'I'm not in charge of visa stamps at the Yugoslav border,' I said and walked off to get a drink. We hardly spoke for the next three months. Which was nice.

As the staff at the Hyatt had suggested, there were indeed about twelve Western reporters who'd stayed on, but each day a few more arrived. The army took over responsibility for us and the Radicals were ordered to leave us alone. Down at army headquarters near Republic Square, we were issued with 'war press cards'. To get them we had to sign a document saying pretty much that we wouldn't complain if we got killed covering the war. I found this rather reassuring. The getting killed bit was a little unsettling, but at least the piece of paper showed that there was a semblance of law and order about the way we were being treated.

More amusing were the permits to film. Each morning for the first few days we would fill out a yellow application form and wait for it to be turned down. Can we film bomb damage? No. Can we film an army unit? No. Can we go up on the roofs at night to try and film cruise missiles? No. Can we interview President Milošević? No, stop asking stupid questions.

Successful applications were made to film in a shopping street for half an hour between certain times. For the first few days that was about it. Eventually it all changed and we were allowed reasonable access. In the short term, we just did what we could, despite being confined within the city limits.

One morning we were out gathering street reaction to the bombing when a hostile crowd gathered round us. A few insults were thrown, then a few coins. It was getting more unpleasant by the minute. The less emotional among the crowd gave us interviews. Most were along the lines of 'How stupid are your leaders? Don't they know they have made Milošević even stronger?' Everyone we met, liberal, fascist, communist, said the same thing: 'Fuck NATO, fuck your leaders.' We knew very early on that the Serbs would not crumble easily, they never had done before. When a few people began spitting at us Veljko decided we should leave. It was frustrating, we were trying to convey the mood of the people to our viewers and to gauge the validity of some of the more outlandish claims the Yugoslavs were making, but it was an uphill battle. They were difficult days, but the weeks ahead would be both easier and harder in very different ways.

For the Kosovo Albanians things were getting very bad, very fast. Their treatment at the hands of Belgrade in the spring and summer of 1999 has been well documented and is a stain on Serbia's history. What is less known is the Serbian story of that time. They haven't even really written their own story yet. There's some stuff about how they took on nineteen countries and sort of didn't lose, and there is a lot of material about the politics of those years. Even now what is less documented is the ordinary lives lived in extraordinary circumstances, and the war crimes committed in their names. The few Serbs prepared to take on the challenge remain voices in the wilderness. What Serbia did has yet to be confronted by Serbians. Their actions are not comparable to the Nazis and I hesitate to equate the two. Nevertheless, while the majority of Germans eventually accepted their crimes in the Second World War, Austrians did not. Germany produced Helmut Kohl, Austria produced Kurt Waldheim. The Austrians, who have still to confront their past, chose a former high-ranking, Nazi SS officer as their president. Serbia never went through a root-and-branch peace and reconciliation process. Even so, their own story, from their own perspective, was a harrowing one, and in each death, it was as individually sad as anything that happened in Kosovo.

CHAPTER 9

'A time to love, and a time to hate,
A time for war, and a time for peace.'

Ecclesiastes 3:8

O N 17 APRIL 1999, AT 9.30 IN THE EVENING, THREE-YEAR-
old Milica Rakić was in the bathroom of her apartment on
Dimitrije Lazarev-Raša Street in Batajnica near Belgrade. She'd
already said she wanted to go to the toilet twice before, but
changed her mind. Her parents, Žarko and Dušica, were in the
living room along with her brother, nine-year-old Nikola. Since
24 March they usually gathered there because they'd boarded
the windows up, and so felt safer from bomb blasts. Like everyone else in the neighbourhood, they felt the explosions from the
nearby airbase rock their home almost every night.

NATO was making statements about the accuracy of its
smart bombs, but the population wasn't about to take the word
of the organization which was bombing it. For many the feeling
was, 'I might not like Milošević, but at least he never bombed
Belgrade; how crazy are these democracies?' The blast from the
missile came through the bathroom window. When Žarko and
Dušica recovered, they ran through to the bathroom. They saw
Milica lying in a pool of blood and broken glass.

According to Žarko's statement to the investigating judge,

Milica was still alive in the ambulance on the way to hospital. He'd gone with her and then waited as she was rushed to the operating theatre; he then collapsed, was given an injection and driven home. Once there, at 2 a.m., he was informed that his daughter had died. Four days later he swore an affidavit to investigating judge Pavao Vujasić and ended with these words: 'I am aware that no one can bring back my child, but I wish, although I know it is going to be difficult, that those who are guilty of this crime, whether directly, or indirectly, be punished no matter when. Therefore, I am prepared to make my statement at any time, and before any court or institution and to lodge an indemnification claim to such court or institution.'

Someone killed Žarko Rakić's daughter – he wants to know who. What parent wouldn't? The phrase 'accidents will happen' must ring a little hollow for him.

The missiles hit Jovan Radojičić and his wife Sofija at 9.30 p.m. as well, though it was a different night, 5 April. The couple, both in their seventies, were playing cards at their house in Dušana Trivunca Street, Aleksinac, central Serbia. A few houses down, Vukoman Djokic was with his wife when they both heard the sounds of the planes overhead. In a statement to Aleksinac Police Department he describes turning to his wife and saying, 'It's Aleksinac's turn now. They are surely going to bomb us.'

The sound of the planes' engines faded, then came back louder and louder, until they seemed to be on top of the house. NATO planes released seven bombs. Two hit the empty army barracks on the outskirts of town, the rest hit the town centre.

We got there at about two in the morning: myself, Jakša, Veljko and our soundman Milan Antić. A team from Mexican TV was also there along with a couple of Serbian reporters. It was fairly dark, but by torchlight and car headlights we could make out street after street of devastated buildings. Whole blocks of flats had their windows blown out, there were chunks of masonry all over the place, the windows of the cars were broken, and glass littered every surface.

We filmed what we could, phoned in a couple of reports to Sky and waited for light. It was quite a scene. In the road behind the blocks of flats at least twelve residential houses had been flattened. The result was ten deaths and fifty-two injuries. Among the fatalities were Jovan and Sofija.

We clambered over the ruins of their house, stumbling on bits of brick and pieces of furniture. Local residents emerged from their basements, or the ruins of their houses, and stared at us. Many of them were clearly in shock. I looked at Jovan, or what was left of him. Then, I had no idea who he was, or even if he was male or female. His body had been crushed by falling masonry. Parts of him oozed out of the slabs of concrete. One metre away sat his wife, upright in her chair, a card still in her hand. Her autopsy report concluded that it was 'a case of violent death by suffocation . . . the result of the house collapsing in the bomb explosion'.

All the police reports of the night quote witnesses describing the screams of those in the rubble, and the shock of people running in the darkened streets. Slobodan Sekulović lived in one of the damaged flats overlooking Dušana Trivunca Street. He testified to the Municipal Court two weeks later that 'the scene was horrific and it cannot and will never be forgotten . . . I remember my granddaughter couldn't understand how a house made of bricks could be blown away, since this wasn't possible in a tale for children she had read'. NATO had huffed and puffed and blown down ten lives. Collateral damage.

The Yugoslavs say that based on radio intercepts, the planes which attacked Aleksinac were British. The British Ministry of Defence says the RAF was not in action over the town that night.

Varvarin was different. In most of the mistakes NATO made when they killed civilians, you could argue that they were trying hard not to.

In Varvarin, the planes attacked the town's small, crowded bridge at 12.53 p.m. on market day. Fourteen minutes later they came back and did it again. From what we saw, it really looked as if they weren't trying hard enough not to kill people. All the spy satellites, forward air controllers, drone aircraft, pilots, targeters and intelligence officers seemed to have missed the fact that the bridge was crowded with people at the time. There were no sirens, and no warnings, just a sudden roar overhead as two planes screamed along the Morava River, then the explosions, and the sounds of part of the bridge collapsing into the water.

Several people died or were injured in the first attack. Fifteen-year-old Sanja Milenković was blown into the water but was unhurt. She began crawling up the riverbank to help friends who were lying injured on the remainder of the bridge. People rushed to help the dead and dying, emergency first aid was given, the authorities began to arrive. According to eyewitnesses, the planes came back at 1.07 p.m.

The second missile strike killed and injured more people. Among the dead was a priest, Father Milivoje Ćirić, who had emerged from a church service after the first blast to try and assist those on the bridge.

Sanja was hit in the back by shrapnel. Her father helped to load her into the ambulance and encouraged her to fight for life, but she closed her eyes. As her father said, 'I knew it was for the last time.'

I stood at the end of the road in Varvarin, stared down at the bridge and wondered why, in 1999, NATO didn't have the equipment, technology or just plain common sense to bomb the target at one in the morning, instead of one in the afternoon. The bridge had been too narrow for a tank to cross, and there was a bigger bridge 2 miles upriver, which was left untouched. I was told by NATO sources later that it was hit because it had a fibre-optic communication link running through it.

To the right was a hotel, which had been badly damaged; behind us was the church.

After a few seconds I realized I was standing in a pool of liquid. I bent down, and touched it, and saw the dark red spread across my finger. I noticed a small bone, like the wishbone of a chicken, lying in the wet. I moved a respectful distance away and then went up to the morgue along with a couple of dozen other correspondents.

Looking at corpses was a necessary function of the job we were doing then. The Serbs were making ridiculous propaganda claims, so it was necessary to see the evidence. Father Milivoje's headless body was on the front slab; next to him was a man whose leg was blown off. It had been placed alongside him, but upside down, so that his foot was next to his hip. There is very little dignity in the body of someone who has died a violent death, but it still seemed wrong not to at least place the limb in the correct position. There were twelve corpses.

Sanja's body was still at the hospital. She'd gone for a walk on market day, telling her mother not to worry.

'Don't be crazy, Mum. Who's going to drop bombs on a small town?'

It is thought the pilots were from the United States air force. Whoever it was didn't try hard enough not to cause 'collateral damage'.

The handful of trees just before the railway bridge outside the village of Grdelica bore strange fruit on 12 April. Pieces of burnt and twisted metal were lodged in the bark, strips of crimson flesh hung from the branches. There was a familiar smell in the air. Few of us spoke as we climbed up the embankment towards the remains of the three-carriage passenger train, which had been crossing the bridge at 11.40 that morning. It had left Grdelica three minutes earlier. The bridge crosses a small river, which runs through fields, heading out into the countryside proper. The nearest houses are perhaps 200 yards away.

Sixty-eight-year-old Petar Mihajlović was in the middle carriage. He'd left Belgrade that morning in order to avoid the bombing campaign, which was intensifying in and around the capital. He felt he'd be safer in the countryside and was travelling down to a summer house his family owned in southern Serbia. The first USAF plane arrived at such speed that one survivor described it as making a 'piercing, hissing noise'. Immediately, another plane dived in and fired two missiles. The first hit the front part of the bridge; the second hit the middle carriage of the train. A road bridge a few hundred yards upriver was also attacked. In his testimony to the investigating judge, Petar Mihajlović said: 'For a while I was not completely conscious and through a kind of mist I saw chaos all around me. I was in a destroyed carriage with only its skeleton left. Suddenly a young man was beside me offering help.' They got out just in time. All three carriages were on fire, survivors spoke of hearing the screams of those inside.

Twenty-eight-year-old Jasmina Veljković may have been one of them, or she may have already been dead. The explosion had torn off her left arm and she lay in one of the carriages as the flames swept through them. Her autopsy report concluded: 'Violent death, the result of the brain and all the vital centres in it being destroyed.' Her relatives, who had seen her off at the station, identified her because they recognized an unburnt fragment of the dark brown leather jacket she had put on that morning.

Twelve bodies were identified, five were so disfigured that identification was impossible. Three people were missing, sixteen were injured. A few days later NATO, which apologized for the tragedy, issued cockpit footage of the attack. In Brussels, spokesman Jamie Shea pointed out the speed at which the train came on to the bridge; it was so fast, he said, that the pilots couldn't abort their mission. Even at the time this seemed odd. Not only did the film look too jerky, but also trains in Serbia rarely moved anywhere at speed, especially having just pulled out of a small village station three minutes previously. After a few more days NATO admitted another mistake. When officials had transferred the cockpit footage on to video to release to the media, somehow it had been played at triple speed.

I left the scene after a few minutes and made my way to the nearest house. The mobile phones didn't work in this rural area, and the battery on my satellite phone had faded so I was looking for some mains power.

An elderly couple was sweeping up the broken glass and debris from the blast, which had shaken their home. Their clock had stopped at exactly 11.40 a.m. They had no electricity because the attack on the road bridge had cut power to the whole village, including its medical centre.

These were the type of stories the Serbian public was receiving day after day. They heard little about the slaughter in Kosovo, and from their perspective they were once again the plucky little fighting nation standing up against aggression.

There were several hundred other examples of civilian deaths. The cluster bombing of the city centre in Niš, the casualties from hitting schools, hospitals, monasteries, churches, television buildings, factories and oil refineries. The Yugoslav military and political machines managed to protect themselves and emerged from the war more or less intact, but there was little they could do to safeguard the civilian populations. In certain cases they endangered them. On several occasions troops and equipment were hidden in schools or placed next to hospitals. That meant NATO could not legally attack those targets. Article 50 of the Geneva Conventions makes that clear, but Belgrade encouraged NATO to break the law, and after the first couple of weeks of bombing, when the air campaign was clearly having little effect, NATO didn't need too much encouragement.

Some of the other Serb defensive tactics were less reprehensible; in fact, some of them were ingenious.

CHAPTER 10

*'The height of cleverness
is to be able to conceal it.'*

François de La Rochefoucauld

O N THE MORNING OF 24 MARCH, GENERAL NEBOJŠA
Pavković was a nervous man. The Yugoslavian high command had been told by a spy inside NATO that 'Operation
Allied Force' would begin at nightfall. Pavković was out inspect-
ing his troops. As commander-in-chief of the Yugoslav Third
Army, based in Kosovo, he had to make sure everything was
in place.

Belgrade had been planning for this moment for almost
as long as NATO had. The Alliance blueprints for bombing
Yugoslavia were mostly drawn up in the late spring of 1998, but
the defence of Yugoslavia was part of a strategy much longer
in the making. It had been conceived during the Cold War, and
it had also been rehearsed. The best equipment began to be
moved into a network of secure underground bunkers. Planes,
computers and radar systems were hidden deep below the surface. The bunkers were built to withstand a nuclear blast of
medium strength. Saddam Hussein was so impressed by their
quality that he commissioned several for Iraq and referred to
them as 'my Yugo bunkers'.

Between January and March 1999, senior officers had visited Iraq, Ukraine, Russia and Belarus in a partially successful attempt to upgrade their air defence systems, buy cheap oil and get cash advances to sustain the coming war effort. Alternative lines of communication were put into place, and by January, military units in Kosovo had been put onto 'random order movement' to confuse the American spy satellites and drone aircraft.

In February, sympathetic former Yugoslav officers in Slovenia and Macedonia had fed NATO agents with misinformation on tactics, and Belgrade had begun constructing plastic decoy aeroplanes and tanks.

Pavković knew the Yugoslav military had done a professional job; nevertheless, he was still nervous. Richard Holbrooke had told Milošević that the air strikes would be 'sustained' but other information leaking out of Brussels and passed to an agent in the Paris embassy suggested it would be a short campaign. No one in Belgrade, or for that matter in the Western countries, knew for sure.

At least Pavković, along with the rest of the high command, did have NATO's list of targets. A few months earlier a French army officer, Pierre-Henri Bunel, who was working at NATO headquarters in Brussels, had leaked them to Yugoslav secret service agent Jovan Milanović.

Bunel said later he was acting on orders from French intelligence. If that is true then French President Jacques Chirac either sanctioned the betrayal of allied military secrets, or was unaware of what his intelligence chiefs were up to.

Pavković's mobile phone rang. On the line was a British intelligence agent calling from a number in Brussels.

'General Pavković?'

'Yes, who is this?'

'I represent the people who are going to bomb you. I appeal to your good sense, please, even now you can stop what will happen. If you begin to pull your troops out of Kosovo today, we can still prevent the bombing.'

The man calling knew it was a hopeless demand. Pavković was a career officer tasked with defending his country. To ignore orders from Belgrade, and begin moving troops, would have been tantamount to treason. The general hit the 'end call' button, put the phone in his pocket, and carried on with his inspection.

When the first of that night's fifty or so missiles struck, the barracks were empty, the airfields mostly clear, the radars hidden, the vehicles camouflaged and the dummy targets in position. It went on like that for seventy-eight days and nights. By the end of it just thirteen tanks, a few radars and a handful of artillery pieces had been destroyed.

The camouflage operation was used all over the country. The Straževica hill near Belgrade housed a major radar complex. It had been built during Tito's regime by a Croatian firm and was designed to withstand nuclear attack. NATO's planes hit it several times and smashed the barracks on the surface, but the complex itself wasn't even scratched. Every time they knocked down the radar antenna, the Serbs rushed out and erected another. Much of the deception was an open secret. Maya Ćivić a civilian, was a keen cyclist and each day on her 20-mile-long rides she could see what NATO was looking for.

'Some of the anti-aircraft guns were placed on the top of apartment blocks in New Belgrade. We used to bring coffee to the guys manning them. In the fields along the Sava river there were choppers and tanks under camouflage, but there were loads of civilian buildings around there and I was furious that the government felt that we were just pawns in all this.'

Not everyone was hiding. At 8.10 p.m., as the early warning system picked up the first enemy jets entering Yugoslav airspace, Captain Zoran Radosavljević scrambled his MiG-29 fighter jet from Batajnica airfield. Accompanied by two other MiGs, he headed north to meet them.

He knew that neither the radar nor the radio on his jet was functioning. This, in combat terms, left him effectively blind. The days of the eyeball-to-eyeball dogfight in the sky had long gone; he probably never even saw the jet that killed him. The missile that blew him out of the air was launched from several miles' distance.

Why did he go up? He was under orders. He was also a top gun, which means he had enough experience to know that he was on a mission which could not succeed. That night there were between twenty and twenty-six NATO planes in the skies – they were from the Dutch and US air forces and everything on board their aircraft worked. A satellite may have picked up his movement from the runway, an AWACS plane will have certainly spotted him on the radar once he was in the air, and the Dutch and American pilots will have tracked him as he came within their range.

A Yugoslav air force contact said, 'You can call him a hero, or a fool. It's up to you.'

The experts knew they couldn't win a war against NATO; all they could do was try not to lose it. A journalist, then working at the independent B92 radio station, met two military intelligence officers a week into the bombing: 'We went to the Cafe Ruski Czar near work. They were in plain clothes and were friendly but they were at the end of their tether. First they talked about my work at the radio station and told me they didn't consider it unpatriotic, then they asked my views on the situation. Remember there were no foreign diplomats in town, so they had limited access to alternative views. I told them: "You will lose this war. The only way out is to find an honourable negotiated settlement as soon as possible." They said to me, in a sort of desperate way, "We know, we proposed the same, but were flatly rejected by the man at the top." "So now what?" I asked. "Nothing, we will try and save as many people as we can, and try and defend ourselves."'

Milošević's attitude led what were described as 'a few good men near the top of the regime' to try to save the country by feeling their way towards negotiations. Unreported, and virtually unnoticed, they travelled to Sofia, Vienna and Bucharest for negotiations with third parties and occasionally with the British, Germans and Americans. They included some senior people from the Foreign Ministry and a handful of directors from large companies.

At the time Aleksandar Vučić from the Radical Party was Serbian Minister for Information. He later told me that Milošević didn't really have a game plan. 'Slobodan Milošević seemed to be just hanging on for one more day, every day. He didn't know what to do during the war. At the beginning and at the end, some of his high-ranking officers were trying to persuade him to do a deal.'

A couple of weeks into the war I was approached by a Yugoslav cabinet minister and asked what I thought the outcome would be. I told him I didn't know exactly how things would happen, but that one way or another, NATO would not allow itself to lose. 'Look at it this way,' I said. 'You might think Yugoslavia is a really important strategic nation, but for the big NATO countries you're just a small, irritating pimple and they'd rather you didn't cause an outbreak of acne in the region. NATO is now committed, its reputation and future as an organization is at stake, its leaders will do whatever it takes until you surrender.'

I think a lot of people at the top accepted that line of thinking. Most people believe that Milošević's idea of strategy was to stumble from one crisis to the next, trying to buy himself time with short-term solutions to long-term problems. That would explain some of the ideas he came up with in early April. A Yugoslav army source says Milošević wanted to widen the war into Bosnia and Macedonia: 'He asked for US troops in both countries to be attacked. But we needed the assistance of the Bosnian Serb leadership for an operation against a US barracks in Bosnia. Some of the leadership was by now pro-American, and the others were still angry with Milošević because they felt he'd sold them down the river at Dayton. So they got their revenge and refused to help. By the time that was sorted out, we'd managed to talk to the president and make the argument that we shouldn't risk going into Macedonia, and later on that we shouldn't risk attacking the Apache helicopters and troops arriving in Albania. The politicians agreed that taking the war over the borders would alienate neighbouring countries which at the time were actually helping us by being open to trade and turning a blind eye to smuggling.'

With nine MiGs shot down and limited ground options available, desperate measures were undertaken. Perhaps none so desperate as that of the chief of the air force, Lieutenant Ljubiša Veličković.

His contribution came after public support for continued resistance began to crumble. Once NATO began targeting the civilian infrastructure of the country, everyday living became even tougher. Gas, water and electricity supplies were switched off by the bombing. So many bridges were down that travel was difficult. In Novi Sad, people were using barges to cross the Danube, something they hadn't done since the Middle Ages. Hundreds of civilians had been killed.

The Serbs were now concentrating on deception and ground-to-air defence. They knew if they could just shoot down a few more planes, NATO pilots might be forced even higher than the 15,000 feet they routinely flew at. But to hit them, you had to see them, and in modern warfare, that meant 'painting' them with a radar beam. The problem was that over the past few weeks, bitter experience had taught the Yugoslavs that turning a radar on for more than three seconds risked the radar installation being blown up by NATO missiles. Nevertheless, Belgrade needed a success.

General Veličković held a meeting at a command post and proposed a tour of air defence locations. He concluded with the words: 'OK, I'm going to do it, anyone want to come with me?'

A senior army officer, who was present, says his commanding officer excused himself on the genuine grounds that he was exhausted, a decision which saved his life. A colonel went with Veličković accompanied by the general's driver. They went up to an anti-aircraft/radar site next to the Pančevo oil refinery near Belgrade.

The general entered a large mobile radar unit, a container mounted on a truck, which could be moved at speed. He ordered the radar to be switched on. The operators were silent but reluctantly obeyed. They already knew there were twenty-six planes above them. After three seconds one of the operators began to say, 'General, we—' He was cut short.

'Keep it on.' Veličković needed a few more seconds to lock onto a NATO jet and get a missile away. After six seconds several of the soldiers in the unit got up from their chairs in front of the bank of screens, and after another second they began running out of the container. Two seconds later the missiles struck the container. Veličković died along with the colonel. A warrant officer was among the injured and he later died of his wounds. The general's driver was among the survivors.

A civilian with contacts at high levels in the army takes up the story: 'I remember that night. We heard the explosions and I was listening to Radio Pančevo. The mayor came on saying there had been an attack but, unusually, he didn't say what had been hit, if it was the oil refinery or whatever. They usually came back on within a few hours or even minutes to say what it was. A few days later a rumour went round that some arrogant officer had insisted a radar was switched on and had got himself and others killed. Then it was announced that the general had died. It was only later we found out the real circumstances, I tell you, that man died a hero.' As with Captain Radosavljević: 'A hero or a fool. You decide for yourself.'

An army officer who was at the meeting when Veličković decided to go believes the general's pride got the better of him: 'Earlier some of the army generals had been teasing him. "Hey Veličković," they joked. "Where's your air force? Where's your air defence?" I think he took it too seriously.'

It wasn't all failures and futile gestures on the Yugoslav side. Two NATO planes, both American, were shot down, including, early on in the campaign, an F-117 stealth fighter. The Stealth was 'Sambushed'. On the night of 27 March Captain Ken Dwelle of the US air force had been flying alone for several hours when he appeared a few miles north of Belgrade and readied himself for his bombing run. He maintained radio silence and dropped his speed to 500 miles per hour when suddenly the warning lights began to flash; surface-to-air missiles, or 'SAMs' were on their way up. The F-117 was supposed to be 'invisible' to radar, and the Yugoslavs knew about the problems of switching their equipment on. Nevertheless, somehow they knew the Stealth was coming. The air defence soldiers fired thirty SAMs into its path. One hit the jet, and at that moment there was no way out. An anti-aircraft gunner, Dušan Berdić, saw the plane the moment the SAM hit it, and gave this account in a Sky News documentary:

'There was a big fireball, falling, it fell for about a minute. The moment we saw it we all opened up on it, maybe twenty guns around the field we were dug into. We cut it in half. At that moment we all cheered and said "Yes!" but, well, later you think maybe the pilot has a family. My personal opinion is that he had no chance to survive. I don't know if they rescued him, I don't think so, although we did hear a lot of helicopters that night, in fact not only that night.'

As soon as Dwelle put out a Mayday call, several American AH-64 helicopters scrambled from a location in neighbouring Bosnia. They were full of US Rangers and their job was to rescue Dwelle.

At the same time, the elite Yugoslav Cobra Brigade was rushing to the scene. Each side was desperate to get Dwelle before the other. According to the Americans the Cobra was beaten to the prize by a few precious minutes. A Yugoslav army captain, specializing in military equipment, was on duty when the news came in that the plane had been downed: 'I was in an underground bunker when the loudspeakers began blaring "We have hit one!" When I saw the first pictures I said, "If that's a jet fighter then I'm an old woman", then I looked more closely and said, "Hang on. It's a Stealth!"'

The media arrived at the site in the morning. The Yugoslavs were not about to pass up the opportunity to demonstrate their firepower.

We dragged our equipment over ploughed fields near the village of Budjanovci until we came upon the wreckage. In most countries the whole area would have been sealed off, but this was Serbia. This meant that every child in the neighbourhood had rushed out to see the fallen wonder from America, and were climbing all over the twisted metal and tangle of wires. Proud parents stood in their muddy boots watching as a boy, about six years old, carried his plastic gun onto the wing of the F-117 and began to wave it at the foreign journalists while giving the Serbian three-fingered victory sign. A local farmer decided he needed a souvenir. Taking a knife from his belt he carved a bit off the wing. Soon the whole village, aided and abetted by some of the media, attacked the plane as if it were a roast chicken. I couldn't bring myself to do this, but was secretly pleased when a colleague gave me a little bit of history to hold. It was about two inches by one inch, a strange piece of metal the likes of which I had never seen before. It was about a centimetre thick and the inside was a fine honeycomb of criss-crossed metal and fibres. I've still got it in a desk at home. If the US air force wants it back, they only have to write and ask. I worry that it might glow in the dark.

Within a few days postcards and T-shirts appeared on sale in Belgrade depicting a Stealth and bearing the now legendary phrase: 'We're sorry, we didn't know it was invisible.' These were snapped up by Belgraders on their way to the daily anti-NATO rock concerts in Republic Square. At about the same time a Russian 'trade' delegation showed up in Belgrade. Its real purpose was to take a look at this 'futuristic' American technology that had fallen into the hands of Belgrade. They went away with a few pieces and a degree of disappointment. This was first-generation Stealth technology. The Russians were concentrating on developing anti-stealth weapons and wanted access to the more recent equipment the Americans were making. They did want the 'black box' flight recorder and opened negotiations with Belgrade. These faltered when the Russians would not pay the asking price, which was military assistance.

The Chinese took a different view. They were years behind Moscow and Washington and here was a SAM-sent opportunity to catch up. Many analysts suggest that parts of the Stealth made their way to Beijing; however, a Yugoslav intelligence source denies this. Some of it is definitely in the Yugoslav Aerospace Museum, other bits are in children's toy boxes around Budjanovci and one piece is in my front room.

The Stealth incident was a rare but real success. Several Yugoslav sources suggest that another Stealth came down in Bosnia and that a third had to make a forced landing in Zagreb. There are also persistent rumours that at least one US air force pilot was captured and then handed over when US envoy Jesse Jackson came to Belgrade to negotiate the release of three captured US servicemen. There is no hard evidence for any of this.

Apart from the Stealth and the shooting down of an F-16 fighter, the Yugoslav's other 'hits' were, for NATO, pinpricks, albeit expensive ones. Twenty-one pilotless drones were destroyed. On one occasion the Yugoslav air force brought one down by flying alongside it in a helicopter while a soldier used a mounted machine gun to blaze away at it through an open side door. Dozens of cruise missiles were hit, most of them during daylight when they could be seen. The tactics were simple. The air defence teams left them alone until they were into their final trajectories and then opened up with their Bofors anti-aircraft guns, which fired hundreds of rounds per minute into the path of the incoming missile.

Against the jets, the ground teams sometimes fired cheap missiles (they are called 'bait') at where they thought the planes were. They knew they had no chance of hitting them, but it caused NATO pilots to fire off anti-missile missiles, and take more time to home in on their targets. On occasion this gave the aircraft's position away, allowing the anti-aircraft gunners to pour fire towards them. Technicians had modified some of the Yugoslav SAM-6 batteries by removing their Russian-made radar systems and installing a type of closed-circuit television system. This allowed them to fire off a SAM and then guide it towards the light emitted by the jet's engines by using a joystick and a TV monitor. This then meant the pilot couldn't lock onto the source of the missile, and also gave the Yugoslavs a picture of the skies.

Even that low-tech approach was sophisticated compared to that used by Serbia's farmers. Every agricultural village in the country has a radio link with a weather station. It alerts farmers to the danger of hailstorms, which can destroy their crops. The farmers fire small 'anti-hail missiles' which emit a chemical which breaks up the hail into rain. It was a simple task to link the farmers, the radio contacts, the missiles and the military. Within days of the war breaking out, farmers all over Serbia were enthusiastically firing their little missiles up towards NATO's jets. It had probably never been done before, and it was an unusual air defence system. It had a limited effect, but occasionally would make a pilot abort a bombing run and return to base.

There were some very strange machines in the air. On day five of the war the Yugoslav air defence system picked up three small planes flying in the Vojvodina region and throwing out a white dust cloud. The on-duty officer at the radar system headquarters says he informed his commanding officer: 'He in turn contacted the NBC [Nuclear Biological Chemical] chief who began to calculate how long it would be before this cloud reached Belgrade. I asked a reconnaissance unit to check the reports. They phoned back and said, "Yes there is a cloud, but it's coming from three agricultural planes". I reported to my boss that three stupid Serb farmers were out spraying their crops. It's amazing that NATO didn't shoot them down.'

The Yugoslavs were also listening to almost all of the NATO pilots' cockpit communications. One afternoon the information minister, Goran Matić, 'invited' me for tea at his large, gloomy mansion up in the exclusive Dedinje suburb of Belgrade. First, though, he gave me a test. He took me outside for a brief walk, ending up at a junior school. It was quiet because all schools had been closed due to the bombing.

'Look,' he said, pointing at two army communication trucks, hidden beneath camouflage, and parked underneath a slight overhang of the school hall. I politely reminded him that this was forbidden under the Geneva Convention. He, less politely, reminded me that bombing factories, hospitals, apartment blocks and electricity supplies was also forbidden, then reminded me that NATO had broken its own constitution by attacking a sovereign state which was not threatening a NATO member.

There wasn't much point in arguing that equipment was also hidden in the factories and hospitals. Anyway, I believe he showed me the trucks to see if I would either report their presence on air, or pass the information on to 'interested parties'. I did neither, as both could be classified as spying. Three days later, having passed the test, I was back having tea. This time Matić took me out onto a veranda looking down into Belgrade.

'Mmm,' he said. He began most sentences with this. 'Mmm, Tim, you know we can hear everything the pilots say?'

I asked how, and he waved a hand in the vague direction of Belgrade.

'Mmm, we have so many civilians listening in on short wave as well as our official equipment, all these people out here, they are calling us day and night with what they pick up.'

At the time I was sceptical, but it later transpired that NATO was communicating on open, unencrypted lines, in English. English is the official NATO language for combat operations; it's also the second language of many highly educated people in Belgrade, and the other major Serbian cities. The Americans had a secure encrypted digital system, but all the other air forces were a decade behind them. As most of the air raids were joint operations, the Americans were forced to use the open system. Even worse, for NATO, the Yugoslavs appeared to know the targets and their code words in advance. This suggests that the flow of information to Belgrade did not stop with the arrest of Pierre-Henri Bunel shortly before bombing started. In fact it only dried up once access to the target list and code words was cut from 600 personnel to 100. After the war, the Americans wanted to know exactly why 600 people needed to know in the first place. They received the answer that representatives of all member countries needed to be told, in order for it to be a partnership of at least educated equals. They still wanted to know why that meant 600 people, and concluded that they wouldn't bother with NATO on something they took 100 per cent seriously. Like Afghanistan. The US military, and to a lesser extent the politicians, hated doing 'war by committee'.

NATO's make-up ensures that the Supreme Allied Commander is an American. There is no way they are handing that power to anyone else. The political leader can be, and is, a European, but the power from the barrel of a gun remains with Washington. The Kosovo War may have safeguarded NATO's immediate future by giving an answer to the often-asked question: 'What is NATO for in the post-Cold War world?' But the war in Afghanistan appears to suggest that NATO only has a small, possibly geographically defined role; it had wanted a global one. Even during the Kosovo War, the Americans didn't play by NATO's rules in the first few days of the conflict. One of the NATO ambassadors from a major European power later said: 'General Wesley Clark didn't tell us about certain things. Of course we knew about them from other sources. We demanded that he must go through the correct procedures, we argued that if not, it would be difficult to forge a political policy direction.'

That was one of the occasional problems at the political level, but at the military level NATO was having problems on an almost hourly basis.

On several occasions NATO pilots used the code words for specific targets as they moved in for the kill, and the targets were immediately moved. If 600 people at NATO had access to the target list, it's no surprise that Belgrade had access to it as well, and that they used it to play NATO at a deadly game of 'Now you see me, now you don't'.

What were left in place were the hundreds of wooden rocket launchers, plastic tanks and dummy planes. NATO hit all sorts of things, but little of it belonged to the Yugoslav army.

On the outbreak of war, Predrag Ristić was drafted into the army as an anti-aircraft gunner and sent to Kosovo. He gave the following story in a documentary for Sky News: 'One day we were in a little village near Podujevo and there was a tractor with a pipe for spreading silage. A spy plane was overhead and it watched as we pushed the tractor into a barn, they probably thought it was a tank. We moved to some nearby houses and then counted as NATO dropped fifty-three bombs on that building.'

The elite Yugoslav units in Kosovo had spent a few days, each side of 24 March, smashing the KLA. Pockets of resistance were left, but it wasn't until NATO's air campaign began in earnest that the KLA was an effective force again. Some MUP units were involved in rounding up the Kosovars and forcing them out of the province. The heavy armour was already hidden, and bit-by-bit the rest of the forces joined them in bunkers, woods, hills and a variety of buildings.

We were allowed into Kosovo a few weeks later. The authorities checked we'd signed our 'don't blame us if you get killed' papers, put about forty of us on a double-decker coach and drove us down to the province. There were few other vehicles on the road. About 50 miles north of Priština, a MUP armoured personnel carrier appeared in front of us, and then another behind. On top of each was a mounted machine gun and gunner. They constantly swung round, scouring each side of the road in case of KLA sniper fire. This almost amounted to a convoy, which, in Kosovo equalled a target. I was more concerned about a NATO air strike on the coach than sniper fire.

Before we'd entered the province one of our British colleagues had phoned NATO and asked them not to bomb a coach if they saw it on the road. Given the number of mistakes being made I thought this was the height of folly. There is only two letters' difference between 'don't' and 'do'. There was a joke doing the rounds at the time: A US pilot over Yugoslavia radios in for target instructions. 'Bomb Kragujevac' comes the order. 'Where?' says the pilot. 'Kragujevac' says the man at base, again pronouncing this difficult place name wrongly. 'Where?' says the pilot. 'Kragu . . . ah, forget it,' says the controller, 'just bomb Niš'.

For almost an hour, the only people we saw were small units of police at makeshift roadblocks. There were well over 100,000 troops in the region, thousands of artillery pieces and hundreds of tanks, but they had almost vanished. Northern Kosovo had a majority Serb population so most of the houses were undamaged. Some locals had painted Serb symbols on their homes to make sure they were left alone by the ethnic cleansers. Just outside Priština we rounded a corner and drove past an oil depot, which had been hit a few hours earlier and was burning out of control. Dense clouds of black smoke rose into the mid-morning air. We wanted to stop and film, but the army 'minders' refused.

It may have been a sunny day, but as we drove into the suburbs above town, we entered the twilight zone. The city was completely quiet, the streets were empty. A few dogs lolled around the broken shopfronts. The retail premises had mostly been smashed and looted, their contents spilling out into the road; pieces of cloth, discarded food and empty boxes lay amid the broken glass. That day, in a town that had housed 200,000 people – the majority of them Kosovar Albanians – we saw about fifty civilians. In the smaller streets we noticed police and army vehicles, and men in a variety of uniforms. Not all of them looked as if they were in regular units; some of them were young, wearing bandannas, sunglasses and as many weapons of death as they could carry without falling over. Rambo was in town. This went on all the way into the centre. Here too the streets were empty but the scene changed. The damage was not from the Serb forces, but from NATO's bombs.

The multi-storey post office, a department store, a government building and about twenty houses were in ruins. The windows in several streets were blown out, and the skeletons of still-smouldering cars lay scattered around. In the distance we could see the black smoke still billowing out from the oil depot.

We got out and began filming, and putting questions to the Priština authorities.

'Where are the people?'

'They are hiding in case of a NATO attack.'

'What, all 200,000 of them?'

'Yes.'

This fanciful explanation was almost as stupid as one given a few weeks earlier, when the Serbs were denying that hundreds of thousands of Kosovar civilians were pouring into Macedonia. The information minister, Goran Matić, had actually said into our microphones: 'They are not refugees, they are actors, paid by NATO to walk round and round in circles to make it look as if there are large numbers of them.' He didn't even blush.

We inspected the ruins, many of which were still in flames. Sparks flew, and the wood cracked as we ventured through them. We were supposed to stay together and be watched by the minders, but there were four of them and forty of us. Veljko, Milan and I slipped away into an undamaged street of apartment blocks.

'Are you crazy? Are you animals?'

The questions rained on my head from three storeys up.

Three women had gathered on their balcony and were pouring down invective.

Holding a variety of babies and toddlers in their arms, they screamed that Clinton and Blair were war criminals, and demanded to know how NATO's leaders could drop high explosives onto a residential area. The city had been bombed almost every night for weeks and for long periods was without water or electricity. Many missiles had missed their target. A few had smashed into the Orthodox cemetery on the outskirts of town. I counted about twelve wrecked graves; the bones of the occupants were lying in the earth.

One woman was so angry she could barely speak, another was crying, the third shouted at me in Serbian. This was not the time to engage in a debate about the rights or wrongs of NATO actions.

We filmed them for a couple of minutes, they refused a request for us to come up and speak with them, and so we moved on. After a while we were back on the main street. About 200 yards down the main thoroughfare I noticed the large frame of the BBC's John Simpson. For a portly figure, he was going at a fair pace. A hundred yards behind him was ITN's Julian Manyon, who had broken into a trot. The thought hit me immediately: 'The Grand Hotel!'

The Serbs were still preventing us from using our satellite phones on the grounds that we might use them to call in air strikes. Mobile phones didn't work, and the phone system in Priština had been taken down by the bombing. This meant we would have to wait perhaps eight hours to report what we'd seen. Simpson and Manyon both had the same idea at the same time. If anyone could get a phone to work here, it was the Grand Hotel.

I asked Veljko and Milan to carry on filming, and broke into a run. I'd given my fellow Britons a head start, and I was handicapped by my back problems, but then again I was ten years younger than them, so it was a fair race.

Priština's main street is very long. After about a minute I had them in my sights. Manyon was catching Simpson, and I was catching them both. After two minutes, as we were rounding the curve leading to the Grand, I was within 50 yards of the competition. Simpson and Manyon made it through the hotel doors at the same time, with me about ten seconds behind.

As I puffed my way in, they were both talking animatedly at the front desk. There the reception clerk was shaking his head and explaining that their phones were also out. Simpson wouldn't take this for an answer. I watched in admiration as he picked up the reception phone and hit the buttons a few times. Then he went round to the public phone by the lift and did the same thing. He gave up and we retired to the bar, which happily, was working, had electricity, and cold beers.

Naturally, Jakša had scooped all of us. As we raced through the streets, he had calmly walked round to a friend's house. There were individual phones, which were somehow routed through lines which weren't down.

He phoned through to Sky and gave the first live eyewitness report of conditions in Priština.

On my way back up to the coach I noticed that my favourite restaurant in town had been burnt to the ground. It had been two things: a very good place to eat pasta, and an Albanian-owned business. The quality of the food wasn't enough to save it from the criminals in uniform who destroyed it. I hooked up with Jakša and the crew, got back on the coach and we made our way across some train tracks towards the graveyard. I was sitting next to a well-known British news-paper journalist, a man I liked and whose work I respected. We noticed, about 80 yards away, a group of perhaps ten civilians walking away from us along the tracks. They looked as if they might have been gypsies and were carrying bundles of some-thing, possibly clothes. We saw them for around eight seconds. Two days later I read the online version of the reporter's trip to Priština, and was interested to see that the unknown group had turned into 'a group of Kosovar Albanian refugees fleeing Serb brutality'. From our fleeting glance, I had no idea who they were or what they were doing.

The graveyard was a mess, and to the Serbs an atrocity. Any culture would have been angry about a cemetery being bombed. But the Serbs take these things more seriously than many. When thousands of Bosnian Serb civilians left Sarajevo in 1995, many dug up the remains of their relatives, took them with them and re-buried them, so that future generations would know where their ancestors lay. The NATO officials will have known they made a mistake hitting a graveyard, but they will not have known just how much anger the mistake caused.

The minders rounded us up; they wanted us out well before dark, as that was when the planes usually came back. Most of the PR officials were OK. After an uneasy start, we had devel-oped a working relationship. Not all of them were what you would call 'regime people'. The most popular was Vesna, a former journalist. One day she showed up at army headquar-ters wearing full camouflage uniform. She took such a ribbing from the media that she never put it on again. Vesna was with us as we set off for the eight-hour journey back to Belgrade. The coach was packed, hot, sweaty and full of cigarette smoke. As it got dark, some of the journalists and photographers fell asleep; others were writing their reports or looking through their photographs. Somewhere north of the city of Niš, a massive lightning storm broke out. We drove up the deserted motorway in heavy rain with the whole skyline to our left lit up by the flickering of forked lightning. I had never seen, or heard, a storm like it. The thunder was immense, great cracking noises followed by rumbling, which went on for seven or eight seconds. To add to the sense of drama we could see heavy anti-aircraft fire going up to our right where the storm had not yet reached. It was like driving through a tunnel of both man-made and natural fury.

NATO hit a military target near Niš that night, but it was also busy bombing plastic, as it did every night. Two companies in Western Europe built dummy military targets. International sanctions meant Belgrade couldn't buy them on the open market, but a few had found their way into Yugoslavia. They didn't have enough and so the military went to a civilian company near Zemun with a request for more. Decoy planes and tanks can just be a few pieces of wood, and these were built, but so were other far more sophisticated versions.

When a NATO drone plane or spy satellite is over a tank, it can sense the heat coming from a tank engine and calculate when it was last switched on. To counter this, the Yugoslavs built heat-generating equipment and fitted it into the decoy tanks. They also put together planes, which from the air looked like the real thing. One of the Zemun technicians was on the project from the first day of the war: 'We made dozens of false planes, it took a team a day's work to make just one, but we didn't estimate the cost, we just built them. About thirty were hit so we did our job and I think it was worthwhile because the decoys saved lives.'

The same company also repaired Yugoslav air force radar systems. One of the engineers was in a team working twenty-hour days:

'Our forces had a number of American Westinghouse systems. On the second day of the war, one of them was hit. It took us a week to get it back in working order. When the cabin came in there were holes in it and bits of shrapnel from a Tomahawk cruise missile. There was also blood on the floor. One of the guys inside did survive, his cap was still there soaked in blood, he's still injured now, and he always will be. Soldiers used to come and deliver equipment which had been hit, they were always exhausted. Sometimes, if we had a bit of paperwork to do, they'd just lie down on the floor, go to sleep for a few minutes, then get up and go back to their work.'

Another tactic the authorities came up with was used at Batajnica military airfield. An army expert in camouflage explained why NATO hit the airfield night after night: 'Our engineer corps bought vast amounts of black plastic sheeting. Some nights, after the bombing, they would go out and lay it on the runways. The next day, from the air, it looked as if we had laid asphalt. We overheard one pilot say: "How the hell did they mend it so quickly?". So they came back time after time, which of course meant they weren't bombing something else more valuable to us.'

All most people saw of all this was the nightly tracer fire heading up in a lazy, swaying, arc of metal towards the planes at 15,000 feet. For many Belgraders, the war was absolutely real, in the sense of the explosions, the damage and death, and yet unreal, in the sense that you never saw the enemy. They felt, as anti-aircraft gunner Dušan Berdić said to me, as if they were 'fighting with ghosts'.

They were also fighting with their fear.

CHAPTER 11

'Ere we will eat our meal in fear, and sleep
In the affliction of these terrible dreams
That shake us nightly.'

William Shakespeare, *Macbeth*

SOMEWHERE IN SERBIA, A VILLAGE WAS MISSING ITS idiot. He didn't look dangerous, despite the pocket-knife he was waving towards me. In fact his manic grin, hair and clothes were more Forrest Gump than Freddy Krueger. We were filming at an anti-NATO rally in Kragujevac, at the spot where the Nazis had massacred 6,000 Serb men, women and children in 1943. Apart from the village idiot, there were about 15,000 other people present.

'You are NATO pig,' he said, pronouncing NATO as 'Nah-toe'.

'You are NATO fascist aggressor,' he continued. 'We kill all NATO,' he went on, and he would have gone on and on, but I brushed past him and caught up with cameraman Veljko Djurović and soundman Milan Antić. At least they were only crazy in the way that all Serbs are, not in the village idiot sense. They were also two of the bravest people I've ever met.

We'd already filmed a bit of bomb damage to a local bar-racks; the Zastava car factory was also on the itinerary, and now this rally.

Here I sensed, en masse, what I'd already felt around town in Belgrade. Defiance, yes, but also fear. It wasn't there in the first few days of bombing. The people were so angry then that they forgot to be scared. Eventually they thought long and hard enough about where they might be heading to realize that there could potentially be a ground war in every one of their cities and municipalities. Few people would say it openly, but in private, many were deeply concerned.

They would have fought a ground war, even if they were frightened of doing so. As crazy as it seems to some people in the West, they would have taken on the American, British, German, French and other armies. Knowing they would be beaten, they would have fought. Like I said, they're crazy.

One hot afternoon, Veljko, Milan and I were in a cafe in Belgrade when talk turned to a ground war. Despite Bill Clinton, it was beginning to look possible. President Clinton had dropped a huge clanger on 23 March by helpfully telling the Yugoslav political and military elite: 'Don't worry, we're not going to have a ground war, so you guys hold out for as long as possible.' The words he actually used were along the lines of 'My fellow Americans, don't worry, I am not about to send American ground troops to a war in a place most of you have never heard of.' It just sounded like a reassurance to Belgrade. 'Since when did anyone win a war through air power alone?' they asked. 'The US in Vietnam? The Russians in Afghanistan? Half the world in Iraq?'

The military establishments in all the NATO countries collectively uttered a massive 'D'oh!' For domestic political reasons, Clinton had given away a major military weapon: the threat of a ground war.

British Prime Minister Tony Blair was among those who

were stunned. When what the US State Department had briefed would be a three-day war dragged on to its second month, he saw that Clinton's statement had been the huge error everyone feared. Blair became the prime mover to get the threat reinstated, and the hardware in place to carry out the threat.

Milošević was trying to ride out the storm, gambling that NATO public opinion wouldn't hold up – a miscalculation from a second-division chess player. It was the latest in a long line of miscalculations, and it was connected to the worst mistake he made. Milošević expelled the Kosovar Albanians from Kosovo. Nothing else he could have done so guaranteed his eventual defeat. And yet, understanding the West, and Western public opinion, so little, he handed the US, NATO, the EU and each individual country victory in the battle which in modern warfare is so crucial: the battle of public relations.

The moment the first images of the hundreds of thousands of Kosovars pouring into Albania, or trapped in no-man's-land on the Macedonian border, hit the TV screens was the moment the leaders of the NATO countries knew they could go the long haul. Without those images, public opinion may or may not have turned against the bombing campaign, but with them came what some of the waverers feared was lacking: justification.

John Raven, the British military intelligence officer, is convinced that the resolve to continue was solid: 'The determination of Whitehall and their Washington counterparts never wavered from the plan or the strategy. Yes, on an almost daily basis there were problems, but we never wavered.'

So by mid May, as Milan, Veljko and I sat in the Belgrade cafe, the language used by Tony Blair, backed by the military build-up in Albania, made the possibility of a ground war seem very real, and very scary. Then they both stunned me.

'Tim, we need to tell you. If there is a ground war, we can no longer work with you as we will put down our equipment, take up a gun and go to fight the invader.'

The fierce Serbian sense of culture, history and identity I had read so much about and seen en masse suddenly revealed itself to me in a very personal manner. Two people I admired and liked so much, men who loathed Milošević and worked against him, would fight for Serbia. Not for Milošević, he was just the Yugoslav president, but they would fight whoever invaded Serbia. At that moment I understood, more clearly than previously, that if a ground war came it would be a very bloody affair, for both sides. In Kosovo there were tens of thousands of well-equipped Yugoslav army soldiers. They were in their own country; many had five years' combat experience in Croatia and Bosnia. And behind them were tens of thousands like Veljko and Milan.

After the war we interviewed Miloš Gagić, a volunteer of the front-line 'anti-terrorist unit' in Kosovo. I suggested that to resist a ground war would have been suicide. He smiled, paused and said, 'Yes it would have been suicide for them.'

Another veteran, Predrag Ristić, thought the ground war was coming when in May all the anti-aircraft units in Kosovo began receiving large stocks of anti-tank missiles: 'Every night when we heard planes, we weren't sure if they were for bombing, or if these would be the ones bringing the parachutists. We were always on alert for them coming.'

NATO would almost certainly have won, but the losses might have been immense. The Yugoslav army was not the undernourished, ill-disciplined, under-equipped, unmotivated army rolled over by Operation Desert Storm in Iraq in 1991. But none of this meant the Yugoslavs weren't fearful for the future, and the futures of their families.

So, at Kragujevac, amid the fiery rhetoric at the monument to the victims of Nazism, I saw the anxiety.

That was fairly early on; by May it was more intense. One evening I went to a party hosted by Maja Marsenić, a Serbian woman who ran a school for teaching English as a second language. The electricity was out so we ate and drank by candlelight, and the occasional glow of a bomb exploding a few thousand yards away. About twelve of us sat outside her apartment which was situated fairly close to one of the NATO targets which was bombed almost every evening. Throughout the evening, our conversation was punctuated by very loud explosions. Each time, much to the amusement of all the guests, I flinched slightly.

'I can't help it,' I said, and then to cover my embarrassment joked, 'And I can't help it despite having been bombed in better towns than this.'

This was the opportunity one of the guests had been waiting for. He launched into a ferocious verbal assault, accusing me of bombing him, his family, his city and his country for no good reason. I tried to explain that I wasn't a pilot, that I was nervous about flying, and certainly couldn't bomb anyone, but the more drunk he'd become, the more he was waiting to fight me, and I'd given him his excuse. The other guests, all Serbs, were embarrassed. These were educated people who understood the difference between me as a person and NATO as an organization. They attempted to calm him down, and having failed, bundled him into a car and drove him home. After that, our conversation was more sombre and again I sensed the anxiety they were feeling. They seemed to be intellectually hunkered down, waiting to see out what was, for them, a terrible experience. Never knowing when to quit, I got into another argument, this time, though, a dignified one. Someone ventured that the world didn't know how the Serbs were suffering under the onslaught.

I launched into a speech about how the people who endured the three-year siege of Sarajevo in Bosnia underwent more in one weekend, than Serbia had gone through in two months. My job title at the time was 'Diplomatic Correspondent'; I never really lived up to it.

I got back to the hotel at about midnight. I was still awake at 1 a.m. when Jakša rang. He rang most nights, at midnight, at one, at two, to phone in details of everything that had been hit; I would then phone the foreign desk and update Sky on what was going on. I'd been drinking a large glass of red wine, with my feet up, the curtains drawn and the nightly show in full view. The anti-aircraft artillery fire arced upwards through low cloud, snaking its way toward the sound of the planes. Sometimes, when more than one battery was in action, the two sets of tracer would wind round each other in a sort of orange and yellow DNA double helix swirl. Occasionally, if the units were placed far apart, the tracer would form a gigantic X in the sky. You could tell where the gunners thought the planes were by watching as the DNA or X patterns moved along the city skyline, following the jets. With a few glasses of wine inside you, you could forget what was really happening, and just watch the dots making pretty pictures.

'Meet me downstairs in two minutes,' said Jakša.

Five minutes later I was in reception. We went out to our car, picked up Veljko and Milan and set off across Branko's Bridge in the direction of Pančevo.

'They've really smashed the oil refinery,' explained Jakša, 'and we've got permission to go there.'

We drove in silence through the darkened, deserted streets, heading out of town. After a few miles we pulled over, got out and waited underneath the last bridge before the refinery. Given that dozens of bridges were already in rivers and canals all over the country, that was probably the most stupid place we could have waited, but it was where we had been told we would meet our official escort. We waited to see if a NATO bomber, or the escort, would arrive first.

'Listen,' whispered Jakša. 'Planes.' I don't know why he was whispering; the pilots certainly couldn't hear us. We looked up, and for only the second time during the whole seventy-eight-day war, I actually saw a formation of NATO jets. Their engines droned ever louder, but they were a mile to our left and heading away.

The only other time I saw them was when we were filming in a Belgrade orphanage. It was about eleven at night and I was outside in the playground getting some air. The clouds broke, a full moon shone through and suddenly there were several planes, darks spots against the silver of the moon. The sirens sounded, and the children also began to wail. There were about thirty of them, aged between two and six, sleeping in the basement for safety. They always cried when they heard the sirens, or the explosions, except for one three-year-old. He'd been told the noise was a great big giant crashing about in the clouds, with his boots on. I remember him, sitting on his potty, pointing at the ceiling and smiling.

At the Pančevo bridge a police patrol drove past, turned and came back. The officers questioned us for a while before making phone calls to get assurances that we were not NATO forward air controllers.

At about 2 a.m. our escorts showed up. We followed

them across the old steel and iron bridge, which leads towards Pančevo, and drove into hell.

Visibility was down to about a hundred yards. It looked like fog, but with the windows down just an inch, it was apparent that this was a mixture of smoke, burning oil and something which gave the air a chemical smell.

We passed through this for a mile before, for whatever reason, it cleared enough to see across some fields and to the refinery. The whole complex was a blaze of orange and red flame, black smoke and the blue flashing lights of fire engines and police cars. We drove slowly down a road bisecting two different parts of the complex. Flames a hundred feet high leapt towards the sky on both sides of us. Amid the crack of burning materials, and the roar of burning oil, there was the occasional groan, or shriek, from metal towers twisting and bending amid the intense heat. We got out and shielded our faces as Veljko and Milan began filming.

Within ten minutes the local authorities ordered us back to the main gates of the complex. We sat underneath some trees watching exhausted, sweating, firemen swigging water and preparing to go back to the inferno. There was little they could do, but a few outbuildings and parts of warehouses could be saved. Suddenly, a number of people began shouting, and everyone scattered.

Jakša shouted across to me, 'Split up! They say there's more cruise missiles on the way.'

Tomahawks had shattered the complex, and now the early warning system said more had been launched from the ships out in the Adriatic.

Nothing happened, the latest salvo was headed elsewhere.

By 4 a.m. we had enough material and we headed back to Belgrade. On the journey I was torn between conflicting emotions. We had another exclusive, the latest in several we'd scooped since the beginning of the war, but I was disturbed by some of the images I'd glimpsed next to the refinery.

Local residents were gathered by their houses, some dressed in their nightclothes, a few holding small children. All were breathing in the acrid air of the aftermath of the bombing, and all would be for weeks to come. We hurtled back across the bridges. These were often the worst moments of filming trips. All of us hated the sixty-second dash across the Danube or Sava Rivers. At night our vehicle was normally the only one on the bridge, so Milan, who always did the driving, would put his foot down and get it over with as soon as possible.

By 6 a.m. we had sent our report to London. Jakša and I walked from the office up to the Hyatt. Across to our right was what looked like a glorious sunrise, except it was in the wrong place. The world really had been turned upside down. It was Pančevo. Even from ten miles away, the fires outshone the dawn light.

NATO was hitting everything. They turned the lights out, and the heating down. They hit the main TV building in Belgrade, killing sixteen civilians and crushing the idea that they wouldn't deliberately target a non-military building. It was a flagrant abuse of the rules of war, and totally failed in its stated purpose, to take Milošević's propaganda machine off the air. The building and its occupants were smashed late at night; by 9 a.m. RTS was back on air.

US planes accidentally bombed a convoy of Kosovar refugees, causing a huge loss of life, and wrecked a barracks full of KLA soldiers.

They even hit Bulgaria, Hungary and the Chinese embassy in Belgrade. Firing cruise missiles into neighbouring countries was definitely a mistake; there is a question mark about the embassy. Some of the remnants of the cruise missiles we saw suggested that when they were fired they were already past their use-by dates. That would explain hitting Bulgaria, and also why one of the Tomahawks went missing in the first week of the war. NATO's radar operators eventually found it, going round and round in circles over Serbia. It hit a field, but it could have hit anything.

The embassy was different. Bombs from a B-2 jet hit the target, which was partially destroyed. The question is, did they know in advance which building it was? The official explanation is that it used to be a Yugoslav ministry, but that the Americans' maps were out of date, and so they hit it not knowing it was the Chinese embassy. They killed four civilians, and caused a massive diplomatic incident resulting in violent anti-American demonstrations in China.

Mark Kirk was one of the pilots who took part in the operation to bomb the building on 7 May. Kirk, who went on to become a US senator, was also a former navy intelligence officer. He visited the CIA's Belgrade station shortly before war broke out. He supports the official explanation and gives this account:

'I took a look at what the CIA were doing. The A team was up against Slobo, finding where he was, what he was doing, how he was protected. The B team were all younger guys; we called them the Young Turks. Well, they all liked jumping in four-wheel-drive vehicles and getting down into Kosovo to see the KLA. That left the guy who made the coffee, and he was the guy in charge of making the maps for targeting. Can you believe that? Nobody in the station wanted to do it. It's boring and it does nothing for your career. It's an important function, but it's dull, so I can believe how the screw-up happened.

'Anyway, that night I was flying an EC-130 Compass Call over Belgrade. I was in the "Star Warriors" from VAQ 209 Squadron. I was responsible for putting electronics into the Serb radars, you know, blanking out their communications and SAMs, electronic warfare stuff. The moment we landed back at Aviano and opened the doors, the ground crew was there. The first thing they said was:

"Do you know what you guys just hit?"

"Nope," I said.

"The Chinese embassy!"

"Well," I replied, "sometimes people miss."

"No," they said, "you hit it three times."

"Well in that case," I replied, "we hit the target. Blame this one on the target list people."'

They are the ones who took the blame, and the US apologized repeatedly to the Chinese. What is less known is the alternative theory for which there is circumstantial evidence, but no proof. This version of events suggests that the Chinese had a sophisticated communications and electronic eavesdropping system in the embassy and was passing the military information it gathered to the Serbs. The Americans, who suspected that the Chinese might have had access to their stealth technology, were furious and took the risk of bombing sovereign Chinese territory. A CIA operative in the Balkans says that a few days into the anti-American demonstrations, a senior US diplomat showed up in Beijing. He showed the Chinese a dossier detailing what the Americans knew about the bunker. He says that was why the demonstrations were turned off like a tap. In his version of events, both sides decided that was the end of the matter.

The 'Star Warriors' flew 150 combat missions during the Kosovo War. On 149 of them the aircrews were not told what the target was. They were given the longitude and latitude, which were known as 'BE' numbers, and they dropped bombs on those coordinates. However, on that particular night, and only on that particular night, next to the BE numbers were the words 'Federal Ministry of Supply'. It is a strange coincidence.

Privately many Serbs were delighted at the embassy bombing and the subsequent rows, but overall, weariness set in. There were vague rumours of discontent among reservists in the southern towns, and everyone was heartily sick of the power cuts, the noise, the death toll and the growing threat of the ground war. Others were sickened when, in the middle of the war, the editor and publisher of the *Dnevni Telegraf* newspaper was murdered. Slavko Ćuruvija had been warned his life was in danger, but even during the bombing he continued to publish articles critical of the Milošević regime. Many people believed that someone in the regime was responsible for the killing, and that the true face of the regime was on display.

According to a conversation I had with Ćuruvija's widow, Branka Prpa, he had been warned to stop publishing by a friend, the former Minister of Culture, Nada Perišić. She had told him that 'people at the very top are very angry'. The Montenegrin secret service had also warned him that his life was in danger. Branka asked her husband to flee: 'He told me "I'm not going to run away." I didn't say anything more because people make that decision only once in their life and I thought he had the right to make it.'

The secret police were following Ćuruvija the day he was killed, but mysteriously, they pulled off minutes before he was shot. The report of that day, from the state security headquarters files, is both chilling and mundane. Titled 'Operation Turkey' it shows how at 1.53 p.m. 'the object and his wife leave the flat. They walk to Knez Mihailova Street where in front of the Russian Emperor Restaurant they meet an older man and a woman.'

It goes on like this, listing every street the couple walk down, everyone they meet, everything they do. And then, at 4.58 p.m. the surveillance is stopped. The only reason given is 'as agreed with the head of the department'. The couple were walking back towards their apartment. When the assassins came, Branka had little idea what was happening:

'In the last few seconds of normal human life we were in this passage outside the house. He took my arm, maybe he felt safer like that; people sometimes know when danger is coming. I felt for a moment a breeze, and there was dust, and I heard the sound, it was bullets, bullets all around us. Slavko started to fall down, and I thought maybe he tripped on a stone. But the killers kept firing. They fired about seventeen bullets and they were ricocheting, and I began to understand what was happening. I tried to turn around, and at that moment a man, whose face I didn't see, hit me in the head with his gun. I fell, and my face was next to Slavko's. A man in a black jacket and hat walked up and shot him in the head. Then they all just walked calmly away. No words, no nothing.'

Fear swept through the independent media and the opposition. If Slavko could be killed, anyone could be killed. Even muted criticism was now curtailed. The regime watched the funeral to see who was there, and what they did. The main opposition leader, Zoran Djindjić, had to make an appearance. Ćuruvija's death could not be ignored, but even as he threw earth onto the coffin he too was warned he was in the gunmen's sights. As he finished the ritual, a voice whispered, 'You are next, you have to leave now.' Two secret service agents opposed to his assassination had warned one of Djindjić's friends, who now passed on the message.

The hit team was to have been from the police, but they were nervous, and unhappy about being ordered to kill a fellow Serb, even one they didn't like. Djindjić was concerned that the warning could be a ploy to discredit him. Leaving Serbia at a time of war would damage his credibility. The friend argued that the risk was too great: 'I told him, "Who needs dead heroes? I want you alive. You have a wife, two kids, forget politics."'

The following year Djindjić told me he took the advice: 'My security and I decided to leave straight after the funeral. We knew we had at least two cars on our tail and that the phones were tapped. So we changed cars three times on the way down to Montenegro. There were eight security people and myself. The first change was near Požarevac at the pay toll, the next at Užice. We got through the border because a contact from the Montenegrin police knew the police at the Serbian side.'

Ćuruvija was murdered, Djindjić had fled, and some of the more liberal Serbs, even the anti-NATO ones, asked themselves what sort of a society they were living in, and who was to blame. The daily rock concerts in Republic Square had been attended by thousands of people in March, now there were hundreds, sometimes just a few dozen. Yugoslavia's infrastructure was being systematically smashed, people had almost had enough. NATO had announced it had moved from Phase One to Phase Two of its campaign. This meant more targets being hit more frequently. Phase Three was an option, as was a ground war.

The queues at the bread shops and petrol stations grew longer. The power cuts made life difficult for everyone. By late

May, the US air force began to use graphite bombs on the electricity grid. The graphite could knock out power without destroying the infrastructure of the grid. It had a huge psychological effect on the population. People were left in the dark for long periods. The Americans had asked their allies what they thought of this weapon before deploying it. One senior British diplomat was flying back from Washington when an American general asked him for his opinion: 'I told him I thought it was a very good idea. We had moved to what I called Phase Two and a half by then, Phase Three would mean an extended menu of targets, here was a way of hitting Serbia hard.'

The walls were closing in on Milošević. On 27 May the president was indicted by the UN war crimes tribunal for alleged crimes against humanity. This gave him another reason to find an exit. If the ground war came, then the tanks would come all the way to Belgrade, and he might be arrested. There had long been behind-the-scenes negotiations, but now Milošević had an inducement to actually listen to some common sense. He was running out of options and time while the public was running out of patience. International mediators were working hard to give him a way out, and NATO a reason not to invade. We would soon be back in Kosovo.

CHAPTER 12

'They make a desert and call it peace.'

Tacitus

'DON'T SHOOT! DON'T SHOOT, IT'S CHERNOMYRDIN'S plane!'

The Yugoslav air defence communications system crackled as the panicked voice of an officer came on the net. Several anti-aircraft batteries, waiting for that night's attack, had heard the plane. It was the first for more than sixteen hours, and so they turned their guns towards the sound. The information that Russia's Special Envoy, Viktor Chernomyrdin, had left talks with Milošević and was heading for the airport hadn't filtered through to all of the anti-aircraft batteries dotted around the greater Belgrade region.

NATO didn't want to embarrass Chernomyrdin, or accidentally kill him, so it had authorized a pause in the bombing in that area. When the roar of a plane's engines suddenly broke the relative calm, some gunners went onto full alert. Chernomyrdin had a narrow escape: the battery next to the airport knew what the plane was, but others, further away, could have hit it on its flight path towards Russia. He got out OK, but Belgrade didn't. That night NATO came back, and hit harder than ever. They always stepped things up after the

Russians left. This led to the joke: 'Oops, the Russians are here, let's go to the shelters.'

The first Russian into Belgrade had been Prime Minister Yevgeny Primakov. He turned up as early as 30 March. President Yeltsin needed to get Milošević to understand something, so he sent people that Slobo would listen to. The message was quite simple, but Milošević had to hear it from 'grown-ups'. Living, as he did, in 'Sloboland', he still believed that the old ally, the fellow Slav, the brother Orthodox, the Russian, might rescue him. Yeltsin wasn't going to go as he and Slobo weren't equals, but Primakov was high up enough to ensure that Milošević would believe what he was told. In very plain terms Primakov told President Milošević: 'Sorry, we can't help. I'd give in now if I was you.'

Just in case he couldn't quite understand, Primakov brought along Russia's Director of External Intelligence and the chief of staff of Russia's military intelligence agency. They explained to him why he couldn't win. They told him about NATO's resolve, NATO's weapons and what they could do, about how eventually he could face a ground war, about how his army would be overrun in five days amid heavy casualties and what would happen to Serbia. And then Primakov said again, 'and we can't help. I'd give in now if I was you.'

Milošević had spent years waiting for the Russians to ride to the rescue. Not the Yeltsin people, but those he hoped would soon be in power, Gennady Zyuganov's Russian Communist Party. His grasp on the enormity of the collapse of the Berlin Wall was tenuous. Slobodan Milošević wanted Primakov's SS-300 air defence missiles. Instead he got a slap in the face. The SS-300s would have changed the war. NATO would have lost a lot of planes. But he didn't get them.

'Sloboland' was a strange place, populated by a handful of people, and he had created it along with the help of his wife Mira. For years he'd been sacking people who disagreed with him. Those who valued their jobs more than their pride began telling him what he wanted to hear.

So, in the real world, anti-NATO demonstrations in Moscow attracted 1,000 elderly members of the Communist Party, and ordinary Russians struggled to survive daily hardships. In 'Sloboland', 20,000 people were on the streets and Russia was in turmoil over the outrage being perpetrated on Yugoslavia. The Russian intelligence men were sent to put the beef into Primakov's unpalatable sandwich. They also met with senior Yugoslav military staff. These meetings hit home – they were 'soldier to soldier'.

The Yugoslav high command wasn't that surprised. They'd thought that there was an outside chance the Russians would back them, but they wouldn't have bet on it. During the decade of international sanctions against Yugoslavia, Russia had stuck to the military embargo. This was why the MiGs which went up against NATO on 24 March did so without functioning radios or radar. Russia could have given SS-300s to Belgrade, but President Yeltsin, in his more lucid moments, understood well that NATO would almost certainly win the war, and did he really want them as an enemy afterwards? Over something he really cared about, maybe, but not for President Milošević. Yeltsin knew what the Russians knew, which was what the Americans and British knew. In fact most people, except Milošević, knew in advance that Russia was not going to rescue him. The president floundered about for a while as the bombs dropped, but eventually, so did the penny. Public opinion was in free fall; he needed a way out, so he needed to negotiate.

There were private ways to do this. The Italians had kept their embassy open throughout the campaign; discreet contacts were made there, and with the Greeks. The populations of both countries were deeply concerned about the bombing. Their politicians walked a tightrope for three months. In public they murmured words into microphones, designed to show their electorates they shared some of the misgivings. In private they murmured to NATO that they would not withdraw their approval, or in Italy's case, its airbase at Aviano.

The Greeks and the Italians were used as a 'back channel'. Then, in mid May, the EU appointed the Finnish president, Martti Ahtisaari, as its peace envoy. Together with Chernomyrdin, he began working on the deal to end the war.

The British Defence Secretary, George Robertson, had pretty much stated NATO's terms in a press conference: 'Serbs out. Kosovars in.' He had not meant that the Serb civilians in Kosovo would have to leave along with the military, but that is what happened. When you boiled it down, the deal was simple. Milošević would agree to pull his troops out. The bombing would halt. When the Yugoslav forces were out, NATO's troops would come in. The refugees would come back, and NATO would police the province to prevent the two sides from killing each other again.

NATO could say it won, because it forced the Serb authorities out of the province. Milošević could say he won, because NATO troops could not enter the rest of Yugoslavia, could not control the Yugoslav media and could not take over the state resources, all of which had been in the Rambouillet document. It allowed Milošević to make statements to his dwindling band of believers who, being believers, wouldn't laugh when he announced that Yugoslavia had beaten NATO.

At a military level, the Yugoslav military still takes great pride in the fact that it was not taken apart by NATO. The country may have been, but the army, as a force, survived almost intact. That, perhaps, was a hollow victory, because at a human level the army suffered serious losses. Getting the figures is difficult. In the last week of the war, a rumour went round the Serbian, British and American media that a US air strike in southern Kosovo had killed several hundred Yugoslav troops in a single attack. A NATO ambassador was at the Brussels headquarters when the reports began to come through: 'I heard about the event and I found it credible. I personally took the view that we needed to hit the troops on the ground anyway.'

At a political level there was something in the deal for both sides. Ahtisaari and Chernomyrdin got the headlines, but someone else was working in the shadows. Peter Castenfelt, a Swedish financier, ran a financial firm called Archipelago Enterprises in London. He had contacts with the Russian government. Castenfelt knew Chernomyrdin well and had advised him on various matters in the past. Milošević wasn't listening to Chernomyrdin, and the US negotiator, Strobe Talbott, was on the verge of nervous exhaustion. Talbott flew to the US to rest and Castenfelt flew in on or about 28 May. He told Milošević the outline of the Ahtisaari/Chernomyrdin deal, which was pretty much what the NATO countries and Russia had concocted. Castenfelt told Milošević: 'This is your way out, it won't get any better than this.'

Bodyguards from the elite Russian *Spetsnaz* unit accompanied Castenfelt to Belgrade and their presence gave his words extra weight. Milošević's own personal protection team had been trained by the *Spetsnaz* and members retained their links with Moscow. The bodyguards of Kim Il-sung and Saddam Hussein had gone through the same training.

On 3 June, Yugoslavia accepted the terms brought by the hand of Ahtisaari and Chernomyrdin. The following day Castenfelt left Belgrade.

On 7 June, detailed discussions between NATO officers and Yugoslav commanders began, and were then suspended after the Yugoslav side would not accede to some demands. That night, NATO intensified its bombing across the country. It was one long explosion which sounded like 'you still don't get it do you?' But they did. The Yugoslavs knew they would sign; it was just a question of which day that week.

Also on 7 June, we'd been taken to one side at the army headquarters and told there would be a media convoy going down to Priština the following day, and that we would be in it. We were given a pass, and a number to stick in our car window in order to get through the checkpoints. Those pieces of paper became the hottest tickets in town. By this late stage of the war, there were at least 300 members of the foreign media in Belgrade, in addition to our Yugoslav colleagues.

At 6 a.m. on Tuesday 8 June, the thirty or so of us with permission to travel arrived at the headquarters, packed, and ready to go. So did about one hundred of our colleagues. By 8 a.m., another hundred had showed up. They were also packed, ready to go; some had brought dozens of bottles of mineral water, boxes of food, two vehicles even. What they didn't bring were the necessary permits. The Tower of Babel must have been a beacon of calm and clarity in comparison to what followed.

I made my way up to the balcony overlooking the square outside the headquarters, where the vehicles, which would make up the convoy, were beginning to assemble. I took a coffee, a chair and ringside seat above the seething mass of belligerent, anxious, sometimes even hysterical journalists. I couldn't blame them; without the comforting feel of the permit nestling in my pocket, I'd have been down there in the front line.

Every single reporter, from the smallest newspaper in Media Nowhereville, to the national networks, was demanding a place. The phrase, 'Do you know who I am?' was tried in a variety of languages by reporters attempting to intimidate officials into believing they were important and therefore should be given a press pass. This is always a stupid thing to say to an official with power over you. There are two responses. The official will either become even more irritated and determined not to cooperate, or they will turn to a colleague and say 'You better fetch a nurse, there's someone here who doesn't know who they are.'

Reporters from Canada to Brazil were telling harassed press officers how many viewers they had, how their radio station was the country's most listened to, or how the president of their country formulated foreign policy according to their articles. Photographers from South Korea to Australia were explaining how many awards they'd won back home, or how their editor would sack them if they didn't get into Kosovo. News photographers are a notoriously boisterous lot. It was no surprise, as departure time drew nearer, that a few engaged each other in pushing matches with at least one punch thrown. As far as I know, not a single extra place was granted on that first convoy.

As I drank my coffee a familiar figure shambled onto the balcony and looked down at the melee with a bemused expression. It was Boris Johnson of the *Daily Telegraph*, later to become Conservative MP for Henley and then Foreign Secretary. I didn't know him to speak to, but with his shock of white hair, ambling gait, portly stature and Oxbridge accent he was immediately recognizable from a thousand picture bylines, TV talk shows and radio interviews. Boris was a young, talented, opinionated columnist. He looked like a young fogey intellectual who was far too busy being enormously clever to bother about things like fashion, or football, or paying the gas bill. He wasn't a hard news hack, and he certainly didn't come across as your average war reporter. The *Telegraph* had sent him to do a series of personal essays complete with personal views and idiosyncrasy. He beamed at me from underneath his white eyebrows.

'Bit of a rough scene down there,' he said.

We introduced ourselves and chatted about various things and I liked him immediately; he was good company. Our attention was diverted by a screaming match between two journalists below about who had asked first to be on a reserve list, which the press officers were pretending to draw up in case anyone dropped out.

'Er, Tim,' asked Boris, hesitantly, 'do you think I should try and get myself down to Kosovo?'

'Certainly, Boris,' I replied, warming to his total honesty in a situation, the likes of which he appeared not to have seen before.

'And just how dangerous is it there right now?' he said.

'Well, for us more dangerous than it has been for months, because the Serbs are about to lose and they are going to be raging mad.'

'Ah,' said Boris, nodding sagely. 'I suppose I should have a flak jacket then?'

I pretended not to be surprised that he hadn't brought one, and agreed that yes, perhaps that would be a wise precaution.

'And where would I find one of those?' he asked.

I began to tell him there was a flak jacket shop just next to the baker's across the square. For a few seconds he gazed enquiringly in that direction and then began to amble off towards it. Perhaps I could have got him to go all the way across to the non-existent shop, but I doubt it. Either way, I stopped him, apologized, and said that if he could get himself down to Priština later in the week, he could ask around the bigger TV companies to see if anyone had a spare jacket they would lend him.

It was almost time to leave. I fought my way down the packed staircase to find Jakša, Veljko and Milan. We loaded up our cramped Opel, claimed our place in the convoy and at about 10 a.m. set off along with about fourteen other cars. We were the only British broadcaster to make it into the convoy and left our colleagues seething on the steps outside army headquarters.

The journey down was uneventful. It should have taken about four hours, but due to bombed roads and bridges took about eight. We followed the progress of the talks on the radio and arrived on the outskirts of Priština at around 6 p.m. Little had changed; there were lots of police, army and militia, few civilians, and no smiles. There were still a couple of hours of daylight left, so we checked into the Grand Hotel and went out to film.

We went back up to a Kosovar Albanian quarter and climbed into the burnt-out shell of a row of shops, which had flats above them. Everything was charred to a cinder. Nothing inside was left intact. Soot and ashes fell from a staircase which felt as if it might give way as we went up to the first floor. I did a quick 'report to camera', holding a pile of smashed crockery and picture frames and said something about 'broken lives'. Outside, down an alley, we found an elderly man wearing the traditional Albanian skullcap. He didn't want to give his name, or say anything about who had burnt and looted the district, but did give us a quick interview about how 'difficult' things had been. He'd been living in a basement with some of his family for three months, venturing out every now and then to forage for food. As we filmed, a MUP armoured personnel carrier cruised by, its occupants staring out coldly. The man ended the interview and disappeared back into the shadows.

From there, we travelled down to the city's main hospital to see a couple of Israeli journalists. Their car had been peppered with sniper fire from an unknown gunman as they approached Priština. Both had gunshot wounds in their legs; it had been a lucky escape. As it grew dark, we went back to the Grand. We'd made it to the city in time for the end of the war. We weren't sure what the coming days would bring, but we knew it was a crucial time.

The Serb population in Kosovo didn't yet know that they had lost. They only knew what RTS told them, and it had not fully begun to prepare the population for what would be regarded in Priština as a great betrayal. That night, at the hotel, there was a taste of the anger to come. I was glad I missed it, but Jakša, Veljko and Milan were less fortunate. At about 10 p.m. a raging drunk Serb civilian staggered into the restaurant, which had about ten locals and ten foreign media people in it. Taking a gun out, he began waving it in the air, screaming hysterically about NATO, and fascists, and bombing, and foreigners. Then picking on a German journalist, he forced him out of his chair and made him kneel, and then lie down on the floor. He had the gun to the back of the reporter's head, and his finger on the trigger. No one moved for a few seconds. Then a waiter approached slowly and talked to him in a soft voice. The drunk muttered a little, then shrugged, and still holding the pistol, wandered towards the reception area and out into the night.

The next day, the talks between NATO and the Yugoslavs continued in the town of Kumanovo in Macedonia. They dragged on, but progress was made. As at Rambouillet, the Americans again had to spell things out to the KLA leadership. The KLA were now on the winning side, and wanted to chase the Yugoslavs out of Kosovo, firing on the withdrawing troops. The Yugoslavs needed a guarantee that any retreat would be peaceful. The Americans told the KLA to grow up, and Belgrade got the assurances. The Yugoslavs left the talks three times to consult with Belgrade, before late in the day a 'Military Technical Agreement' was signed by both parties. All that had to happen now was proof of withdrawal and the bombing would be stopped.

We were up early on 10 June, and got our reward. We were cruising around various roads looking for army columns heading north out of the province. After about an hour all we had seen was the odd one or two vehicles, but nothing suggesting that Belgrade wasn't playing games with the West as had happened so many times over the past ten years. As we drove over the brow of a hill, we got lucky. In the distance we could see a column of about thirty military vehicles heading away from us in the rough direction of Belgrade. Milan accelerated towards them. As we neared the tail of the column we could see, amid the lorries and jeep-type vehicles, heavy artillery pieces, and tracked vehicles. Some of the trucks were carrying twenty to thirty soldiers. This looked like the real thing.

No army likes being filmed retreating, and we were still unsure of the situation, so we followed the convoy for a few minutes, filming surreptitiously. We overtook a few vehicles, filming out of the side window for a tracking shot, went up ahead, turned round and caught them head-on.

Jakša and I both made phone calls to different sources to make sure that what we were looking at was the first evidence of the retreat. Reassured, I made a live report into Sky before sending our pictures into London. The team back home turned them round within a few seconds, using the headline 'World Exclusive' on the screen. NATO already knew what was happening, but they were the first pictures to hit the air.

The NATO Secretary General Javier Solana suspended the air strikes, the UN adopted Resolution 1244 allowing an international security presence to enter the province, and as the day drew on, more and more Yugoslav vehicles emerged from hiding. Tanks, heavy artillery, anti-aircraft guns all were soon trundling north. On top of the vehicles sat the Yugoslav police and army; among them were a few militia members. Some were so happy to be going home alive, and not in a box, that they waved cheerfully at us and gave the Serb three-fingered salute. Others stared sullenly and gave us the internationally recognized one-finger salute.

By dusk we were back in Priština. It was a hot, sweaty, thick evening. The air hung heavy over the darkened city, which was still without power for long periods after NATO bombed the electricity grid.

Then RTS officially broadcast the news that the Yugoslav forces were pulling out of the province. Kosovo was where the Serbs had first settled, over a thousand years before. It was where their oldest churches were, it was considered as much a part of Serbia as California or Texas are considered part of the United States. Now it was over. Legally it remained part of Serbia, but everyone understood that without the armed forces, the reality was different. Kosovo would soon belong to the Albanians.

Within minutes of the news broadcast, the firing began. I was lying on my bed in the Grand on the sixth storey, which was the top floor. At first there were just a few gunshots, then from all over town came the sound of more, and more. A machine gun opened up in the street outside. I crawled to the window and looked out. Tracer fire was rising from dozens of different sources. They were shooting into the air in pure anger. Some journalists reported this event as celebrations, which hinted at a gap in their understanding of the psyche of the Kosovar Serbs.

All over the city hundreds of guns were fired. Amid the cacophony I could hear men shouting in fury, then a few bottles being smashed. A terribly loud cracking noise just above the window made me dive for cover. It scared me so much that I pulled my flak jacket on and lay on the floor for a few seconds. When I stuck my nose above the sill I saw what it was. A few streets away, an anti-aircraft gun was blasting away, the gunner venting his blind fury into the night sky. The tracer swung towards me, and again the shells smashed against the top of the building.

I ducked down again and crawled for the door. Just then there was a knock on it. I stood up and opened it. There was Milan. He smiled when he saw my flak jacket.

'Tim, Jakša asked me to come up and tell you not to worry, they are just shooting into the air.'

'Tell Jakša to come up here and not worry.'

Milan didn't understand, but I didn't want to explain. I just wanted to get out of the room. As we went down to the restaurant I wondered if we would get a repeat performance from the mad drunk who'd offered such terrible service on Tuesday night. Happily, the Grand now had some real muscle on the front door to stop people like him getting in. As for us going outside, large sums of money would not have tempted me. The gunfire lasted almost an hour, and then petered out. The Serbs went to bed to sleep off the alcohol, but they can't have had sweet dreams. They were about to swap one nightmare for another.

CHAPTER 13

'Ah Lazar, Lord of Serbia,
this has never been and can never be:
one territory under two masters'

Unknown Serbian poet on the
battle of Kosovo Polje, 1389

THE WOMEN COULDN'T STOP CRYING AND THE CHIL-
dren couldn't stop laughing. The kids were having a great
time. 'Look!' they shouted excitedly. 'Tanks, in our village, and
hundreds of soldiers!'

The tanks were revving their engines to go, the troops were
boarding their lorries and the women were weeping quietly into
their handkerchiefs. The children saw, and heard, a carnival of
engines, guns, shouts and a volley of ceremonial shots into the
air. The women saw the end of their way of life. They knew that
shortly after their army left, the revenge would arrive.

It was 11 June, about nine in the morning. A column of
Yugoslav army vehicles were lined up, their wheels and tracks
crumbling the rutted track which led through the village into
dust. Some of the soldiers were in high spirits, happy to be
going home. Others cast sympathetic looks towards the women
lined up outside their houses. They were intermittently waving
their handkerchiefs then crying into them again.

Earlier at a different location the Belgrade army PR people, who were also keen to leave, had organized a 'photo opportunity' of the retreat to give the media some pictures. We went along and they presented us with three cranky lorries and about twenty bored soldiers. This was not the reality of the Serbs' departure from Kosovo after a thousand years.

We went looking elsewhere and found the village. It saw the drama of the day, an act being played out all over the province.

Jakša had been very cautious. We'd already driven to one village off the beaten track, but turned back. It just hadn't felt right. There were no houses along the way, and the track was shaded on each side by bushes.

If you wanted to do some nefarious deed here it could be done without witnesses. We noticed a couple of military vehicles hidden in the undergrowth, guarding the approach to the village. We didn't know which unit was ahead preparing to leave, but it wasn't worth the risk of finding out.

We were on the road back to Priština when we noticed a village on our right, with a lot of activity inside it. We pulled up, parked the car, and I stayed behind as Jakša walked up into the village to talk to the commanding officer.

After a couple of minutes he came back and said to me, 'OK, we can go in, but you have to stay here.'

I knew better than to ask why; he would have regarded it as a superfluous, stupid question. Jakša, Veljko and Milan walked into the village and began filming. Eventually, Jakša came back out and said I could now come in, but I mustn't speak to anyone, not even my twenty words of Serbian.

'They are not very happy with foreigners right now,' he said.

I walked in, and hung around in the background. If anyone caught my eye, I tried to look as Serbian as possible, which was to say, not at all.

An elderly woman approached me. She was wearing enough black to make it clear she was a widow. She said something pitiful to me. I had no idea what, but she was clearly a frightened, tearful old lady. I smiled as sympathetically as possible, nodded, patted her hand and walked away. In different circumstances I could at least have talked with her, but I'd been told not to speak the language of the 'NATO fascist aggressor' army, which was about to enter Kosovo.

In 1995, I'd spent a few hours with the last seven hundred ethnic Serbs in Croatia. They had taken refuge in a UN refugee camp in Knin after the Croatian 'Operation Storm' in Krajina. The other 200,000 Serbs had fled into Bosnia, then Serbia. Most of those in the camp were elderly, with no close relatives, or were very poor, and had no form of transportation. They'd been left behind.

Croat militiamen were outside the complex and wanted to get in to 'deal' with them. The ethnic Serbs were so grateful to have someone to 'tell their story' to that they searched around until they found someone who could speak to me in English.

Now though, speaking English could get me in trouble.

The tanks gunned their engines, the lorries started up and the troops began to leap on to the vehicles. The officers, who appeared to be from different units, gave each other bear hugs, kissed each other three times in the Serbian way and slapped each other on the back. The women cried harder, and the children skipped about.

A squad of twelve men fired a volley of shots over the roofs of the houses, and then they too jumped on board a lorry and the convoy set off.

As the tank roared past me I seized my chance and asked Veljko to film a quick report to camera. I said something about the army heading north and then, pointing south towards Macedonia, said that the revenge was coming from that direction. I had to say it a couple of times to get it right.

An officer strode by and shouted something to Jakša.

'What was that all about?' I asked.

'He was just saying that you speak very good English for a Serbian reporter.'

'What!' I said. 'You told him I was Serbian?'

'No, I wouldn't do that,' replied Jakša, straight-faced, and then added, 'I told him that you were a reporter from Radio Television of Serbia.'

As we walked back to the main road, I was still wondering whether to laugh or be angry. The children had raced down on their bicycles, or had run ahead to see the convoy leaving. They waved the Serb salute, three fingers for the Trinity, and watched as the convoy headed north. Then they ran back to the village to see what else they could do, on this swelteringly hot June day.

The convoy snaked its way onto the highway temporarily halting the traffic. It was all one way, north. The Serb civilians weren't waiting for the Kosovars to return, or for NATO to show up – both options were considered too dangerous, and so tens of thousands were preparing to leave and hundreds were already on their way.

Once the column had left we watched a few refugees slowly driving past. There were battered Volkswagens, old Yugos and occasionally the car of someone who'd done well and could afford an Audi. Slower still were the tractors. Up front, the father would be driving. Behind him, in a trailer would be his family, his wife, their children, grandparents and sometimes friends who didn't have their own transport.

They would be bumping along, sitting on top of their belongings, staring silently at the passing land. A few even hoped they might see it again one day. Most knew this was the last time. There would be no going back to their houses when things calmed down. So a few set fire to their own homes, to prevent a Kosovar living there.

It's difficult for some people in Western countries to understand such a deed. But we have not experienced war on our territories for sixty years. That some Serbs wilfully destroyed their own houses shows how deep emotions run in war, in any country.

So the civilians, baking on their trailers, comforted the children. Their exciting game of 'retreat' had suddenly become too real. Most of the adults didn't know where they were going. They would head for Belgrade, but would they get there? The Milošević regime's track record in taking care of its fellow ethnic Serbs wasn't great.

The bitter irony for some was that they were now experienced refugees, with a war in Croatia to learn from. Among those packing bags in Priština were many thousands who had fled Krajina in 1995. Milošević had just cut them loose. After abandoning them militarily in Croatia, he now failed to take responsibility for their welfare as they poured out of Kosovo.

He'd shipped them there in 1995, to live in poor conditions; some had been camping out at the Priština sports stadium. Now they were again heading for Belgrade on tractors. The term 'uncertain future' barely covers what they must have felt.

The cars were also laden; every available space was packed. If it wasn't with small children, then it was bags, candlesticks, toys, blankets and water bottles.

I was working; I didn't stop to think about what I would take nor whom in my extended family I would have room for if I had to choose.

I asked Veljko to flag down one of the cars. A Yugo slowed to a halt in the middle of the road, its back end weighed down by whatever was crammed into the boot. The mother sat in the passenger seat, next to a man of about thirty-eight years. Milan asked him where he was from, and what was happening there. He shrieked at us, 'I am the last Serb in Djakovica! I am the last Serb! And shame on you for filming a fellow Serb's disgrace!'

I looked in the back window. Amid the piles of belongings were three children, a boy and two girls aged between five and nine. They were hot, sweaty and exhausted. The man drove off, his exhaust spluttering. The wind blew the plastic sheeting he'd tied over what remained of their family life, and rattled it against the roof of the car.

The Serbs from the towns and villages of southern Kosovo were on their way. Most of the others would join them within days. Within weeks the returning Kosovars would fall upon the remaining Serb civilians, shooting some, burning others houses, and dynamiting their churches.

We filed a report and set off for the airport. I didn't think we'd make it, but the guards had either joined the retreat, or didn't care anymore. For me, Priština Airport is only really memorable for the location of one of the silliest things I've ever done.

We drove in, parked a couple of hundred yards from the terminal and began filming. The buildings were shattered. It was never a very nice airport, but now it was a wreck. The windows were blown out, twisted steel shutters hung from them, and weeds grew everywhere. It had ceased to be an airport seventy-eight days previously and the entire staff had gone.

The road we were on was strewn with debris. I opened a packet of chewing gum, began to throw the paper over my shoulder, then, in a Pavlovian reflex action drummed into me by my grandparents, I stopped, and put the paper in my pocket. Jakša looked at me with incomprehension on his face, but even among the debris of a smashed-up airport, in a war zone, I couldn't litter.

Above us, a NATO drone arrived. It was one of the latest generation and could relay quality, live images back to its base station in Macedonia. During the war, General Wesley Clark occasionally had the pictures patched through, live to his office in Brussels. Allegedly he occasionally made decisions based on what he saw.

This didn't overly impress the men and women in the drone units. They argued that commanders were now using technology to make snap decisions, which should not be made until expert analysis of the image was undertaken.

I didn't know that then, but I knew someone was watching so I couldn't resist waving to it. In fact I think at least three of us did. Perhaps General Clark waved back. I wouldn't do it again. The latest generation of pilotless drone aircraft can fire missiles. This means someone can make a decision about what they are about to fire at from thousands of miles away. Using old technology, bombing was authorized after a period of studying the image, to make sure what you were looking at was a target. Waving at a flying camera is only fun the first time you do it. I began to get the feeling you get when you know someone is looking at you. Which of course, they were.

In real life, at least you have the choice of turning round and saying 'What are you looking at'. But in this circumstance you'd either have to be able to fly or be 3,000 feet tall. Eventually, after being really irritating for about ten minutes, it went away. Perhaps some commander had said, 'Ah, looks like some stupid journalists down there at the airport.'

A few minutes later, there was a tremendous roar of jet engines. Three MiG-29s, hidden inside a hill, took off. There were at least two secret exits opening onto roads. They'd revved their engines inside, and then taxied out. Using a short take-off technique, they were up and away.

Others were to leave, but we didn't see them. The Yugoslavs had all sorts of things in that hill and although they didn't get it all out the Russians did.

Late that afternoon, after we got back to the hotel, a rumour went round town that the Russian army was coming and would beat NATO into Kosovo. Allegedly, one of its units had left its peacekeeping duties in Bosnia and was now driving across Serbia.

There was nothing official, just conflicting rumours about what was happening; one rumour said the Russians would arrive around midnight. At about six, Priština's Serbs began to line Main Street; dozens of them stood patiently waiting for what they thought would be their saviours.

I went out for a walk on my own. A short way up the street I found a group of about fourteen Kosovar women and girls. They were carrying baskets of flowers and were receiving sullen stares from the Serb civilians and occasionally shouted at or pushed. I asked them why they were there.

'We wait for NATO,' said a young girl of about twelve.

Here was one mixed-up bunch of people. I explained in a variety of languages, including my own hand signals, that 'no, NATO was not coming tonight, it's the Russians. And if you value your lives, go home, and wait one more day.' They left. I assume that twenty-four hours later they were back and this time threw their flowers onto a British armoured vehicle.

By nine, thousands of Serbs were lining the street. I went up to my room for a couple of hours' rest, arguing that I would need it, in case they really did come. I kept thinking they wouldn't on the grounds that believing 'The Russians Are Coming!' is akin to getting into a taxi and shouting, 'Follow that car!'

It was a sweltering night, so I left the window open.

I awoke to the sound of gunfire. Up and down Main Street, men were firing Kalashnikov rifles and pistols into the night air. Most of them were civilians, all of them were ecstatic. Beside them were women and children. Amid the cheering, I could make out the sound of tracked vehicles.

I scrambled for the window and looked out. All I could see were the cheering crowds. I quickly dialled my office. They could hear me, but I could barely hear them above the cacophony from outside.

'The Russians may be in Priština!' I bellowed down the phone. I could only make out the odd word said in reply so bellowed again, 'The Russians may be in Priština!' then to my relief heard, 'OK, I understand that and am putting you through to the sound department.'

As my colleague was transferring me, the first vehicle hove into view. It was a Russian troop carrier, flying the Russian flag. That was good enough for me. Within seconds I was speaking to the on-air producer, and this time bellowed, 'The Russians are in Priština. Confirmed.' A very calm voice came squelching back through the sat phone 'OK, coming to you next.'

I could barely hear what was being said on our programme, but made out the words 'our correspondent, Tim Marshall . . .' so I just started talking, giving a live commentary on what I could see. I was later told that President Clinton was informed of the confirmation of the Russians' arrival on the basis of that report.

All I could think was 'thank goodness I got it right'. What I didn't know was where the Russians would end up. They might have tried to control Priština, but there were only two hundred of them. They were after something more valuable, the airport. Who ordered the Russians in is unclear. They may not have gone to Yugoslavia's military aid, but here was a chance to exercise a bit of power in the region. At the time Yeltsin was in all sorts of trouble back home, not least with a bitter and impoverished army high command.

A man who 'freelances' as a go-between for Moscow says the army took the decision to move without consulting the politicians: 'Yeltsin had lost the confidence of the army and was suffering massive economic problems. The high command wasn't listening to him anymore and the secret services were also extremely unhappy. He had played the whole Kosovo War very badly; he had no leverage with Milošević because they hated each other. He'd discovered that Milošević had put thirty million dollars into a Cyprus bank account to help the attempted coup leaders in Moscow in 1993. When the army saw the Kosovo ceasefire about to be implemented without them involved they simply ordered units in Bosnia to move down into Kosovo.'

What is clear is that the Yugoslavs had no problems with the Russians coming. A Yugoslav army source received a phone call as the Russians were about to cross from Bosnia into Yugoslavia, even though they had no jurisdiction there.

'I was in a restaurant when I got the call from one of the Russian "advisers". He said, "We know what you've got at the airport, and we know the Americans are coming, how far do we go?" I made a call and asked the same question. The answer was "All the way. Tell him he has our full support and tell him to march to the airport." They didn't just get the airplanes out of the caves, they got some state-of-the-art communication systems, which otherwise would have fallen into the hands of the British, who actually turned up before the Americans.'

The Russians rolled down Main Street, the crowds cheered, and then to everyone's surprise the vehicles just kept on going.

We filed a couple of reports and got to bed at about three. It was too dangerous to follow the convoy in the dark. We'd go and find them at first light. Or, perhaps, as soon as we'd finished breakfast.

CHAPTER 14

'You know how to gain a victory, Hannibal,
but you do not know how to make use of it.'

Livy, 'History of Rome'

AT DAWN ON 12 JULY, THE RUSSIANS WERE AT THE AIR-
port, the British were at the borders, and the Americans
were late.

The US army was supposed to take the lead in entering
Kosovo but it wasn't ready. So, despite not being invited to join
the race, the Russians won it. The British, who'd been ready
since the day before, were not happy. They could have made
it to both the airport and Priština first. The Americans insisted
they wait so that they could go in. It makes much better television in the US if their army is seen to be the most important.

In 1944, the US stopped at the gates of Paris, and allowed
the Free French army to chase the remaining Germans out. It
was a political decision designed to strengthen General de
Gaulle's position among the French public. The Americans may
have found him 'a pain in the ass', but at least he'd stand up to
the communists. There was no TV then, so it was a small price
to pay. In Kosovo, they wanted prime time.

With the airport in Russian hands, Moscow could fly more
troops in, and secure Priština as its sphere of influence. The

US Deputy Secretary of State, Strobe Talbott, had ruled out a 'Russian Sector', a clear warning to Moscow. 'Oh yes, sorry,' said the Russians, but only after the troops were already at the airport and NATO was demanding to know what was going on. Foreign Minister Igor Ivanov called the deployment an 'unfortunate mistake'.

The Russians got away with it because it was only Kosovo, and because they had a good excuse. They were there for the same reason that the Americans were coming, to help bring peace. 'Why did it matter who got here first?' they could plausibly ask.

When the British heard that the Russians were driving through Priština, and that the Americans still weren't ready, they moved. A rumour was going around that the 10,000 Russian paratroopers were in the air heading for Kosovo. In the event, Bulgaria and Romania denied the Russians permission to over-fly their airspace.

An elite British unit called the 'Parachute Regiment Pathfinder Platoon' helicoptered in, and landed at the airport at about the same time as the Russian column arrived. There was something of a Mexican stand-off between the two forces. The British had some of their best troops on the ground, but the Russians had armour.

This was dangerous stuff, and it was going to get more dangerous.

The British radioed in the situation to headquarters. Britain's senior general on the ground, 'Iron' Mike Jackson, and his commanding officer, General Wesley Clark of the US army, were informed. Clark's opinion was that the NATO soldiers should take control of the airport. It seems to have been unspoken but understood that this might have involved shooting the

Russians. Jackson thought that the decision on whether or not to commit British troops to potential action against the Russian army was one Prime Minister Tony Blair should make. This led to what diplomats call 'an exchange of views' between the two generals, and what everyone else calls a 'stand-up row'. It concluded with the words of General Mike Jackson: 'I'm not going to start bloody World War Three for you!'

To Clark's anger, Jackson phoned London. Tony Blair agreed with Jackson, it wasn't worth it. Perhaps it wouldn't have resulted in conflict with the Russians, but the risk was too great. Clark appeared to have been prepared to take that risk without consulting Washington. As a safety precaution, the British ordered a special forces unit in the region to board a Hercules transport plane and get to the airport. It was loaded with Land Rovers, which were armed with heavy machine guns. Unfortunately for the British, it crashed on take-off, bursting into flames and slightly injuring the crew. A Dutch special forces unit backed by a medical team flew in from Albania to secure the area and get the Brits out.

General Jackson prefers not to talk publicly about the airport incident, but General Clark mentions it in his memoirs and in December 2001 gave an interview to the journal of the Royal United Services Institute. He felt the situation 'wasn't ever going to be a crisis'. The following February General Jackson replied and, using the same forum, went as far as he was prepared to go: 'Subsequent analysis [of war] by those involved is often characterized by equally sharp differences of recollection and, more importantly, understanding of what was going on.'

He continues: 'General Clark may have felt able to dismiss a potentially serious confrontation with the Russian contingent on the ground at Priština airport as "it wasn't ever going to be a crisis" – many others, including myself, had a less cavalier attitude.'

The British general appears to accuse the American of lacking an understanding of the gravity of the airport stand-off, and of having a dangerously cavalier attitude towards it. A British diplomat active in the war was in London as the situation unfolded: 'My first thought was "We really don't need this one after the last seventy-eight days." I was ringing Solana [the NATO Secretary General] and Clark. Solana was anxious to avoid the confrontation, but Clark really believed that because the Russians had deceived us he had to move. He probably exaggerated the significance of the situation, but that's understandable. The intelligence reports we were getting in about the Russian unit were confused, and of course the unit turned out to be crap.'

While all this was going on, we were grabbing three hours' sleep. It was about 8 a.m. by the time we got to the third checkpoint, which was also the one we were stopped at.

Two Russian troop carriers were parked across a back road, which led into the airport. The gun turrets were pointing outwards, and there were a few Russian soldiers lolling about in the shade. It was already hot, and they were already suffering. They'd moved in such a hurry, they didn't have water supplies. Or petrol. The night before, the mighty Russian army had been reduced to asking local Serb officials in nearby Kosovo Polje to find them enough fuel to get all of the vehicles to the airport. They won the race, but it was a close thing.

Even though we were refused permission to go through, I gave the sergeant a litre of water for goodwill. When that still didn't work and I realized we really weren't getting in, I gave the unit a bag of sweets and we drove off.

On the way back to Priština we saw a few plastic decoy tanks and a fake wooden bridge. We tried to film, but a Serb police-man, who for some reason still cared, ordered us away. As we crested a slight hill, the plain surrounding Priština lay spread out before us. I could see plumes of smoke rising from at least seven houses. The burning had begun. The Kosovar houses had been burnt weeks before; now a few Serbs were torching their own property.

We drove down into the plain and stopped outside one of the houses. It was set back from a country road and surrounded by trees. It was deserted, but the fires were just beginning to catch, suggesting that the occupants had left that morning. Jakša warned me not to touch anything in case of booby traps, and we walked slowly down the driveway.

The right-hand side of the front of the large building was beginning to burn, as was the side on the left. The wooden parts of the front were already cracking and hissing, and flames began to leap up towards the roof. Veljko went as close as he could to film, while Milan kept a look-out on the road in case any armed men arrived. We only stayed a few minutes, and then returned to Priština to find out what was going on.

At the Grand Hotel's 'media centre' the TVs were tuned to Sky, and a variety of other international stations. Sky had their satellite trucks over the border and were advancing alongside the British troops with the reporters doing live broadcasts as they went.

There had been a mad scramble at dawn as several thousand journalists attempted to go across the Macedonia–Kosovo bor-der at the same time as the soldiers. There was an immediate traffic jam of armoured vehicles, Land Rovers, satellite trucks and anything with wheels which the media people had hired.

Dozens of vehicles squeezed through but the rest ground to a halt and had to watch as the British army Chinook helicopters leapfrogged them, carrying military vehicles as they went.

The Sky coverage made for compulsive viewing. At one point, reporter Jeremy Thompson was doing live commentary as army engineers gingerly approached a variety of booby-trapped shops. At times his words were drowned out as Warrior fighting vehicles thundered past. The British had been told their entry would not be opposed, but they weren't taking any chances, and had been given the order to 'hammer very hard, anyone who gets in your way'.

Most of the world's broadcasters were reporting that the British had crossed the border. One of the American twenty-four-hour channels had a different view of what was happening. It had set up its operation at an American base in Macedonia, and was broadcasting live reports of the US army gearing up to move. It was several hours before the station reported that NATO had gone across. I only managed to flick around the channels every now and then, but it was the most bizarre piece of ethno-centric news broadcasting I have ever seen. Focusing on the US army is one thing, but giving the impression that the NATO operation wasn't underway is another. Reporters from a variety of countries in the media centre were incredulous.

We sent a couple of lives and reports in, then at about 2 p.m. decided to drive south and meet the Brits coming the other way. Priština was still quiet. On a few roads we could see Serbs, loading up their belongings and preparing to flee. In one apartment block, a family was throwing mattresses out from a fifth-floor window onto a flat-bed truck. There were now hardly any Serb police or Yugoslav army on the streets.

On the Priština to Skopje highway, there was a steady flow of Serb refugees heading north. It was baking hot and there was no shade. We drove up and down the highway for an hour without seeing any military movement.

At about 4 p.m., we were five miles out of town, driving south, when I spotted two familiar-looking Land Rovers coming the other way with about eight soldiers inside. As they passed us I shouted to Milan: 'It's the Brits! Turn round, turn round!'

He spun the car around and we followed for a couple of minutes before the Land Rovers pulled over. We went past to get a good look at them, then turned again and pulled up.

With Veljko filming we walked across. One of the Land Rovers was flying a Union flag and a British army captain was standing beside it looking at a map and then staring down the highway towards Priština through a pair of binoculars. I offered him my hand and said:

'Hello, I'm Tim Marshall from Sky News. Welcome to Priština.'

He seemed a little surprised, but shook hands, said he'd had an interesting trip up, and then asked to borrow our satellite phone because his communication system wasn't working.

'Sure,' I replied. 'You probably want to tell your mum you're OK.'

He must have thought I was serious as he gave me a very odd look. I quickly phoned Sky to tell them the British army was now within sight of Priština before handing him the phone. I presume he called his base in Macedonia, although it is possible he phoned his mum.

We told the captain the road into the capital was clear, but he preferred to wait. We couldn't hang around, so we bid them good luck and headed back to Priština to get the pictures out to London. Shortly after that, the mobile phone system came back on, and working became much easier. The time lost pulling over the car, setting up the sat phone and dialling London was annoying and we were now able to phone in updates almost constantly.

By early evening we heard that the Sky teams were getting closer to town. Jakša had booked all the rooms he could, and about thirty-four colleagues were heading our way. Even so, we would still be eight to a room.

The first satellite truck and cars arrived and we organized parking, rooms and then food. Twelve of us were just starting to eat for the first time that day when my mobile rang.

'It's Jim Rudder here, they're shooting at us!'

Jim was our then deputy head of news and had come out to oversee the special programmes we would be making once everyone was in Priština. I knew that his sat truck and cars had pulled over about three miles from town, to allow Jeremy Thompson to do a live report, using the city as a backdrop.

Even over the phone I heard the crack of a sniper's bullet.

'Who's shooting and where exactly are you?'

'I don't know, we're up on the road into Priština from Macedonia,' said Jim. 'We're under fire, we're all hiding behind the sat truck.'

'OK, hold on, we're coming,' I said.

Milan and I hurried out of the restaurant and ran to our car. We took the flak jackets out of the boot, and headed up to where we thought our colleagues were.

I jammed the flak jackets up against the side of the front doors. As we tore up a hill I saw two satellite trucks, one with its dish still pointing skywards, and two cars. One of the trucks had a driver crouching behind the wheel and its engine running. Behind the vehicles were about ten people, all flat on the ground. The trouble was, I didn't recognize any of them. It wasn't Jim and our team. But whoever it was, they were in trouble.

Milan threw the car around and I opened the door and half got out. Crouching beside the car, I shouted: 'There's no point in staying there, follow us into town, we know the way.'

Understandably they were very nervous about going into town, as they didn't know the streets, and could end up in all sorts of trouble. There had been sporadic sniper fire over the previous couple of hours, coming from apartment blocks. A couple of people jumped into the truck which had its engine on, and it moved off with us. I looked back and noticed the other sat truck and the cars spin round and head in the other direction away from Priština.

We guided the vehicles into town, left them at the Grand and then set off again to look for our team. London rang, and told me Jim had phoned in to say they had made it into Priština and were looking for the hotel. By the time we got back to the Grand, they were there.

The sniper fire had been coming from a field across the highway. It was probably a lone Serb taking potshots at the satellite dish, which would have made a very inviting target.

As we milled around the car park, I saw a British army convoy driving up Main Street. Serb civilians gazed at the four Land Rovers in silence. I was mightily pleased to see them. The Yugoslav police and army had left, and left behind them a power vacuum. Occasionally we could hear gunfire echoing round the streets.

We went back to our meal, and were joined by Jim and the others. This time I was disturbed, not by my mobile, but by Robert Fisk of the *Independent* newspaper. I'd first met Robert in 1986, and knew him to be a totally committed journalist who threw his pen at every story he came across. He had a few Kosovar Albanian friends still in town. One of them had come out of hiding and called him to say that a gang of armed Serb men had surrounded his house, were threatening to burn it – could Robert come and help?

Robert, being Robert, said yes. Then he asked me to come with him. I was embarrassed but I decided I'd had enough excitement for one day. I also had the responsibility of briefing my colleagues who had just arrived.

He went off on his own. I don't know what happened, but at least he came back later.

Jakša called a meeting in what used to be my room. It was still booked in my name, but now there were about eighteen of us crammed into it, eight of whom would be sleeping there that night. Our bottles of water and flak jackets took up most of the space, so we sat on our bags and listened to the expert. Jakša is a very mild-mannered man, but when it comes to safety he can be quite abrupt.

'Right,' he said, jabbing a finger at myself, and reporters Andrew Wilson and Jeremy Thompson. 'There are people in this town who watch satellite TV and know who you are. They don't like you. They may even try and shoot you. Be aware of that at all times. Everyone else, keep your curtains drawn, and stay away from the windows, there will be a lot of shooting tonight.'

Two of our colleagues, perched on the windowsill, shuffled off and stood by the wall.

'You, my friend,' he continued, pointing at one of our sound technicians, 'take that shirt off if you don't want to get into trouble.'

Tom was wearing a T-shirt he'd bought in Baghdad. It had Arabic writing all over the front. The Arabic script is of course very beautiful, but that's not how many Serbs viewed it. Some believed there were Arab mercenaries in Kosovo. They may have been right; there had been hundreds in Bosnia, and there are links running from the KLA to Al Qaeda.

Jakša explained how for another twenty-four hours things could be dangerous for the foreign media, but then NATO would be in Priština in force. What he didn't say was how dangerous it would be for Serb journalists.

Jeremy, Milan and I went back out to help the team with one of the satellite dishes which was parked in the bus station on the outskirts of town. The British had set up a temporary base there and had a variety of armoured vehicles and sandbagged bunkers already in position. The commanding officer was very welcoming and said we could stay and broadcast from the site, but warned us that there was at least one sniper in an apartment block about 300 yards away. He had a couple of his own men high up in a tower above the station, and they were just waiting for the gunman to show himself.

There were a handful of civilians at the bus station who were leaving town the only way they could. They were mostly elderly and were carrying their few belongings in those large, sturdy, blue and red checked plastic bags now seen everywhere in places where people are not well off. Hidden among the elderly was a young soldier. He had his kitbag but no rifle and somehow he'd been left behind when his unit pulled out. It seemed a strange way to retreat, on a creaky old 1960s Yugoslav bus, but he had no choice. With the army gone, there were parts of town that were no-go areas for Serbs. Even if he made it out of town, hitching a lift in the countryside would be equally fraught. No one had any space in their cars, and the KLA had already moved to take control of some rural areas.

Milan and I left and joined Jakša and Veljko for a beer and to talk over our plans. An old Kosovar friend, who had contact with the KLA, had phoned Veljko. Milan, Veljko and Jakša all had Kosovar Albanian friends. They'd helped each other in the past and a stupid war between Kosovars and Serbs wasn't going to change that friendship.

Veljko's friend warned him that his status as a cameraman wouldn't save him. If some units of the KLA or some civilians caught him, his friend said, they would kill him. He was, to them, a Serb, first and last. Veljko and Jakša had seen the man in a cafe that afternoon, but all three knew better than to speak to each other in public. Speaking in Serb was already beginning to become dangerous, and neither of the two Serbs knew the Albanian language. The threat was not exaggerated. The following month, a United Nations worker from Bulgaria made the mistake of saying a few words of Serbian in public. He was beaten to death by a mob, right there on Main Street.

We talked it over and agreed that we should pull out the next day after we had shown our colleagues around town. It was a good time to leave. Not only were our lives in danger, but also the toilet in my room was blocked. With eight people in the room, it was very quickly unbearable.

We went along to see Veljko's wife, Katarina. She was the producer for a German news channel and was staying in the Grand. It was her birthday so we organized a few beers, a bottle of wine and a cake. It was more of a bun really, but it didn't matter. We set up one of the TV editing machines in her room and played some music through it. Amid the madness outside on the streets, and the media hysteria inside the hotel, we found half an hour to be normal people.

Around midnight I went back to the six feet by three feet of my room I still had jurisdiction over. In an act of chivalry, I'd given the bed to camerawoman Deb Lyle. There had been some risqué jokes about her sleeping with seven men in one night. Debs replied that she wouldn't want to sleep with a single one of us, as we were as sweaty, dirty and exhausted as she was and the toilet wasn't working and there was no water in the taps.

I lay down on the carpet, closed my eyes and listened to the man next to me snoring all night, about eight inches away from my face.

His name was Lucky; I'd never met him before. He was a Macedonian and was 'fixing' for one of our teams. In the mayhem of crossing the border, he'd found himself in Priština. Being a Macedonian Slav, he spoke a language very similar to Serbian, and although he wasn't frightened, he wasn't planning on staying too long. In the morning, when he woke up I said to him, 'Now I know why you're called Lucky.'

'Why?' he asked.

'You're lucky because you don't have to listen to yourself snore,' I replied, and then regretted it as he seemed rather put out.

After breakfast, I gave an interview to a young reporter from *SKY Magazine*. He was in the same position as Lucky. He'd been in Macedonia to do a feature about the Sky operation there. Being the sort of guy he was, he was happy to help out, and so had gone to get some supplies for one of the teams.

Before he knew it, the vehicle he was in was charging across a gap in the border, and here he was, in Priština.

He came along as Jakša and I showed a few of the team around the city centre, explaining what the damaged buildings were, and what had happened where. They were all professionals, and quickly got the hang of the geography and background. In many respects they were better placed than us to report the coming days and nights. They all had experience with the refugees now beginning to pour back across the borders in their tens of thousands.

Every now and then we could see groups of cars and tractors filled with departing Serbs. It was time to join them.

We left our colleagues doing live broadcasts in front of the Post Office centre which had been smashed by NATO's bombs. When we got back to the Grand we heard the familiar sound of tracked vehicles coming up the road. About three Warriors and a couple of Land Rovers growled past. By now there were a few Kosovo civilians about, and they felt safe enough to clap, cheer and throw flowers.

One of the Serb officials from the media centre came rushing out to watch. His name was Radovan; he had never lied to us about events and we believed him to be a decent man. He was also very angry.

A Warrior clipped a section of curb on a traffic island crushing it and leaving a hole in the concrete. 'What the fuck are you doing, you NATO bastard?' he screamed at the soldier sitting at the top of the vehicle. 'You're wrecking everything, you bastard!'

It was an extraordinary moment. All around Radovan were the signs of war. Army vehicles, smashed buildings, bomb craters, damaged phone lines. His country had lost, his people had lost, and thousands of people on both sides had lost their lives. Here he was, an unarmed man facing a giant piece of metal with a large gun attached to it. All it had done was clip a curb, but it was enough to send him temporarily mad.

He followed the Warrior up the street, running alongside it. 'Fucking NATO killers, you come and wreck our cities, you bastards!'

I watched him as he came back. He was still raging mad, but his shoulders had dropped, and there was just the hint of tears in his eyes. Radovan went back into the Grand and started making his own plans to leave.

I had told our team in Kosovo, and the office in London, about our imminent departure and everyone agreed we could leave. However, that morning the London office rang and said that some of the team in Kosovo had been on the phone and were a little concerned that the four of us with local knowledge were pulling out so soon. A request was made: could we stay a couple of extra days? I said absolutely not, and London agreed.

We packed, said goodbye and drove up Main Street, straight into a howling mob of about 600 Kosovars.

They were up at the top of town, in the devastated area we had reported from a few days earlier. They were waiting for Priština's Serbs. Most Serbs got out via a road skirting the south west of town, which went past the bus station. Others weaved their way through town, avoiding Albanian areas as much as they could.

We just went straight into it. The moment they saw the Belgrade number plates on our car, a collective scream of anger went up. The crowd surged towards the car, chanting the Albanian for KLA, which is UCK. It sounds like 'Ooh chi ka'. Right then, it sounded dangerous.

Milan was driving and for once I was in the front seat. For months I'd been sitting in the back seat in case the car was stopped, so that I wouldn't have to speak in English. Now I was up front, so that Jakša and Veljko wouldn't have to speak Serbian. We'd feared something like this might happen, but not so soon.

Some of the men and boys began spitting at the vehicle. A few were kicking the doors. Milan tried to edge through them without slowing down too much. I could hear him muttering obscenities under his breath. I wound down my window and leaning out, stuck my hands in the air, made the V for victory sign and shouted back, 'Ooh chi ka! Ooh chi ka!'

I doubt that it helped. Perhaps the mob never intended to do more than jeer as we passed. Either way, we made it through, drove past a Warrior parked a few hundred yards up the road and left the town behind us.

We drove steadily for about thirty minutes, then reached the end of the refugee column. Ahead of us were thousands upon thousands of vehicles.

The road was narrow, just big enough for two cars to pass each other. But up ahead were retreating Yugoslav army convoys, which included vehicles so wide that cars couldn't overtake. An added problem was the bombed bridges. From time to time, the column had to leave the road and travel over dirt tracks to get to a temporary bridge, before rejoining the road.

Milan cut the engine and, like everyone ahead of us, we got out into the heat and stood by the car. Now it was my turn to keep quiet again. The younger men were stripped to their waists, the older ones to their vests. The women sat fanning themselves by the side of the road, or trying to divert their thoroughly hot, and bored, children. From time to time the column would advance a few yards. Most of the men would push their cars to conserve their petrol. No one wanted to get left behind, and there wasn't a garage in Kosovo with any fuel.

Getting to the border from where we were should have taken an hour. It took around five. Eventually the line began to thin out and we headed towards Niš. From there we took the Belgrade road. Every now and then we passed columns of tractors and trailers. At two toll-booths we saw groups of farmers who had been prevented from going further north. The Milošević regime was again abandoning Serbs to their fate.

Belgrade had decided it didn't want the embarrassing spectacle of angry Serb refugees clogging up the capital and protesting that Milošević had betrayed them.

Some who did make it as far as the outskirts of Belgrade were stopped by the police and led to a hillside a few miles away. There they were more or less dumped. A small tented city grew up away from sight of Belgraders. RTS wasn't in a hurry to publicize their plight. As we passed them on the road, I could see their tragedy, but I couldn't help thinking of myself, and a feeling of total relief washed over me as we sped up to Belgrade.

Compared to situations some colleagues have experienced, this trip hadn't been so bad. The four of us had all seen worse things in the past and would do again, but it wasn't a competition, and it had been physically and emotionally draining. We hardly spoke once we were through the refugees and moving. We drove back in silence, lost in ourselves. Although we thought of friends and family, comfortable beds, showers and good food, we also wondered, 'What now for Serbia and Milošević?'

PART THREE

AFTER

CHAPTER 15

'Plots, true or false, are necessary things,
To raise up commonwealths and ruin kings'

John Dryden, 'Absalom and Achitophel'

THE BALKANS EXPERT SET OFF, ALONG THE MARBLED
corridors of Her Majesty's Foreign and Commonwealth
Office. He had with him a sheaf of papers, and he carried an
opinion about President Slobodan Milošević of Yugoslavia.
Some colleagues shared his views. The meeting he was heading to would help decide if his belief that 'enough was enough'
would become British government foreign policy.

It was late June 1999. Serbia had been taken apart. Its air
force had been proved to be obsolete, its army had retreated
and its economic capability to sustain itself was buried under
the rubble of war.

Even as the meeting took place, Kosovo's Serbs were being
'ethnically cleansed' by the returning Kosovar Albanians. Now
it was the Serbs' turn to have their villages looted and burnt,
women raped, and men kidnapped, tortured and shot. The
Roma weren't spared during the orgy of violence. During the
week of the meeting in London, Kosovar Albanians forcibly
expelled 5,000 of them from the southern part of the town of
Kosovska Mitrovica.

The KLA had also begun to blow up every church, and every symbol of Serbia it could get to. It wasn't just trying to remove all the Serbs; it was attempting to obliterate every trace of them from the landscape.

NATO had said it bombed Yugoslavia to prevent ethnic cleansing. Now, even with 50,000 troops in the province, it couldn't stem the murderous wave of criminality which fell upon the Serb civilians, causing them to flee.

And yet despite all this, despite losing the war, and leaving the Serbs to be killed, there was Milošević. He was in charge, in good health, sitting on top of a large amount of stolen money and he still had the capacity to foment trouble in the region.

The situation in Montenegro was considered to be the most worrying. If Milošević brewed up a civil war there it could easily spill over into Bosnia. That would leave the Dayton peace deal in tatters, and ruin years of work by the international powers. That Milošević still had this power was, as a Foreign Office mandarin put it, 'bloody annoying'.

It was also a little embarrassing. Milošević's continuing presence at the top of the tree, and the inability to prevent yet more ethnic cleansing, took the shine off NATO's triumph in Kosovo. As long as Milošević was in power that victory would look a little tarnished.

With one hand, Milošević gave the Americans the internationally recognized 'spin on this' middle finger. With the other, he stuck two fingers up to the British. All Britons know the strength of this two-fingered sign language. This means it's quite a shock when, as a small boy, you first see footage of Winston Churchill sticking two fingers up at everyone and smiling. I saw him doing it on old newsreel, played as I watched his state funeral in 1966.

Milošević appeared to be doing it the right way round because the British got the message and they didn't like it. The view that enough was enough was agreed at the London meeting.

The Balkan expert had helped to prepare the outline of what to do. Representatives of other government departments were present at the meeting, as were a handful of Americans from the State Department. The State Department officials had received the green light from their boss Madeleine Albright to start turning the screws on Milošević. She was still smarting after the seventy-eight-day war against a country she thought would cave in within a week and she wanted a result before the Clinton administration left office.

One of those present said: 'The meeting worked out an approach which evolved into a strategy. Robin Cook endorsed it and followed what we were doing closely. At the London meeting we agreed that Milošević had survived because he had persistently told two big lies. One, he persuaded the population that the world hated Serbs. Two, he persuaded them that they could only interact with the world through him. So, we had to nail those lies and get to the people. We had to isolate the regime, and engage the opposition.'

Another Foreign Office official put it differently: 'The thinking in 1999 was "we have an adversary, we have to use political warfare to bring him down".'

Not everyone agrees that there is such a thing as 'political warfare'. They point to EU projects, such as the giving of oil to opposition-led towns in Serbia, and say that it was encouraging democracy and nothing more. What is left unsaid is 'we were helping them, because like them, we were also actively working to get rid of Milošević'.

Political warfare has many forms. Individually they don't amount to much, but put together as a strategy they make a powerful weapon.

The most obvious ways had already been conducted for years. Since the early 1990s the British embassy had overseen the arrival of CDs, broadcast equipment and money for the independent media. It had mostly arrived through private, unreported channels. The Foreign Office had authorized support for the opposition parties, and MI6 had been working to find contacts on the ground to help fill an information deficit.

According to former MI6 agent Richard Tomlinson, MI6 had been making approaches to Yugoslavs from early on. In his book *The Big Breach*, which was banned in Britain under the Official Secrets Act, he describes posing as a journalist from *The Economist* and meeting a 'Zoran Obradovic' at a Belgrade cafe.

He writes a distasteful description of Obradovic, implying that his clothes, car and taste in food give him away as someone with connections to the regime. In Tomlinson's version, he has a sixth sense that Obradovic may suspect him of being a British spy, and that therefore he may be in danger. He leaves in a hurry, and drives to the Hungarian border.

Zoran Obradovic is, in reality, Zoran Kusovac. He is a respected journalist from the former Yugoslavia. At the time Tomlinson met him, he was freelancing for Sky News and a number of other journalistic outlets. He went on to work for *Jane's International Defence Review*. His suits, car and tastes were no different to anyone else working at his level of income. If Tomlinson had done a basic check on Kusovac he would have known this.

At the time, Kusovac drove an Opel Astra. This vehicle is about as different from those the regime types drove as his story is to Tomlinson's version: 'We met at the Hotel Moscow, downtown. He wasn't your average idiot that comes here from the UK or the States and wants to be a PhD in Yugoslavian studies in a week. He said to me: "We've been reading your stuff and we want to see if we can cooperate." He meant perhaps I could write for *The Economist*. But after a while he dropped the pretence and said, and I thought this was so clumsy, "I've got to tell you, I'm not from *The Economist*, I'm MI6 and we want you to work for us."

'I looked at him for a while. I don't give a fuck about countries, about Serbia, Yugoslavia, whatever, but I was angry. I said, "I don't like spies; I think you're sleazy. I tell you what, I don't like the police either, but I'll give you three hours and then I'm going to tell them who you are. Now fuck off."'

After Tomlinson came others, but they were far subtler. One in particular drifted through Belgrade, gathering information left, right and centre. Everyone knew who he was, but he was never rude enough to embarrass anyone by admitting it.

Through the 1990s, the approach of the diplomats and the intelligence agencies had been to gather information which would pierce the thoughts of the inner circle surrounding Milošević. Because that circle was so tight, no one was sure what he was going to do. The other reason may have been because Milošević had no idea what he was going to do either.

Charles Crawford was the British ambassador to Belgrade from 2001 to 2003; he had studied Milošević for years and arrived at the same conclusion as several Serb analysts: 'I think he liked wobbling along a tightrope, and I agree that his strategy was to get up in the morning, improvise all day, then go back to bed.'

The British, who had built up a psychological profile of Milošević, were given access to the American version. Both countries employed specialists who had studied hundreds of hours of footage and photographs of Milošević, some of them clandestine, over a period of years. They had interviewed dozens of people who had met the man.

A pattern of weight gain during stressful periods emerged. Milošević also smoked and drank more during those periods, which, in turn, caused his diabetes to worsen.

The profiling had limited but interesting uses. At times of great stress to Milošević the Americans often tried to push him a bit harder. During the war this was behind the decisions to indict him for alleged war crimes and put a $5-million ransom on his head. They may have caused his stress levels to rise even further, but he was still in power.

A few CIA officers came up with half-hearted plans to spirit him out of the country. These never got past draft proposals, which always faltered on the rocks of common sense, especially in light of the fact that he moved around a lot and rarely slept in the same building for more than a few nights.

By late June 1999, the approach changed. The diplomats and intelligence officers became more concerned with finding out who, in the inner or outer circles, would betray or abandon the president and, by doing so, help the isolation process, and bring him down.

They were pushing at a partially open door. Many ordinary Serbs were sick of Slobo; fervent nationalists were angry that he had lost another war, and the Serbian establishment was asking itself what sort of future there would be, as long as he remained in power.

Charles Crawford describes this policy in football terms: 'You pressure the opponent; when he makes a mistake, you blast the ball in the net, or in this case you help the Serb people put the ball in the net.'

An MI6 officer, who worked on the strategy, found that it became easier to talk to people inside the regime: 'Regarding cultivating, we had people so horrified at the system, that they virtually came to us. A lot of people knew who was who as the process built. With others it was a case of "we can make it worth your while", or at least that's what it amounted to. The difficult bit was the calculation of when to offer, the moment to try.'

A Yugoslav military intelligence source says that should not have been too difficult: 'When the outside was looking for people, they looked for those they could either blackmail, pay, or who simply had enough common sense to know that time was running out. It was clearly an operation; the Americans tried to coordinate it in the aftermath of 1999, then it was taken over by the British who had better intelligence.'

Within the Foreign Office, the MOD and MI6, the stepping-up of 'political warfare' was an open secret. One British ambassador, connected to the region, watched the process unfold: 'We were aware that our services were talent spotting. That's the difference between the situations in Yugoslavia and Iraq. In Yugoslavia there was some talent to spot.'

The talent-spotting took three forms. Which media to back, which opposition politicians to support and who inside the regime would cooperate.

Since 1997 the media had been given the most help. In that year the British, and other governments, almost gave up on the opposition leaders after they failed to capitalize on a victory handed to them by ordinary people. They had taken to the streets in large numbers for month after freezing month to overturn local election results stolen by Milošević.

The opposition politicians had looked at this show of strength and said, 'There goes the mob, I must follow them because I am their leader.' Then, when the efforts of students, pensioners and workers put a dent in the edifice of the regime's power, the opposition politicians returned to their preening and bickering. The Foreign Office concluded that the media was the only opposition worth backing.

Now, though, another push would be given to the political parties. One way was to promise people, such as the Democratic Party leader Zoran Djindjić, that Britain, the EU and the US would never again deal with Milošević.

This time there weren't going to be any compromises. No Daytons, no special envoys, no friendly chats, no stern warnings; they were through with him. Instead, training, money, equipment and connections to dissidents inside the regime would all be provided to the opposition. The Americans and British would play the major concerted role while the EU and the German government would help with funding.

According to an FCO field officer they all began to hammer away at those inside the regime who they suspected were looking for a way out: 'The important thing was the message. You've got to keep repeating it, and the message was "you've got to switch sides".'

Not everyone waited to be spotted. In the autumn of that year a Yugoslav cabinet minister had an interesting conversation with a British journalist as they drank coffee on the veranda of his Belgrade house.

The minister said that there were some people in government who were aware that the country was facing difficulties and that perhaps some different people might be required to forge better relations with the outside world. He agreed that it was difficult to discuss the issue, especially as there were no official diplomatic channels to go through. Britain, for example, no longer had an ambassador. He wondered if perhaps the journalist knew someone he could talk to.

His choice of words allowed them to be interpreted as those of a well-intentioned minister of state seeking to further the interests of his country, and not as meaning that he had seen that the ship was sinking and he was looking for a lifeboat.

The journalist gave the minister the mobile phone number of a British diplomat working in Kosovo and returned to London. There he met a Foreign Office official at a branch of Café Rouge in west London and mentioned the conversation. A couple of days later the official called for a chat about various matters and ended the call with the words: 'Oh, by the way. If you see the minister, tell him to get in touch when he's really serious.'

This was duly relayed, and the journalist says that he heard no more about it.

At various levels inside the regime, people knew all this was going on; some even knew the details.

One of those who saw what was coming was a banking executive with close ties to Milošević and army intelligence. He began to hear the reports of who was being approached and what was being said: 'London and Washington sat down and worked it out. Washington put up most of the money and some of the ideas. London put in the planning and they both agreed to build up the opposition by helping organizations such as [protest group] Otpor and [broadcaster] B92. It was also clear that Vuk Drašković would have to go. Senior people in our government would have to be found and then talked into understanding that there was an alternative. It was also agreed that the ideological arguments of pro-democracy, civil rights and a humanitarian approach, would be far more forceful if accompanied, if necessary, by large bags full of money.'

A Serbian businessman who also knew Milošević said he watched the foreigners in action: 'Once they found someone and were confident they were genuine they put the following argument: "Look, with Slobo you can earn X, and yeah sure it's a lot of money. But without him you can earn X, Y and Z." A lot of people got the message, although the banker Bogoljub Karić didn't go for it, and look where he is now, nowhere. The Americans tried to persuade him because they knew that he was desperate to get off the list of people banned by the EU from getting a visa. Those that did go for it? You can see them still doing well in business now.'

Bags of money had been brought in for years. They were about to get heavier. So were the deliveries of broadcast equipment, computers and even small printing presses. There would be training seminars in Budapest, and clandestine meetings in Montenegro, Bulgaria, Bosnia and Austria. The strength of the media and opposition had to be built up if the cracks in the regime were to be widened.

When the London Foreign Office meeting broke up, another wave washed up against Milošević's sandcastle. The tide was beginning to come in from all directions, and he never saw it coming.

CHAPTER 16

'The theatre is irresistible;
organize the theatre!'

Matthew Arnold, 'The French Play in London'

VELJKO DJUROVIĆ FELT HIS HEART BEAT FASTER AS HIS car inched towards the Yugoslav border guards. It was always like this when he was smuggling money in from Hungary. Ahead were cars full of Serbs who had been across to the city of Szeged to buy the type of items which were in short supply in the remains of Yugoslavia. The vehicles were packed with boxes of coffee, soap powder and the small things which helped to make life normal.

Veljko's job as a cameraman had taken him to many front lines; there was no gunfire at this one but it was still dangerous.

'Your heart always goes faster when you know you're in a sniper's range finder. When we took the money across to Serbia, we always tried to look as relaxed as possible. We would tell jokes and read the papers. But we all knew we would be in big trouble if we were caught.'

Veljko had been to Budapest to pick up a bag full of cash. The money came from a journalists' organization based in Western Europe and was destined for Belgrade's Independent Journalists Association (IJA), which he had helped form in 1994.

As usual, he had gone to an anonymous hotel in the Hungarian capital, ordered coffee at the cafe and put a Serbian newspaper on the table in front of him. Before long a man arrived carrying a bag. A few words were exchanged, and then Veljko left, taking the bag with him.

'As a cover story I would always go shopping for the things we couldn't get in Serbia, then I could tell the border guards that was why I had been in and out of Hungary on the same day.'

The money, sometimes as much as £10,000, was used to run the IJA, and to pay the fines of journalists who fell foul of the ever tightening media laws introduced by the Milošević regime. When journalists were jailed, money was found to help their families to buy food and pay the rent.

The organization was set up as an alternative to the Milošević state media machine. Control of the newspaper *Politika*, and the TV station RTS, gave Milošević control over Serbia. Every event was either twisted to support the regime, or ignored if it didn't fit. In 1995, as 300,000 Serbs were fleeing from the Croatian offensive in Krajina, RTS led the evening news with a story about a circus in Portugal.

This type of thought control led to the growth of the independent media, even though it had to struggle against years of closures, fines, raids and the 'confiscation' of equipment. The 'confiscation' was in reality often theft. Computers and broadcast equipment taken from the premises of small independent companies would find their way into the offices of the state media.

Veljko had been a senior cameraman at RTS in the 1980s. He had been in Nicaragua, El Salvador, Northern Ireland and Romania. He was used to conflict, and he was used to reporting it fairly. This was why he was forced out of RTS once Serbia went to war. Milošević's media had no room for independence.

Veljko had resigned a few months after he got back from covering the fighting at Vukovar in Croatia in 1991: 'The bosses had made it clear they didn't like our reports. They didn't fit the rest of the output because we were trying to do honest reporting. But our editor said: "Guys, you seem sick of war already, so you're not going back." They were pushing us to report things that weren't true. For example, on one occasion, that the Croatians had burnt twenty-seven Serb villages and ethnically cleansed the people. But we knew that the Yugoslav army had asked the people to leave for their own safety, as they weren't sure they could hold the area.

'They put me on other duties. The editor said, "OK just follow Vuk Drašković around, and any time he makes any mistakes, make sure you film it," but even the work I did then didn't satisfy them. I knew it was time to leave. I just couldn't do it anymore. You know, some of the people in charge then? They still have jobs now.'

By this time 1,200 media workers had either been fired or had resigned.

The IJA eventually moved from two small, scruffy rooms into the Media Centre off Republic Square. The Media Centre coffee bar quickly became a refuge for those who had been driven from their jobs, or who were vilified by the regime. It connected people who believed that their careers were over, and gave a lifeline to those who thought the world had gone mad.

The Serbian secret police moved in as well. Every day, plain-clothes officers were seen in the cafe drinking coffee, smoking cigarettes, reading newspapers and watching everyone around them.

Committee members used to walk down three flights of stairs and go outside if they had anything sensitive to discuss. They even took the batteries out of their mobile phones after a technician said they powered listening devices that may have been planted in them.

The authorities knew a lot about the British and American efforts to help the independent media. Embassies were monitored, phones were tapped and agents inserted into movements such as the student organization Otpor.

In 1999 Aleksandar Vučić of the extreme nationalist Radical Party was the Serbian Interior Minister. This gave him access to secret material: 'I used to get the police reports on my desk. There it all was, proof. We saw that foreign intelligence agencies were teaching students in Budapest on how to organize. They were also giving money to the students; we knew that because we had people inside Otpor. What you call opposition movements, I call front agencies for foreign interference. The Open Society was one such front agency.'

The international businessman George Soros set up the Open Society – Sonja Licht ran its Belgrade office. Her work to support a free media included bringing in equipment for broadcasters. On one occasion a van full of equipment, destined for Studio B television, drove across from the Hungarian border at dusk. As it set off down the motorway towards Belgrade, the van was stopped by a group of men and the equipment was stolen. Licht is sure they were from the state police: 'So the next time we did things differently. We had a lorry full of stuff for B92 Radio. Well, it was getting dark again, and we didn't want this lot stolen, so after we crossed the border we drove straight to the town of Subotica. We were working with the zookeeper there, organizing school visits. He opened up the zoo; we drove the lorry in and parked it right in the middle of the lions' enclosure. The keeper then let the lions back into the enclosure for the night. Nobody was going to steal that equipment.'

Vučić believes that by cooperating with 'outsiders', people such as Sonja Licht were working against Serbia. In 1999 she was accused of being a traitor and members of her family received death threats: 'We were not helping foreigners; foreigners were helping us. I am Serbian and I am part of the culture. There are people who will never understand. Everything was wrong. We were living under an extremely irresponsible regime, which didn't care for the people, nor for the values we believe in. They were ready to stay in power to promote their own selfish interests and to cut us off from the world. Even if the modern world is not such a great place it's still a sin to cut a country off from it.'

By September the connections back to the world were becoming stronger. The seeds of change were being sown. The independent media became more powerful, the opposition politicians more confident and the student movement more forceful.

In that month the opposition held a rally outside the Yugoslav parliament. The numbers were impressive; the behaviour of one of the politicians was not. Vuk Drašković was about to lose the last particles of credibility he still had with the anti-Milošević movement. By doing so, he eventually cleared the way for a man who really would take on the president.

Drašković was a poet turned politician, who was nicknamed 'King of the Streets' due to his ability to attract large numbers of people to political rallies. He had aspirations to be the real king, and although most experts referred to him as a nationalist, I felt he was more of a 'Draskovist'.

When he felt it benefited him, the tall, bearded party leader took to the streets and criticized the Milošević regime. He was even arrested and beaten up by Milošević's thugs in uniform.

Despite this, when the wind blew in a different direction he joined the government, then left it, then joined it, then left it.

Drašković spent ten years doing a Serbian version of the British folk dance 'the hokey-cokey', and singing its lyrics, 'You put your right foot in, your right foot out, in, out, in, out, you shake it all about. You do the hokey-cokey and you turn around. And that's what its all about.'

It always seemed to be about what was good for Drašković and never what was good for Serbia. The other opposition politicians who also called themselves democrats never danced with the regime; they knew by doing so they would help legitimize it.

Jakša, Veljko, Milan and I went along to film the rally. The streets were already filling up as we walked towards the parliament and the atmosphere was one of anxiety. This was a test of how many people would come. Less than 10,000 would be a disaster for the opposition. More than 50,000 a triumph.

Drašković had failed to say if he would attend or not. He was waiting to see how many people showed up before he would commit himself.

By 8 p.m. there were perhaps 100,000 in front of the parliament. People looked around themselves, saw each other and felt stronger for it. Alas, the opposition politicians were doing what they always did, which was to bore everyone senseless.

They took Andy Warhol's maxim that 'everyone will be world-famous for fifteen minutes' very seriously. Everyone on stage had to make a speech, preferably a long, dull one. People no one had ever heard of were up there, wittering away, ranting about 'Slobo'. They represented so many different groups that I began to feel that there must be ten million political parties in Serbia. One for every member of the population.

This was what it was like for those working towards a coup d'état. You couldn't blame them as they all felt passionately about Milošević. They hated him.

Therefore each passionate person, and passionate group, demanded to be heard. Their passion prevented them from swallowing their egos and uniting around one person. The problem was that until that one person was found, there was no alternative to Milošević. Catch 22.

Serbs, and Yugoslav Serbs, had always had a strong man, a king, to unite them. After the Second World War, the West Europeans gradually invented the European Union as their attempt to prevent them from killing each other again. The Serbs and their neighbours had Yugoslavia, Communism and Tito.

The EU survived, and the other three didn't. When Tito died, the ties that bound the neighbours, almost as brothers, frayed and then snapped. Milošević stepped in, and told the Serbs he was the man to put their faith in. Many of them voted for him.

They then underwent four lost wars and counted their dead in the thousands. Their neighbours counted their dead in tens of thousands. They lost count of their money due to hyperinflation and mass unemployment.

Then they watched a million refugees replace the mainly educated youth, who were doing whatever they could to get out of the madhouse. While this mismanagement of Serbia was happening, those working for the regime were better paid, got the best jobs and were bumped up the housing lists. To make it worse, criminals were benefiting from the chaos and flaunting their wealth around Serbia's major cities. At the same time old people were not receiving pensions, and workers were not receiving their pay.

More and more people agreed 'enough was enough'. It took them some time, but now a lot of Serbs wanted a different leader. But who? There was no Serbian Nelson Mandela, or Vaclav Havel – no one person who stood head and shoulders above any other pretender to the throne.

All this meant that the speeches droned on, and on. I was sympathetic to them as I watched their passion pouring into a microphone and then surging out of the loudspeakers to 100,000 people and anyone else in the world they hoped was watching. Some of them were magnificent.

But it went on for more than an hour, and because they weren't all screaming 'two beers please', which was stretching my knowledge of the language, I was a little bored.

Neither Drašković, who was watching all this from a hall across from the parliament, nor the other main opposition politician, Zoran Djindjić, had yet said a word. But at least Djindjić was on the stage.

At one point someone threw a tear gas canister, scattering a part of the crowd to the right of the stage. This was a frequent occurrence at opposition rallies. Usually they were thrown by someone from the regime to smear the opposition. RTS television, which always vastly underestimated the numbers of people present, would then report the event as 'a gathering of mindless hooligans intent on destroying Serbia'.

As it was the most entertaining thing which had happened so far, on this occasion it may have been thrown simply to relieve the boredom.

About 2,000 supporters of Drašković's Serbian Renewal Movement were right in front of the stage, waving light blue flags and chanting their hero's name. By 9 p.m., he'd decided the event was enough of a success for him to be associated with it. A great roar went up from his supporters as he waded through the crowd and began to climb the steps at the back of the stage.

As the speakers continued their attempt to find a cure for insomnia, everyone waited for either Djindjić or Drašković, who loathed each other, to step forward.

I noticed a commotion at the back of the stage behind the line of dignitaries. Veljko, who was filming the crowd, turned round and focused in on it. Through the suits of the waiting speech-makers, we could just make out Drašković's bodyguards having a fistfight with Djindjić's security team.

We learned later that the melee, which the two men did not take part in, was about which of them would speak first. Eventually they both made speeches but they could barely bring themselves to look at each other, never mind have a dialogue. Everywhere you looked on the stage you could see division and even in the speeches the cracks showed.

It set the tone for coverage of the event. The people had done their bit and turned up, but yet again, those that would lead them failed to show leadership. Particularly, one of them.

Things appeared to go quiet amid widespread disillusionment, but behind the scenes all sorts of things were going on.

Drašković had shown himself to be unreliable. The British and Americans, who had never trusted him, gave up on him entirely. There were far more serious, and equally importantly reliable, players around.

The following month, a group of Serbian activists gathered for a meeting at the Marriott Hotel in Budapest organized by the International Republican Institute (IRI). The IRI is an American organization partially funded by the US government and employs a number of former government officials. They had made contact with the student Otpor movement and paid for senior members to travel to the Hungarian capital.

Otpor was the most exciting of the opposition groups. It showed the flair, wit and enthusiasm that so many of the establishment opposition parties lacked. 'Otpor' means 'resistance', a word which summed up the strength of feeling against Milošević. The group's symbol was a white clenched fist on a black background. Its leaders organized political rock concerts, which had an air about them reminiscent of the passion and anger of British punk rock in its early years.

On one freezing cold night in Belgrade I saw a man in his late twenties stride onto stage wearing a T-shirt with the white fist emblazoned on the front. With his breath coming out in white clouds he approached the microphone, raised a clenched fist in the air and roared at the top of his voice: 'Otpor! Otpor! Otpor! Otpor! Otpor! Otpor! Otpor! Otpooooorrr!' and then he left the stage. He said more in those ten seconds than some of the speakers at September's political rally managed in ten minutes.

But passion and wit were not enough. Otpor needed help, and its supporters had no ideological difficulties in getting it from whichever source they could. Young members were frequently arrested on trumped-up charges, some were beaten, and others lost their jobs. Wearing an Otpor T-shirt became an unofficial offence. This led many of the parents of the young activists to question their own support for the regime. It also failed to suppress the organization and instead the campaign against it spurred members on to greater efforts. When the Americans came calling, it wasn't seen as 'foreign interference' but as 'democratic assistance'.

A retired US army military attaché, Colonel Robert Helvey, chaired the Otpor meeting in Budapest. Colonel Helvey had worked in the American embassy in Rangoon and had seen at first hand how the State Law and Order Restoration Council regime controlled Burma. His experiences there gave him an insight into how to help knock down the various supports holding up the structure of the Milošević regime.

Otpor had already worked a lot of it out for themselves, but Helvey gave them a dimension they lacked. He had experience, an outside view, and the backing of American money.

They agreed with the strategy laid down at the Foreign Office meeting in London four months previously. The 'myth of inevitability' that Milošević couldn't be beaten had to be broken. That myth was the foundation on which the support structure of police, army, media and politics was built. Once the foundation was broken, the pillars of support would crumble.

Helvey chaired several such meetings, some in Budapest, some in Montenegro. Each time the Otpor members would return to Serbia carrying know-how, equipment and large bags full of cash. With this they quickly built a network, which stretched across the country and gradually seeped into the consciousness of the body politic. Their slogan '*Gotov je*!' – 'He's finished!' – was inspired in its simplicity.

Those seven letters, written in white, on a black background, began to appear everywhere. At bus stops, in school playgrounds, on walls, on T-shirts, badges, government buildings, hospitals and even, when an activist was brave enough, inside police stations.

Each time a sticker, poster or spray-painted *Gotov je* was seen, another grain of sand fell away from Milošević's sandcastle.

Almost three million stickers and posters were produced. A Yugoslav military intelligence source says the Serbian secret service tried to find the printing press: 'Army intelligence knew where it was, but didn't talk to the other services about it because it had started to become a national consensus that Slobo had to go. Otpor had a sort of military wing, people who had access to weapons and who knew how to fight. There was only about ten of them but with their connections they could liaise with the army. We knew and they knew, that the regime was going down the drain. Otpor wasn't just a bunch of students, they were organized. They were a revolutionary organization just like any other.'

British and German money was also coming in, along with some low-level training. The BBC was re-transmitting the programming of B92 Radio, and the German broadcaster *Deutsche Welle* paid for newsprint and printing presses for at least one opposition newspaper.

Between them, the three countries spent well over $60 million dollars financing the opposition.

As the end of the millennium approached, Otpor was up and running as was the wider operation to get rid of Milošević. The next hurdle to overcome was that of agreeing on the name of the man who would be king.

CHAPTER 17

*'Change is inevitable. In a progressive
country, change is constant.'*

Benjamin Disraeli

THE TEMPERATURE WAS WELL BELOW FREEZING AS WE
stood in Republic Square watching a giant electronic clock
count down the days, hours, minutes and seconds to the end
of the twentieth century. Europe's last Cold War dictator was
also running out of time, even if for most people it didn't look
that way.

Jakša, Milan, Veljko and I went for coffee at one of the
cafes in the square and talked about the future. All around
the world the approach of the new millennium was provid-
ing the stimulus for such conversations and for many people it
was a time of hope. In Serbia, however, things looked bleak.

Intellectuals wondered if their country's fate was to become
the land that time forgot, a sort of new-millennium version
of Enver Hoxha's Albania or Kim Il-sung's North Korea. The
military and police feared that Serbia would be the scene of
an eventual civil war. Ordinary people felt the hardship even
more keenly as they fell further into poverty, and much of the
younger population either headed into hedonism or out of
the country.

Veljko and his wife Katarina were thinking of leaving. They'd agreed they would wait another year and if things hadn't improved by then they would head west in search of a better future for their young daughter. They both had exportable skills. In addition to her work for a German TV channel, Katarina was a university professor. Both of them were exactly the sort of people the country needed, but after ten years fighting the regime they were emotionally exhausted.

A cloud had settled over Serbia. You could feel it in the air of despondency about the place. Instead of looking ahead, people looked towards the ground, their heads bent as if under the weight of the increasingly harsh conditions in which they lived. The opposition activists and regime insiders could feel the first faint tremors of change, but most of the population just hunkered down for the long, dark winter nights and the power cuts that inevitably came with them.

As the clock counted down, final efforts were made to try and get rid of Milošević the easy way. British intelligence sources indicate that at least one message was sent to Milošević offering him the opportunity to retire gracefully; Yugoslav intelligence sources indicate that two attempts were made. One was by the Americans and the other by the Greeks acting as messengers for a third party.

A Serbian reporter who has good journalistic contacts with Yugoslav army intelligence says that an attempt was made in the Hungarian capital: 'The message was passed in Budapest to senior Yugoslav government representatives by people from the UN, but really the offer was from the Americans. The deal was: "Tell Slobo not to worry about The Hague War Crime indictment. We'll make sure that they don't come after him, but if he doesn't want to play ball then we'll keep pushing. All he has to do is call an election, lose it, and then retire gracefully. He can even keep some of the money, but he has to understand that it's over."'

Milošević was told that even though he would not be pursued, his son Marko would still be wanted for alleged drug trafficking. Milošević ignored the offer.

One of his former advisers observed another attempt via Milan Milutinović, who was the Serbian president and a fellow Socialist Party member: 'Milutinović was a link via the Greeks but it didn't work because Milošević just wasn't receptive. There were attempts to establish reliable channels, but there was no point.'

The adviser went on to explain that Milošević point-blank refused to cooperate. This had been predicted by the CIA psychological report on the president, which indicated his reversion to stubbornness under pressure.

As with so many leaders he couldn't bring himself to admit that he would be replaced. He stuck his chin out in defiance of the outside world and said he was acting on behalf of the Serbian people. Eventually those same people, assisted by the outside world, said 'enough is enough' and gave him a right hook.

Milošević only had one strategy, which was to hang on until something came to the rescue. When he refused the offers to step down he didn't have any other moves to make, but his opponents had a fall-back plan and simply continued to undermine him from within.

The former Serbian information minister, Aleksandar Vučić, watched this from his position as a coalition cabinet member: 'There were many problems in the Socialist Party at the time and in the leadership. Everyone knew what was happening but no one wanted to do anything about it.'

The offers came and went and the giant digital clock in Republic Square ticked down to midnight, then to the first second of a new millennium, and on into the remaining time Milošević had in power.

The New Year celebrations in Serbia were muted. Many people were too busy surviving week to week to take on the regime. Across that winter it seemed as if nothing would ever change, but under the surface Otpor continued to chip away at the Milošević edifice, and the opposition politicians continued to receive training in campaign techniques and economic practice from the American, British and German specialists.

They were helped by a series of high-profile and unexplained murders including the shooting of the paramilitary leader known as Arkan. The deaths deepened the unease ordinary people felt about the state of their country and also created a climate of fear among the regime members and caused them to ask themselves, 'Who's next?'

Arkan was gunned down on 15 January. A month later the Yugoslav defence minister Pavle Bulatović was killed as he sat in a restaurant. His murder was followed by that of the head of the Yugoslav national airline, and then a senior official in the Socialist Party.

I was in Brussels the night Arkan was murdered. Jakša phoned me and by way of saying hello told me: 'Arkan has been shot, I think he's dead but I can't confirm it yet.' He gave me the few details he knew before hanging up to call Sky News and report the situation live. I made a few calls myself, went on air to sum up what I knew about the man and then headed for the airport.

Arkan was big news. He was a larger-than-life figure whose name was known and feared throughout Europe. He had charm, courage, wealth, a beautiful pop singer for a wife, a plausible manner and lots of guns. This heady cocktail made him a folk hero to many Serbs and a source of fascination to the outside world. However, it failed to hide the fact that he was a gang leader and had been indicted by the UN war crimes tribunal.

Arkan's real name was Željko Ražnatović. In the early 1970s he had been a small-time criminal and football hooligan. Within a few years he had progressed to bank robberies in Western Europe before returning to the Balkans to carve out a full-time position as a name within the Balkan mafia. During the 1990s he formed his militia – the 'Tigers'. They operated in Croatia and Bosnia and were known to be an utterly ruthless group of men guilty of committing a string of atrocities.

By the time of the Kosovo War, Arkan had branched out into business, bought a football club and formed a political party.

Whenever I met him he always wore a suit and spoke politely. He never touched alcohol or cigarettes. During the Kosovo War he used to come to the Hyatt Hotel in the evenings. Rumours had circulated that his Tigers were operating in Kosovo and he suspected that NATO was targeting him. It was no surprise when a hotel he part-owned in New Belgrade was hit by a cruise missile.

On several occasions as I walked through the entrance of the Hyatt a nervous doorman would approach me with an offer I felt it better not to refuse:

'Arkan wants to see you.'

I would make my way to the tea room whereupon two athletic-looking blonde women would draw themselves up to their full height of six feet and bar my entry to the area around him. They were part of his team of bodyguards and were both expert kick-boxers.

Arkan and I would talk about the current situation but I would always steer the conversation around to the alleged war crimes of his paramilitary group. He never gave an inch on the subject.

'My Tigers are true soldiers who have never killed a civilian and never raped a woman. When I am with them in the field if they so much as steal a piece of bread I punish them. They are warriors and I am a warrior and warriors do not do such things.'

He said this with such sincerity that for a second I would almost forget about the volumes of evidence to the contrary from people in Bosnia and Croatia. Almost.

One of my colleagues criticized me for spending time with him but my view was that if you want to understand what's going on in the world it's no good just talking to the good guys. He used to tell me all sorts of little snippets, which were very useful to put together with what other sources were saying.

On one occasion Milan, Veljko and I went along to his football club, Obilić, to film a game against Čačak, which had been organized to raise money for families who had lost their jobs after NATO bombed a series of factories in the town. After we had enough footage we were invited up into the directors' box. Arkan and I talked about football and he revealed a good knowledge of the game in England. I told him about a series of coincidences that had resulted in my playing cricket for France against Italy in Rome and joked that if only I could manage to do the same for Leeds United my life would be complete.

His response was to offer to let me come on as a substitute for Obilić during the last ten minutes of the game. It's not often you get a chance to play for the Yugoslav champions and I was sorely tempted to accept.

Fortunately my judgement came to the rescue. To be seen talking with Arkan was one thing; to play for his football team would be quite another.

Towards the end of the Kosovo War he came to the Hyatt to watch the Bayern Munich versus Manchester United Champions League final on the giant screen in the bar. Like most Leeds United supporters I was churlish enough to want Bayern Munich to win. Arkan said he was in two minds as both teams represented countries which were bombing Serbia. He ended up backing the English side, which duly won with a last-minute goal.

Arkan had spent years making his own luck, often at the expense of others, but no one who lives life the way he did can have luck forever. I knew he wouldn't die in his bed and often when sitting with him I felt I was talking to a dead man. That night was the last time I saw him alive.

His luck ran out eight months later in the foyer of the Intercontinental Hotel, which is opposite the Hyatt. A man he appeared to know approached him to say hello, then took out a pistol and shot him several times. He died along with a friend who was also hit.

The first thing Jakša had to do when I arrived to cover the funeral was call the editor of one of Serbia's national newspapers. A reporter had written about the coverage of the death and in quoting some of my comments made on Sky News the night before described me as 'more than just a friend of Arkan's'. We were both furious. I was neither a friend nor 'more than a friend' of Arkan and to suggest otherwise could get me in trouble with all sorts of people.

Jakša took a strong line with the editor who immediately apologized saying that he had not seen the piece and would reprimand the reporter. He offered a retraction but Jakša advised that to do that would only draw attention to the matter so we dropped it.

The following day Veljko, Milan, Jakša and I went to cover the funeral service, which featured flags, patriotic songs and uniforms. As well as family, friends and many members of the Tigers, several thousand people turned up to pay their last respects. It was a comment on the state of the country. For many Serbs, Arkan was a hero. Among the younger generation there were those who glamorized his gangster lifestyle and hoped to emulate it, while among the older Serbs were those who believed him only to be a defender of the country.

There were dozens of armed men from Arkan's organizations mingling with the crowds and several of them were close to where Veljko had set up his camera. We stood on a makeshift platform for my 'report to camera' and I said something about how for some Serbs Arkan was a hero and defender of the state, but for others he was a murdering gangster. It seemed a fairly accurate description, which explained to viewers why so many people had gone to pay respects to what most people regarded as a war criminal.

After we had filed our report Milan, Veljko and I went for a drink in the bar of the Hyatt, which was empty apart from the three of us. We were halfway through a beer when two large men in leather jackets came in and looked towards our table. It was obvious they were looking for us so it was a little alarming when they went over to the barman and asked him to leave the room. They only needed to ask once and he immediately disappeared while one of the men closed the doors behind him.

By this point the three of us were almost frozen into our chairs. There was no doubt these men were from either the secret police or one of the Belgrade gangs. They approached our table and one of them spoke to me.

'Mr Marshall, could we have a word with you?'

'Certainly,' I replied in as confident a manner as I could.

'Could we speak to you alone?' said the man. I could feel Veljko and Milan breathe an inward sigh of relief, which suggested they were thinking, 'Phew, at least they're not going to shoot us as well.' I couldn't blame them; I would have been relieved if it was the other way round.

It turned out that the Ražnatović family had already seen our report and the two men had come to pass on a message from Arkan's son, Mihajlo. I immediately jumped to the wrong conclusion and thought there was going to be trouble because I had used the words 'murdering gangster'. I began to explain that I was just putting across two views when the man doing the talking smiled and said that Mihajlo felt it had been a fair report and wanted to know if I would like to come up to the family house to join the funeral wake.

This put me in a difficult position. Whatever one thought of Arkan, the fact was that Mihajlo, who was not known to be involved in criminal activities, had lost his father. To turn down the invitation might be considered rude by some rather frightening people. On the other hand, as a journalist I couldn't be seen to be participating in the mourning process.

I thanked the man for the invitation, asked for Mihaljo's number and rang him to explain why I had to turn down his offer. When I later told this story to some colleagues they said I was mad not to have taken up the opportunity to be the only reporter allowed into the headquarters of the Arkan operation on that day of all days. These things are subjective; you can be criticized for having sources such as Arkan, and criticized for not getting closer when you have the opportunity.

The murder of Arkan made international headlines, but for the Serbs it was just one of many which caused shockwaves to roll through Serbian society. A Yugoslav industrialist who has contacts with both the British and Yugoslav secret services says the fear factor the killings induced should not be underestimated: 'The bizarre sequence of political murders was important leverage in persuading people that there had to be a change. There were also the abductions of people on The Hague wanted list. They were carried out by mercenaries who were paid DM50,000 each; those operations were organized by the NATO forces in Bosnia. Concerning the murders, the government said the CIA carried them out. I still don't know who did it but it wasn't smart for the government to blame the CIA because a lot of people started thinking, "Well, if the Americans can get the Defence Minister then they can easily get me." It followed on that people began to look for a way off the sinking ship.'

The lifeboats were being readied and the training of the opposition continued. The National Democrat Institute (NDI) commissioned a US company to gauge opinion inside Serbia. Doug Schoen of the polling firm Penn Schoen and Berland Associates flew to Budapest to brief a gathering of opposition politicians who represented a number of different parties. Schoen demonstrated how the polls showed that enough Yugoslav voters would unite behind a single figure to oppose Milošević as long as that individual had certain credentials.

He or she would have to be a nationalist, have a clean past, have had no involvement with the regime or foreign money, and must be untainted by the petty squabbles of the main opposition leaders. That pretty much ruled out everyone that anyone had ever heard of. A few weeks later Schoen returned, this time bringing evidence that the man who fitted the above criteria and who therefore could replace Milošević as Yugoslav president was called Vojislav Koštunica.

Some of the opposition members present were unhappy with this. They knew who Koštunica was but feared that no one else in the country did.

He was a Belgrade lawyer who headed the small Democratic Party of Serbia, but he was virtually unknown to people outside of the capital. The Americans argued that his relative lack of profile wasn't a problem and that he could be 'made to be known'. The important thing was that the polls indicated that those who had heard of him felt him to be a credible person.

After this meeting in Budapest, the opposition went back to Serbia to mull over the idea. Most of them had already come to the conclusion that their own party leaders were unable to play the required role. They either had skeletons in their closets or were unacceptable to ordinary people. Koštunica's name had been mentioned before but the NDI spelt it out: Koštunica equalled potential winner.

Drašković was no longer part of the equation and the only other major contender was Zoran Djindjić who headed the Democratic Party.

Some of his inner circle wanted him to be the presidential challenger but according to a source who was present when Djindjić was told of the Koštunica plan he immediately understood that it was a good idea.

'One of the advisers exploded with anger, saying, "No one knows who Koštunica is, Zoran is a national figure he must be the name put forward", but Zoran was quiet and then he said, "No, Koštunica can do it."'

According to the source, Djindjić accepted that he might have to take a step backwards in order to take two steps forward later on.

The compromise between the two men was that if things went according to plan, Koštunica would be president of Yugoslavia and Djindjić would be prime minister of Serbia. Djindjić knew that eventually his designated position might be the more powerful of the two.

Koštunica quickly grew in stature. A friend of thirty years' standing barely recognized him: 'I watched as he stepped out of his skin. In those few months he wasn't the Vojislav Koštunica I knew. He played a role; modest, decisive, articulate. He understood he had to play this role and that this was an historical moment. When it was all over he went back to the old Koštunica, but at the time it was a case of "good for us and good for him".'

The opposition finally had a name to sell, a product to push and an idea to believe in. The idea remained '*Gotev je!*' and it was growing. As the beauty of the Belgrade spring turned into the heat of a Balkan summer Aleksandar Vučić saw the mood change with it: 'The important thing was that there was some kind of understanding that one day the opposition will win. You know, in our federal government buildings no one was reading *Politika* anymore; instead they were reading the opposition papers *Blic* and *Danas*. Everyone was trying to find someone to save them, and so many of them caught that train.'

Vučić was scathing about those he saw as 'rats leaving a sinking ship' but he also loathed the opposition media: 'We had our man inside one of the media organizations and so we knew that they were robbing the West and taking far more than they needed.'

With so much money flowing into the country it seems likely some of it will have disappeared. In Bosnia hundreds of millions of pounds in aid was 'lost' in the first few years after the war ended. But the Western countries were not about to allow a small degree of corruption to put them off. Instead the pressure was increased. The British and Americans carried on making contact with people on the inside of the regime while at the same time training more and more Serbs in modern propaganda techniques.

The equipment continued to flow in. At least twenty satellite phones arrived through a variety of routes including the diplomatic bags of the embassy of a Scandinavian country. The sat phones had the advantage of being difficult to monitor thus allowing them to be used for sensitive conversations. Dozens of mobile phones were purchased for the young activists in Otpor along with desktop and laptop computers.

By now, senior army officers were circulating ideas on how to get rid of the man who had overseen their loss of power. Some sections of the Yugoslav military were even discussing the options with their rivals in the police force. The former head of state security, Jovica Stanišić, was among those who were no longer loyal.

The two main British political parties, Labour and Conservative, began to donate money to the opposition, and support for opposition-led towns such as Čačak was stepped up. German cities began twinning themselves with Serbian towns and using the contacts to funnel money directly into the town halls.

A Foreign Office Balkans specialist believes that the seeds for the whole operation were sown in 1997 following the three-month-long demonstrations which forced Milošević to accept local election results: 'In 97 the opposition got control of fiefdoms such as the town of Čačak and that played a role in the push to remove him because Slobo lost at a technical level. Supposing the opposition movement in Čačak hadn't controlled the town hall, the local media, or had face to face meetings with the local security chiefs, then the whole thing may not have got going.'

In late June, with the economy collapsing and support ebbing away Milošević was forced into another short-term, short-sighted decision. If the population had to suffer another cold, dark winter he knew he could face massive anti-government demonstrations. To give himself legitimacy, he decided to call local, national and presidential elections for September. This news wasn't announced until late the following month in order to give the opposition less time to prepare. Milošević believed they were hopelessly divided, but he still didn't want to give them any help.

The people around him had stopped telling him what was really going on in Serbia. This always seems to happen to despots, and is invariably a contributing factor in their downfall. Milošević truly believed he would be standing against several weak opponents and failed to see that by putting his own name on the ballot paper he was personalizing the vote. He also felt that if things did go wrong, he could always steal victory as he had tried to do in the past. What he didn't know was that this time there were enough people ready to stop him. For the first time those opposing him would be carrying guns and they would be prepared to use them. With an election called, the scene was set for the final showdown. There were just a few more details to work out.

CHAPTER 18

*'A man's most open actions have
a secret side to them.'*

Joseph Conrad

IN THE SUMMER OF 2000 TWO YUGOSLAV SOKO G-2A
Galeb jets were to be seen screaming across the skyline of southern England. Below them many people in the
80,000-strong crowd at the International Air Show at Biggin
Hill mused on the fact that just twelve months prior to this
appearance Yugoslavia and NATO had been at war, but few of
them knew just how ironic and important the presence of the
jets was.

The G-2A jets had the calls signs AB and AC. In June 1999
AC had been sitting on the runway at Batajnica military airport
near Belgrade. The aircraft was full of shrapnel holes caused by
NATO's cluster bombs which had fallen during the seventy-
eight days and nights of the Kosovo War. A few months later
a private Anglo/Yugoslav company had bought AC, and now,
fully restored, it was being shown off at Biggin Hill.

The pilots had mixed emotions as they banked and prepared
for another fly-past. Both were ex-Yugoslav air force officers who
had watched NATO's air power take their country apart. Now
they were civilians, and participating in this spectacle was a way

of acknowledging that the Yugoslavs and the British were not enemies. The presence of the two aircraft was also a way for the British government to make face-to-face contact with people representing Yugoslav military intelligence. Such contact was too difficult in Belgrade because there, in addition to keeping an eye on the opposition groups and foreign diplomats, all the secret services carefully watched each other.

The British knew that much of the army high command was sick of Milošević. The president had downgraded their status and led them into a series of disastrous wars. Army intelligence was probably the best connected of all the Belgrade services and its officers found out most of what was going on before briefing trusted generals within the high command.

A Yugoslav industrialist who had been asked by the British to pass messages to Milošević the previous year says that people fairly high up in the regime approved the Biggin Hill mission: 'Someone here allowed them to go because they wanted the contact to be made. It was one of several such meetings.'

The British embassy in Belgrade issued at least nine visas to Serbs for the air show, probably quite a few more. The army intelligence people who came over were unconnected to the commercial company accredited but used the visit as cover. With 80,000 people about, it was fairly easy to talk without being noticed.

The British wanted to know more about the strength of opposition to Milošević inside the armed forces. They received a cautious reply. The Yugoslav side didn't represent the whole army nor were they in England to do any deals. However, they did have the backing of a group of senior officers who wanted to see the lie of the land. They made it clear that the military in Yugoslavia was deeply concerned about the state of the country and its future. Hints were dropped that in the final analysis the army was loyal to the country and not to the president.

The British were too polite to ask about the role of some Yugoslav officers in the criminal activities of the regime, or about Kosovo. On this occasion they were interested in the future not the past and so the meeting was a cordial affair. Nothing concrete came out of it but the contact at face-to-face level had been made. When two sides are suspicious of each other such personal meetings are crucial.

The army intelligence people returned to Belgrade having gleaned a bit of extra information about how serious the British effort was to get rid of 'the problem' and were assured that this was supported at the highest levels. They also now had names to contact for future use if they required more 'clarification'.

The British went back to London with the feeling that in certain circumstances it was unlikely that the army would fire on the people. That was as much as they could have hoped for and they too now had names they could contact in the future.

A few days later the pressure on Milošević intensified with an attack on his ability to move money out of Serbia via the Cyprus branch of the Serbian Beogradska Bank. The branch was run by Borka Vučić, an old friend of the president. The British leant on the authorities in Cyprus, reminding them of the island's desire to become part of the European Union. The Central Bank of Cyprus suddenly discovered that the Beogradska didn't have 'sufficient liquidity' and closed the branch.

This gave Milošević another headache he didn't want to have to deal with. The branch had been used as a staging post for the money the regime's leading lights had been moving into Switzerland. Without Beogradska, it was a lot harder for senior regime figures to keep stealing from the people; this in turn made Milošević a less attractive proposition as leader.

After years of turning a blind eye to the money side of the Milošević regime, the international powers were now beginning to squeeze. Things had been different in the mid 1990s. Then a former British Foreign Secretary could broker a massively favourable billion-dollar financial deal for Milošević without anyone getting upset. In 1997 Douglas Hurd was working for the British bank National Westminster. Hurd, who had been Foreign Secretary just eighteen months previously, oversaw the part-privatization of Serbia Telecom, which earned Nat West $15 million in commissions.

It must be stressed that neither Hurd nor the bank did anything illegal, but the sale helped keep Milošević in power. One of his bankers remembers the cosy days when it was still respectable to deal with the regime: 'People did business with us because no one cared about the democratization of Serbia. The Telecom deal allowed Slobo to finance elections and paid for the Kosovo War. But he became a problem when Kosovo began so he became unacceptable.'

In July the election date was announced. The first round of voting would be on 24 September. If no single candidate got over 50 per cent in the presidential vote then a second round would be held two weeks later for the two most successful candidates.

The campaigning opened to a chorus of yawns. Few people took much notice; most were more concerned about enjoy-ing the summer than bothering with the politicians they had grown to despise. They also missed the other campaign being waged behind the scenes and which was now beginning to knit together the various strands of opposition to Milošević's power structure.

More and more people from the inside had given up on the idea that they could hold on indefinitely and were getting in touch with each other. A CIA agent oversaw some of the meetings which took place at a villa in Montenegro: 'They didn't have to be nuclear scientists to know that time was running out. The guys toward the top of the pyramid, the ones who held the top bit up, worked it out. They were gamblers and they knew the time to hold and the time to fold.'

More satellite and mobile phones, faxes, computers and money arrived, with much of the equipment now coming through the embassy of the Scandinavian country.

The Belgrade industrialist, who had been the go-between for Milošević and the British, claims that as well as equipment, people were also coming through that route using diplomatic passports. He called them 'technicians'.

'By that I mean they were technicians in seizing power. They were people who think and people who do. They lobbied with the establishment, they helped set up the network. Of course some sections of intelligence knew all about it but there were no arrests because there was a paralysis at the top. I didn't want to help a coup d'état but nor did I any longer want to help Slobo. He no longer trusted me anyway, so I also did nothing.'

'Doing nothing' was becoming an increasingly powerful tool as the election approached. Phone calls that could have been made were put off, and intelligence reports that could have been sent to officials at the top of the pyramid instead sat in drawers in the dull, musty offices of government buildings staffed by people who realized that the system they ran had reached its sell-by date.

According to a Yugoslav military officer now working in Western Europe:

'Military intelligence was familiar with the foreign preparations to throw out Milošević. We knew about their organizations, their propaganda efforts, the meeting in Szeged in Hungary and Blagoevgrad in Bulgaria. We used all legal measures to find out and we passed on the information, but at a political level no decisions were made.'

Some of those passing on information to the Yugoslav agencies were well-placed officials working inside the opposition movement. A CIA man who was helping to put together the coup realized there was a leak and, suspecting he knew who it was, began to think of a way to smoke out the mole:

'I was back in Washington one week and was at the Golden Circle, a strip joint in Dupont, when I got the idea. I've joked about this with my wife; I told her there was a dancer who had her groin just inches from my face and for some reason that was the exact moment the idea came to me. She thought it was pretty funny; anyway we put the idea into motion. In Serbia we told two people, just two, a secret, and then waited to see how long it was before it came out. Goran Matić [information minister] eventually came out with it, but it was bullshit because we'd made it up. But he bit, and we knew who had fed the information to him and so we just froze them out of the information loop.'

In September, with the election campaign heating up, Yugoslav army intelligence returned to the UK and to RAF Biggin Hill under the cover of the air show for the sixtieth anniversary of the Battle of Britain. Again a Yugoslav team and two pilots were invited, as were representatives of all Britain's Second World War allies.

This time the message from the Yugoslav side was that one of the circumstances in which the army might not fire on the people was if the people were defending a democratically elected government. They could not yet speak for all the high command but what was clear was that a significant part of it was now ready to see change.

The same could be said of the population. Even in the rural heartlands, which had less access to alternatives to the Milošević media machine, the polls indicated that support was moving behind the opposition.

In the few days before the first round of voting a wave of nervous confidence spread over the opposition movement. It now looked certain that Koštunica would get through to the second round. He wasn't the only alternative standing against Milošević, but he was the only credible one.

The opposition mainstream was confident that if the second round were a straight fight between Koštunica and Milošević then their man would triumph. The world's media was not invited to witness the event and very few journalists managed to get visas. Jakša and I had been told by the Foreign Ministry that Sky's reporting over the previous few years was considered to be fair and that I would be allowed in to cover the election. It was therefore a nasty surprise when my application was denied.

After a few phone calls were made we confirmed what we suspected. Goran Matić at the Ministry of Information had blocked the application. With my nose pressed up against the window to try and see what was happening in Serbia it was little consolation to learn that most of our media rivals were having the same problems. It was clear that the regime realized that there could be trouble on the way and that if they suppressed it with violence they didn't want the media around to see it. We tried a number of routes to get the decision on my visa reversed but as the apologetic people at the Foreign Ministry kept saying, it couldn't be done.

Election day – 24 September – arrived and a tidal wave of votes washed away most of Milošević's remaining defences. The only things keeping him in power were a big lie, a police force and an army.

To the surprise of even the opposition almost all the available figures showed that Koštunica had won outright and that there was no need for a second round. Under the Yugoslav Constitution if any candidate polled more than 50 per cent in the first round then he or she was the automatic winner.

The Centre for Free Elections and Democracy said Koštunica had won 58.67 per cent of the vote, with Milošević beaten out of sight down on 33.59. The Democratic Opposition of Serbia had the victory at 52.54 per cent, with Milošević on 35.01. Vuk Drašković announced that his Serbian Renewal Party's figures agreed that Koštunica had won, and the head of the Orthodox Church supported the idea that the election showed that a new man was now the duly elected president of Yugoslavia. Even the Radical Vojislav Šešelj deserted Milošević and said that Koštunica was now the legitimate president.

The problem was that Slobodan Milošević didn't see it that way. The official Federal Election Commission, which he controlled, put the Koštunica vote at 48.22 per cent and Milošević at 40.23 thereby requiring a second round of voting on 8 October.

It quickly became apparent that the Federal Election Commission had invented a new form of mathematics in which two plus two could equal anything they thought they could get away with. This was the big lie.

On 11 September the commission said there were 7.8 million registered voters. The figure was confirmed on 26 September but two days later they announced that the electorate numbered only 7.2 million people, which would mean that in just two days 600,000 people had officially vanished. However, their voting slips had not and so 600,000 ballot papers could be used whichever way Milošević wanted. The Commission's figures also showed a surprising number of pro-Milošević votes coming in from Serb refugees and Kosovo Albanians living in southern Serbia.

This clumsy short-term attempt to buy more time was classic Milošević. He tried to be smart by not stealing too many votes and even agreed that he'd come second. What he really wanted was an extra two weeks in which to pull enough levers to ensure he could steal the second round.

The next move was with the opposition. At this point they could have compromised and tried to win again in the second round despite knowing that the Federal Electoral Commission would again use its new methods of adding up. But things had changed; the days of giving in, of compromise, were over.

No one was buying the big lie. Suddenly Milošević was an emperor with no clothes, rowing a boat around a pond, and pretending not to hear the shouts from all around of 'Come in Slobo, your time is up'. It wasn't just that the people thought most of what he said was a lie; they now no longer even cared when he was telling the truth. He claimed he had desperately resisted the break-up of Yugoslavia – whether that was true or not it could still elicit the response 'and you failed!'

In a TV broadcast to the nation on 2 October he once again appealed to patriotism, saying that Yugoslavia was still under attack from NATO but in the guise of the opposition leaders who were therefore traitors to the nation.

'As you know,' he said in a far-from-confident manner to a far-from-impressed audience, 'efforts have been made for a decade to put the whole Balkan Peninsula under the control of certain Western powers.'

Milošević was hinting that the mass slaughter in the region was not the fault of those who pulled the triggers but of the West. Here was the patriotism card played in the belief that enough people would still think that he was the man to save them from this foreign bogeyman. Now, however, there was an alternative in the shape of the nationalist Vojislav Koštunica.

A few weeks earlier a photograph had surfaced of Koštunica holding an assault rifle. A few outside commentators thought this was a vote-loser among a population which was sick of war. In fact it was just the sort of image required to woo the nationalist vote away from Milošević.

Koštunica was guaranteed the votes of the opposition supporters. They would have voted for ABM (or 'Anyone but Milošević') but crucially, he could also impress many Milošević supporters. They would vote for a Good Serb when they saw one in order to get rid of the man whose epitaph could be 'and I failed'. Sometimes even complex politics is simply about winners and losers, and Milošević had begun to look like a loser.

Every time Milošević said something about the economy, the defence of the country, Serbian society and how he'd tried to help the situation, people thought 'and you failed!' He even suggested that if the people trusted the opposition and installed it in power then a crime wave would hit Serbia. He seemed to forget that he had overseen an explosion in crime and perhaps he didn't know that most people suspected that half of his family and cronies were enriching themselves with vast sums of money.

As early as 1987 his Socialist Party had begun opening off-shore bank accounts and moving state funds into them. Later on he pretended to privatize a state-owned company called MKS then used it to channel funds out of Yugoslavia. Some of these funds were used to help Yugoslavia once it was hit by international sanctions, but Milošević's entourage also used it to help themselves to hundreds of millions of dollars' worth of the people's money.

On 2 October the Swiss government froze almost one hundred bank accounts belonging to Milošević and his friends. Fourteen months previously the Swiss had said they didn't know if there were any accounts at all; now after intense lobbying by the Americans, they found dozens containing hundreds of millions of dollars.

Few ordinary people knew the details, but the rumours had begun to circulate and the opposition was able to shrug off Milošević's broadcast. They began to describe Koštunica as 'president-elect'. The outside world called on Milošević to accept defeat and the British Foreign Secretary Robin Cook went so far as to remind Belgrade that the West had a 'continuing and significant military presence' near Yugoslavia. This veiled threat suggested that NATO would not just sit and watch if civil war erupted in Yugoslavia. The idea of intervention seems unlikely but Cook was reminding Milošević that all the cards were stacked against him.

Still he wouldn't go. The opposition was not about to participate in a second round and prepared a campaign of demonstrations and civil disobedience. At the same time it began to put into place a plan drawn up weeks earlier for an armed insurrection if Milošević forced the issue. The work put in during the months leading up to the election was supposed to make that unnecessary but they were prepared to fight if Milošević tried to pull the house down on top of everyone.

The opposition, or perhaps what was now considered the government, called for a mass demonstration in front of the Yugoslav parliament scheduled for 5 October. By calling the people to Belgrade the opposition raised the stakes, as everyone knew that this day would be the showdown.

The country was in turmoil and the borders were closing. The electoral process, for a people which longed for stability, was in crisis. The leaders of just about every country most people have heard of said Koštunica was the winner. Some of those countries couched their responses to the election in 'diplospeak', but it was clear that Slobo's serious friends abroad had cut him loose.

Even the Chinese, who had become Milošević's closest foreign allies, failed to support him. A statement issued by the Foreign Ministry in Beijing said, 'We respect the choice of the Yugoslav people,' which translated as 'Sorry Slobo, we're not getting involved in this one.' The position of Yugoslavia's other friends – North Korea, Iraq and Belarus – were irrelevant as the Serb people viewed them the same way as the rest of the world did, i.e. as 'basket cases'.

At the same time the workers at the Kolubara mining complex downed tools and occupied the site, while the opposition leaders called for a general strike. For the first time, Milošević faced an internal opposition which had developed muscle. The industrial workers and even some rural people had joined the big city intellectuals and students and together they would march on the capital.

The opposition leaders who were organizing the masses had a plan of action and they knew that 5 October was their D-Day. If the plan failed, their lives would be at risk amid widespread bloodshed and the probability of defeat. If the armed forces backed Milošević and he won, it would take years to mount another challenge. The British and Americans knew this only too well; it was what the Biggin Hill meetings had been about. Then they had danced around the subject, but now they wanted a straight answer.

On 4 October a meeting was arranged to take place in the Bosnian village of Laktaši, near Banja Luka. There had been several such meetings attended by two MI6 officers and two of their counterparts from Yugoslav military intelligence. This time the British side brought a team of SAS men to back them up. A CIA officer who helped set up the final meeting said the SAS team arrived in front of a cafe in Laktaši in an unmarked van.

'On that occasion they met in the evening and both sides brought some serious hardware because they had tough things to talk about and they didn't want to be naked if there was trouble. It was easy for the British to organize because they had special forces teams working out of what we called the "Metal Factory" base near Banja Luka. The last meeting was to nail down everything for the following day and the British were concerned about security in case they were double-crossed and the Serb side tried to snatch someone and take them back across the Drina [river]. Imagine if Milošević knew about the coup and before it even got going properly he paraded a couple of British or American spies on TV as evidence of foreign involvement.'

The British had long memories and good reasons to be cautious. The day before the Second World War broke out German intelligence lured a British spy to the Netherlands and then whisked him across to Germany where he spent the duration of the conflict. The possibility of having an agent kidnapped from Bosnia was slim but they weren't taking chances.

The SAS team sat in the van listening via hidden microphones as the MI6 officers talked to their opposite numbers in the cafe. This time the army intelligence people spelt it out, saying that even if Milošević called the army onto the streets the high command would not respond.

There were no guarantees and still no one knew if the entire high command agreed but the message was passed on to the opposition leaders in Belgrade. With just a few hours to go before D-Day all concerned were studying their cards intently. The question was: would the gamblers hold or fold?

CHAPTER 19

*'A great revolution is never the fault of
the people, but of the government.'*

Johann Wolfgang von Goethe

AFTER A LONG DARK NIGHT SERBIA WOKE UP. ACROSS the country people rose from their slumber, joined their friends and family and set off towards the capital. The intention was to kick the darkness so hard that it bled light.

Well before four in the morning the lamps were blazing in towns and villages across the country as people loaded up their vehicles and drank a last cup of coffee. With cries of 'see you in the parliament' they set off, streaming in from the smaller roads and joining the river of determination now flowing in towards Belgrade along Serbia's five major highways.

There was an air of revolution; everyone knew this was no ordinary trip to protest in the capital. Only a few dozen people knew the plan, but it was obvious the day would be different to any other. Many people had seen the guns being loaded into trucks, the stones hidden under tarpaulins and recognized that among their ranks were off-duty soldiers and policemen who were prepared to fight alongside them. If things went wrong they knew a civil war could break out by nightfall.

This was a people's army organized into five columns and led by men and women who knew what they were doing and knew the potential consequences of their actions.

Milošević's first lines of defence were police checkpoints set up on the five highways around the capital to prevent the columns ever reaching him. It was supposed to be a ring of steel but it shattered like glass.

The mayor of Čačak, Velimir Ilić, was at the head of a force of 20,000 men. Among them were the truck drivers and industrial workers of central Serbia. At a rally held at six in the morning in the town square of Čačak, Mayor Ilić had told them, 'Victory or death!' This was not rhetoric; it was a genuine battle cry. If the coup attempt failed Ilić would be among those who might be executed by a vengeful regime.

The Čačak column, which snaked back along the Ibar highway for almost fourteen miles, halted at Majdan. A force of about forty policemen was guarding the roadblock. Ilić strode up to the senior officer and told him to get out of the way. Those behind didn't even bother with words; they picked up the police vehicles with their bare hands and threw them into a ditch.

'You're making them angry,' said Ilić as dozens of men began advancing on the police, who didn't bother to wait for orders; they simply fled into the nearby woods.

Similar scenes were being played out at all the checkpoints on the way into Belgrade. The police vehicles were smashed and the officers were threatened. They knew that if they opened fire they might kill a few of these raging mad men from the Serbian heartlands, but they would then be torn apart. Some of the commanders had already held clandestine meetings with the opposition leaders and agreed to allow the columns through. In

Belgrade several units had been briefed by senior officers that they were not to fire on the crowds. This left the regime with little except the elite units they were counting on if the first line of defence failed.

As Ilić and the Čačak column neared the city they ran into another police unit. This time there were 150 officers in full riot gear and backed up with an armoured personnel carrier.

Ilić asked the commander to move but even as he was refusing the men from Čačak unloaded a bulldozer they were carrying with them from a flat-bed truck. The police commander took out his truncheon and caught Ilić with a glancing blow. It was the only one he struck before he was caught and beaten to a pulp.

In Belgrade the coup leaders nervously waited for the first sight of the cars, buses and trucks now descending on the capital. They knew that if the columns failed to reach the city centre the coup attempt would be over before it even got underway.

Their headquarters was a factory on the outskirts of town which was controlled by Nebojša Čović, a former Milošević ally who had a score to settle with the president. Čović had been mayor of Belgrade but fell out of favour with the regime after Milošević slapped him in the face in front of other Socialist Party members. After that his so-called friends were nowhere to be seen. Now he wanted to slap Milošević back.

A Yugoslav military intelligence source believes that Čović has been overlooked as a key player in the day's events: 'The mayor of Čačak, Ilić, received a lot of attention but believe me this HQ was crucial. There were thousands of weapons at the factory and at least 2,000 trained and armed men there. There was a plan to split up and support the crowds in various places and to seize all of the government ministries. But the crowd didn't know the plan.'

Part of the plan was that the Čačak column was supposed to storm the parliament while the men and women from Niš took over the nearby RTS building. On the night of 4 October a police unit, which had switched sides, had hidden itself on the top floors of the building housing Studio B television. The opposition planned to use the premises to broadcast a speech by President-elect Koštunica. They knew that the regime would try to secure Studio B and so got in ahead of them.

The tens of thousands of people now gathering in front of the parliament didn't know any of this and had just one thing on their mind, to take what they said was already theirs.

As each column raced into town people began appearing on balconies or in front of their houses to cheer them on. Belgraders were also organized and were beginning to move into the centre. The Red Star football gang known as *Delije* gathered and made its way towards the state buildings.

While Otpor had the slogan of the coup, *Delije* gave the operation its song. The chant of 'Kill yourself Slobo and save Serbia' had tumbled down from the terraces earlier that year, spilt onto the streets and had been taken up by the whole opposition movement.

By now it was the turn of the regime loyalists to become anxious. The outer ring of defence was breached and the intelligence coming in suggested that the demonstration was going to be massive. The commanders who were still loyal weren't stupid; they knew something was up, they just didn't know what. Phone calls were going unanswered and down the chain of command officers were suddenly experiencing communication problems. Orders to arrest people received the response: 'Sorry sir, there's a lot of interference on the line.'

At the top the realization spread that Milošević might

be going down within hours and that his removal had been planned. There was a choice to be made: use force to smash the uprising, do nothing, or join the coup.

The police on the steps leading up to the federal parliament building watched as the crowd in front of them grew. They had seen the Čačak column arrive and unload the bulldozer. The commander radioed in reports every few minutes to police headquarters. He didn't like what he heard in return: 'Several thousand students approaching parliament, three thousand people heading your way from the railway station, column of vehicles entering city centre.'

The men from Čačak were impatient; they knew what they had come to do. Dressed in ordinary clothes they confronted the few dozen police on the steps who were armed with batons, riot shields, helmets, pistols and tear gas.

The temperature rose and the lines were formed. The Čačak men were hot, thirsty, hungry and angry. Words were exchanged, and then a few bottles were thrown. The first tear gas canisters were fired as the police drew their batons. Those directly in the firing line rolled back into the mass of people before sweeping forward again a few minutes later, this time a little closer to the police on the steps.

The news that tear gas had been fired quickly spread through the city and to those still on their way. It caused the plan to fall apart. People who had been told to go to the airport or a number of other locations headed straight to the parliament. There was dismay at the opposition headquarters but it changed to optimism as reports came in of the size of the crowd now pressing towards the parliament.

Ilić intended to attack in force at 3 p.m. and the skirmishing had intensified with each wave that fell upon the increasingly nervous defenders. Hundreds of thousands of people were now pressing into the area around the parliament.

By 3.30 p.m. the front line was on the lower rung of steps leading up to the double doors which were closed. The assumption was that behind the doors was an elite unit, and that if the gateway to parliament was breached, they would pour out and open fire.

By now the crowd was almost beyond fear. Another wave of people roared up the steps while others attacked from the sides, which were undefended. Some of the police surrendered, others began swinging their batons and were submerged under a welter of punches and kicks. The front line reached the double doors and began pushing. The doors creaked a little then gave way. As people poured into the hallway leading to the Chamber of the Republics a tear gas canister exploded. The front line ran straight through the cloud and was confronted by the sight of another police unit emerging from the chamber, holding tear gas guns and wearing gas masks. The two sides halted just a few yards apart. The police began firing their guns almost vertically, bouncing the canisters off the roof and down onto their opponents.

The front line reeled and began to fall back but with so many people now pressing in from behind it was chaos. People were falling over, choking from the gas and being crushed as some tried to get in and others out.

Eventually they were beaten back by the gas. Some were in despair, believing they had failed, but by now there was more than one way into the building.

The Red Star gang and other groups had gone to the sides of the parliament and were busy smashing the windows then climbing up and through them. The Čačak bulldozer advanced and scooped up a few protestors before depositing them on the first floor. Fires began to break out in several rooms even as another assault was made on the main entrance.

The police were panicking. The front line was now the double doors and they knew there were already people inside the building. The leader of the opposition party Civic Alliance, Goran Svilanović, got through the doors and called out to the commander of the police unit, who recognized him.

A brief conversation took place in front of the unit which had stopped firing gas. As the crowd followed Svilanović into the lobby the officers had had enough; they began to throw down their weapons and look for exits. Some were beaten, others were helped away.

There were other units inside the building but the battle for parliament was more or less won. People swarmed into the great chamber and along the corridors, joining those who had come through the windows. Offices were trashed and set alight. At one point a man got hold of a fire hose and turned it against a few policemen advancing down a corridor; they too surrendered and looked for a way out.

In the surrounding streets police units were attempting to reach their colleagues but were beaten back by the crowds who now could see that this really was D-Day. Smoke from the parliament mingled with the traces of tear gas as different groups armed with clubs, stones and the shields and batons of the police rampaged around the area attacking anything connected with the regime.

The perfume shop belonging to Milošević's hated son, Marko, was wrecked as people moved on to the next target, which was at 10 Takovska Street. The building, which housed RTS, known as 'the Bastille', was about to fall.

According to authors Dragan Bujošević and Ivan Radovanović, the regime leaders were now desperate. In their book *October 5th: A 24-hour Coup*, which gives an hour-by-hour account of the day, it appears that Milošević sanctioned an order to drop heavy tear gas canisters onto the crowd from helicopters. A reluctant colonel who received the order flew over the burning parliament and clearly saw the massive crowd beneath him. He landed back at his base and reported that the smoke was too thick to carry out the assignment.

This appears to be another example of how doing nothing can be a revolutionary act. On 5 October, as Milošević's support structure was kicked from beneath him, the smoke was too thick, phone calls didn't connect and communication links went down. There are many ways of disobeying orders.

It was now decision time for the elite forces. Milošević could continue to rule without a parliament, but without a TV station he really would be finished. The last desperate orders went out.

From the windows of the RTS building the police unit could see their colleagues outside being beaten back under a hail of missiles and Molotov cocktails. The bulldozer came around the corner from the parliament and ground on towards the Bastille.

The unit received orders to 'take further action' and to 'do the logical thing'. This was interpreted as meaning to open fire on the protestors. It was too much for some of them. One officer began taking off his uniform, others looked for ways out of the building, but a few gathered at the front entrance to try and defend it.

At about this time the 'Boys from Brazil' were called in, either directly by Milošević himself or via his chief of secret police Rade Marković. The Boys from Brazil were a top unit from Serbian state security. They were commanded by Milorad Ulemek, a former French Foreign Legion officer who had returned to Yugoslavia when the wars broke out in 1991.

The unit was trained to NATO special forces standards and had a long history of covert operations in the Yugoslav wars, including the Kosovo conflict.

Ulemek, known to all Serbs as 'the Legionnaire', had already been in contact with the opposition leaders the night before. Zoran Djindjić knew that if the Legionnaire was against them their chances of success were diminished.

'How many battles have you lost under Milošević?' he asked him.

'None.'

'And how many wars have you won under him?'

'None,' came the reply again. The Legionnaire didn't reveal his hand, but Djindjić came away from the meeting satisfied that Milošević could not definitely rely on the Boys from Brazil.

The Legionnaire was at his base near Belgrade playing football when he received orders to intervene. He has given this version of events to a friend: 'The top level called and told me about the situation in the city centre. According to this call there were 70,000 people there and cops were being killed at the TV station. We were told to go in and save them.'

The unit tore down into the city in their Humvee-type army vehicles, a sort of armour-plated jeep with an open back. The Legionnaire was in the lead vehicle dressed, as were all his men, in a black balaclava and a gas mask.

'When we got downtown I realized we'd been lied to; it wasn't 70,000 people, more like 700,000. People were fleeing in front of the vehicles as we came in. A few even opened fire on us as we approached RTS but I'd told my guys to keep calm and not return fire. At the TV station I realized I'd been told another lie, so I ordered the guys back to base.'

As their vehicles came into Slavia Square they were surrounded by what was now a raging angry mob. The Legionnaire stood up and looked around him.

'What was I going to do? Shoot all of them?' he asked himself.

An elderly woman approached him. All she could see was a tall figure dressed in black wearing a mask and with two handguns holstered on his chest. She tugged at his sleeve.

'May I ask you something?' she said. The Legionnaire looked down and nodded.

'You're not going to kill all these people, are you son?' asked the woman.

The Legionnaire says that at that moment he thought: 'Fuck it. I've been waging war for ten years for one man, and the thing I always said I would never do is to kill Serbs, not even for the boss.'

He took off his mask and was immediately recognized by some people in the crowd. The cry went up: 'It's the Legionnaire.' As everyone began cheering his men followed suit and pulled off their balaclavas and gas masks. People began to jump up onto the running boards of the vehicles to kiss the soldiers and wave the three-fingered Serb salute.

The Boys from Brazil set off back to their barracks while the Legionnaire went to meet Zoran Djindjić. This time Djindjić was told exactly what he wanted to hear. The Legionnaire understood that Milošević's time was up and that if any other units attempted to keep him in power then the special forces would step in.

Milošević had called people in too late. He was always a strange type of dictator. He used the levers of power more subtly than his counterparts in Africa or the Middle East and gave himself the semblance of respectability. One of his former advisers who turned his back on him in the months leading up to 5 October says the president reminded him of the Shah of Iran: 'He couldn't make up his mind about how much force to use. He used enough to make people angry, but not enough to make them terrified.'

By the time the Legionnaire had turned his men around, the TV station had just about fallen. There had been sporadic shooting by the police and a Red Star *Delije* member took a bullet in the leg as he sprinted through the main entrance. Then the Čačak bulldozer ploughed into the front doors and the mob set the building on fire. As the staff of this most hated of symbols of the regime poured out some were caught and beaten.

In all more than a hundred people were injured on 5 October including five who had gunshot wounds. Two people died: Jasmina Jovanović was run over by a vehicle and Momčilo Stakić suffered a heart attack.

With RTS off the air Milošević looked doomed. Studio B was backing the revolutionaries as was B92 Radio and Milošević could only now be heard by the few people around him. Without his megaphones his voice was small, drowned out in the fury of the hour.

Theoretically he could have attempted to communicate via YU Info, the twenty-four-hour TV news channel controlled by his information minister Goran Matić. The reality would have been different. YU Info was playing a clever game. From about 26 September it had transformed itself from a propaganda mouthpiece of the regime into an unbiased source of news.

Back in London the Foreign Office Balkans team had watched the output with increasing interest. One of the team had arrived in Hungary on 4 October and was monitoring events from there: 'If you're talking about the media, then YU Info was the best thing in the run-up to 5 October. They simply covered what was going on including what was happening in the streets. They were neutral.'

Neutrality was all the coup leaders needed from the media. YU Info might have been a minority channel, but it was state-run and so by its very impartiality it was sending a powerful message.

The only international TV channel to get a live TV signal out of Belgrade on 5 October was CNN. The Atlanta-based organization failed to cover itself in the type of glory such exclusive access should guarantee.

The BBC and Sky had people on the streets reporting live over the phone from outside the parliament as the crowds gathered and the revolution began. CNN ordered its correspondent to stay in his office a mile away so that he could broadcast live 'in vision'. While everyone else was reporting the magnitude of the early hours CNN stayed with the line that this was another demonstration and reported the regime figure of 70,000 demonstrators without pointing out that this was a ridiculous lie.

Just how CNN was the only station to be allowed a visa and permission to 'uplink' their signal is a mystery. Goran Matić, the man who refused Sky and the BBC entry to the country, gave the go-ahead to CNN shortly after a senior CNN executive paid a visit to Belgrade.

The BBC's John Simpson had smuggled himself in via Montenegro while Sky had Jakša Skecic already in town. Both gave running commentary on the day's events.

I was stuck on the Hungarian border with hordes of other journalists, all of us aware that we were missing the biggest story of the year. It was even more frustrating for another bunch of reporters who had flown into Belgrade airport from Montenegro but who were held in the arrivals lounge.

Among them was ITN's Julian Manyon. As the hours passed one of the cameramen present grew bored and began to practise his secret filming techniques by pointing the lens at Manyon as he paced up and down the lounge like a caged beast.

Manyon had already tried the 'Do you realize who I am?' routine to a far-from-impressed immigration official. The ITN man was now muttering to himself and becoming increasingly cross. Eventually, as the cameraman continued to film, he went back to the immigration guard and shouted at him: 'Don't you bloody realize that you've got a collection of the world's most important international correspondents here? Now I suggest you let us all through to get on with our jobs.'

The guard smiled and the doors to the revolution remained closed.

Downtown the coup looked to be a success by the early evening, but there were still a few nervous hours to go. The new government controlled the media and was backed by most of the police and some special forces. There was still a question mark over the army.

As far as the crowds were concerned the day was won. People transferred their torrid emotions into a street carnival of jubilation and relief. The city centre echoed to the sounds of gypsy bands playing outside cafes and techno funk blasting from the speakers fixed on the backs of flat-bed lorries. Serbia danced through the evening, the people high on adrenaline and plum brandy.

At 3 a.m., as people were beginning to drift home, Zoran

Djindjić was in City Hall opposite the federal parliament. He received word that army tanks had been seen on roads outside of the capital. Both Djindjić and other coup leaders had already heard rumours that the army was going to try and reverse the takeover at 5 a.m. as the crowds began to thin out. Because of this people had been asked to stay in front of the parliament building to protect it.

There was a lot of military activity that night. The army was busy moving units and equipment around the outside of the capital, at least one aircraft troop transporter, full of soldiers, landed at Batajnica and several top-level meetings were held between the special forces, the regular army and special police unit commanders.

Some people built makeshift barricades and a few prepared Molotov cocktails but 5 a.m. came and went, the tanks trundled back into their barracks, dawn arrived and with it a new era opened in Serbian history.

The state newspaper *Politika* hit the streets with a giant banner headline proclaiming 'Revolution!' *Politika* had always spoken for those in power; the headline confirmed that power had changed hands.

That morning the chief of staff General Nebojša Pavković telephoned Vojislav Koštunica and, addressing him as president, congratulated him on his victory and placed the army at his disposal. It was over.

It remains open to question whether Pavković was aware of the high-level contacts that took place between the army and the British in the months leading up to the coup. A Yugoslav military intelligence source believes that most of the high command shared a similar view on the question of whether to intervene and save Milošević.

'They didn't want to make promises to anyone until they saw the election results. Once it was clear that Milošević had lost, it was easier for them as they could argue they were on the side of legality because Koštunica had legally won the election. At first they didn't want to get involved for a number of reasons but they knew that neither side really trusted them and so finally they took part in the coup by not taking part in it.'

It was a relatively peaceful event. Few people thought control could be transferred without a blood-letting in Serbia. Many of the coup organizers feared that at the least there would be running gun battles on the streets of the capital.

In the event, the months of planning ensured that half the job was done even before the parliament was stormed. The violence, the burning, the bulldozer and the smoke were necessary theatre. The coup needed two types of critical mass, each of which was dependent on the other.

Firstly there had to be enough people in positions of power who were prepared to switch sides; secondly there had to be enough people on the streets to give the cover required to switch sides. The regime collapsed in on itself but few of those who caught the lifeboats would have had the courage to do anything without the assistance of the opposition and the smokescreen of the crowds.

A former British ambassador to Belgrade said: 'The Milošević regime imploded. Our help was just useful lubrication and it provided encouragement to people who may not have made the decisions they did.'

In the days that followed there were still some tense moments. I got into town late on 6 October. A team of thirteen Sky News people thundered down the highway from the Hungarian border, driving at ninety most of the way.

We were stopped by a lone policeman about 50 miles from Belgrade. He wanted to arrest all of us but saw reason at about the same time as he saw a DM50 banknote.

We turned up at the Hyatt and I fell into the arms of an exhausted Jakša who had been broadcasting almost non-stop for thirty-six hours. We embraced and kissed each other three times before I recovered my senses and began swearing at him for allowing the revolution to start without me: 'Ten years we've been working together and at the end you grab all the glory and cover it live!'

We laughed and went to the bar which was by now packed with reporters. The borders had opened and the world's media flooded in. What many didn't know, as they commented on the last revolution of the Cold War era, was that on 7 and 8 October there were still factions of the previous regime who had not fully committed themselves to the new government.

If you knew where to look and knew what you were looking at you could see them driving round the city centre in unmarked cars watching each other. The cars usually had four men in them, all heavily armed and all checking for any cracks in the surface of the revolution.

They weren't the only ones checking the situation. The Man Who Doesn't Exist drove in from Hungary accompanied by a Foreign Office Balkans expert. They both checked into the Hotel Moscow in the centre of town, put their bags in their rooms and strolled along the boulevards to the still-smoking parliament building.

They looked just like another two foreigners among the legions of media people, diplomats and Serbs who came to see the aftermath of the revolution. They didn't stay long. Two days was enough to gather enough information to report back to London that the coup looked secure.

The opposition coalition had taken power. The Democratic Opposition of Serbia (DOS) moved quickly to dispel doubt about who was in charge. They took control of the various levers of state and by the end of the week even those few people who knew what was going on behind the scenes were confident that there would be no reverse takeover.

Taking control of the finance sector was easier. Officials inside the Central Bank had known long before most people just how big a mess the country's finances were in and how much Milošević's people were stealing. They began to cooperate with an opposition group called G17 from as early as 1998. By late 1999 even the office of the Central Bank Governor was in on the secret even though the Governor, Dušan Vlatković, was a former member of the Socialist Party.

At this point no one in the international media knew how the whole thing had been put together. The international effort still isn't widely known but then even the domestic organization was a secret. A voice whispered in my ear: 'Go to Čačak.' When I asked why, I was told not to ask stupid questions but to go.

Veljko, Milan and I were walking around the dusty main square of Čačak wondering how to get a story out of this backwater town when it fell into our laps. We went to see Mayor Ilić, a man who I'd vaguely heard of. He told us an amazing story about a column of vehicles 14 miles long, about a bulldozer, and about how he had taken weapons, paratroopers and a team of kick-boxers with him to parliament on 5 October.

'I don't suppose the bulldozer is back here, is it?' I asked hopefully. Ilić picked up the phone. Ten minutes later Milan,

Veljko and I were standing in the digger filming as we roared around town with local people waving and cheering in the streets.

We trundled down to the local TV station where I was shown some remarkable footage of the Čačak men hurling police vans off roads and smashing their way through barricades. I realized we had a world exclusive on our hands. Many people in Serbia knew about some of these events, but the footage hadn't been seen outside of the Čačak region and we had found the bulldozer.

I rang Jakša who organized for our satellite truck to drive down from Belgrade. We edited a piece for our evening bulletins, made a live report and travelled back to the capital.

The moment I set foot in the hotel I was pounced on by about six reporters from various countries demanding to know where we got the footage and how to get to Čačak. The next day the world's media descended on the town and Ilić repeated the story to all and sundry.

We quickly discovered that not everyone in the new government was happy with our report or with Ilić revealing so many secrets. Much of Serbia still thought it had been a spontaneous uprising and DOS wanted to keep it that way; they wanted it to be a people's revolution.

The revelation that Ilić had taken weapons and soldiers with him gave things a different complexion; it looked more like a coup d'état.

A friend who knew many of the senior DOS people persuaded one to come to the hotel to look at some of the footage Veljko and Milan had filmed at the parliament building on 5 October. He agreed he would give an interview explaining exactly what the footage showed.

The longer he watched, the quieter he became. We pointed out shots of the trucks with tarpaulins which we knew contained guns. We showed him numerous shots of officials with walkie-talkies including one of himself on a balcony. We had gone over the images for hours with various people and were able to point out footage of the Red Star youths clearly acting in concert and people wearing communication earpieces among the crowd.

The DOS man smiled and agreed that perhaps it did look as if the whole thing was carefully planned, but insisted it hadn't been. He left without giving us an interview.

There was only one more story I wanted to do, and that was to see inside the parliament. It took eight days to get in. Every morning we asked for permission and every day the red tape held us up. Eventually we were allowed in along with a Serbian TV crew and a Serbian newspaper reporter.

It was an awesome sight. The corridors were black from the smoke and our footsteps crunched through the glass strewn over every surface.

The walls were covered in graffiti, every office on the first floor had been trashed and water still lay in small puddles. Parliamentary documents were scattered among the ashes of burnt-out rooms.

We entered the Great Hall of the Republics, the place where generations of Slovenes, Bosnians, Croats, Serbs, Montenegrins and Macedonians had built a country called Yugoslavia.

Furniture lay smashed on the floor of the debating chamber. Whole rows of seats had been overturned, desks were in pieces, pictures had been defaced and the remnants of ornaments were twisted on the walls from where some of them had been torn.

When the others left to film another part of the building I was left alone in the hall. I sat in silence at one of the desks and looked around. The wars had begun here a decade earlier when the last generation of leaders failed to go their separate ways in peace.

What had been built had been destroyed. What was whole was in pieces.

Here was the end of the story and the end of the dream that was Yugoslavia.

CONCLUSION

'Yesterday is gone. Tomorrow has not yet come. We have only today. Let us begin.'

Mother Teresa

AND NOW?
Now we've come a long way. But after the nightmare of the break-up, the dreams of those who wanted to build a modern, stable region, where the ghosts of the old ultra-nationalists would be laid to rest, are yet to be realized. However, the painfully slow trajectory still bends towards this dream. Integration at an economic level is growing, and the EU, Serbia and its neighbours are all still working towards the Balkan countries eventually becoming members of the European Union. In this context, though, 'eventually' has become an elastic term.

Getting to that point has been more difficult than I had thought it would be. On a visit to Belgrade in 2001, Jakša asked me a question – a rarity as I was usually still the one asking questions, sometimes stupid ones. In response I gave what was not necessarily a stupid answer, but an overly hopeful one. The economy was recovering from the war years and a period of hyperinflation; a genuinely open election had resulted in a democrat, Zoran Djindjić, being elected as prime minister; and NATO had stabilized the region following a lightning operation in Macedonia. So when Jakša asked, 'So Tim – how long before Serbia joins the EU?', I replied, 'Maybe ten years.' He smiled gently and said, 'Maybe twenty. Maybe . . .'

By 2018 the Serbian government had accepted that a target of accession by 2025 was 'very ambitious' and possibly 'unattainable'. It was way behind neighbouring Montenegro in the process, with a long list of unfulfilled requirements on economic and social policies. Prime Minister Brnabić accepted that for the region's biggest country, with the largest economy, 'the road is steep and there is much to be done'.

It could have been different. Prime Minister Djindjić had called the EU 'Serbia's fresh air' describing it as 'a family of modern, democratic and developed countries'. He represented a side of Serbia rarely portrayed by the international media – one that opposed military intervention and war crimes on all sides in Kosovo. He had a passion for justice and democracy. He was the future.

Two years after my optimistic response to Jakša, on 12 March 2003, Djindjić was shot and killed by a sniper in Belgrade. A bullet hit him in the back, cut through his heart and his intestines and exited from his abdomen, hitting a bodyguard. He was fifty-one and left behind a wife, two young sons and a divided nation. The Serbian mafia, allied with former paramilitary officers, was behind the killing. Djindjić had announced complete cooperation with the International Crimes Tribunal for the former Yugoslavia at The Hague, and had sworn to root out organized crime from government and big business.

He understood the dangers of crossing the old criminal guard, having already survived an assassination attempt the previous month when a mafia gang had tried to force his car off the road. A member of the Belgrade 'Zemun Clan' was arrested but quickly released after a court stated he was only a businessman, whose sales were being hurt by his incarceration.

Djindjić gambled his life and lost. Taking on organized crime and handing over suspected war criminals to The Hague ensured retaliation. He'd indicated he knew what might come next, saying, 'If some people think they'll stop the implementation of laws and reforms by removing me, then they are awfully mistaken, because I am not the system.'

The man who pulled the trigger, Zvezdan Jovanović, was an officer in Serbia's special operations unit and had been part of Arkan's infamous 'Tiger' paramilitary gang. One of those who organized the killing was 'the Legionnaire' – Milorad Ulemek, the man we saw in the previous chapter who pulled the plug on Milošević. Ulemek had been part of this story from the beginning, operating death squads in Croatia, Bosnia and Kosovo. Both he and Jovanović were connected to the Zemun Clan. Both were convicted after a four-year trial that was marred by threats to court officials and the murder of several witnesses. Both, along with ten others, are now serving long prison sentences.

Djindjić is sometimes known as 'the Kennedy of the Balkans'. Jovanović fired the fatal shot (and a second one) using a Heckler and Koch high-powered rifle from the window of a building 180 yards from where Djindjić stood. There was talk of a 'third bullet' so perhaps the comparison is inevitable. But Djindjić was Djindjić. Flawed, inspirational, his own man, and Serbia's best chance.

Around 100,000 people turned out to follow his funeral cortège through the streets of the capital. Serbia had not seen the like since the death of Marshall Tito in 1980. They grieved and they swore to build on Djindjić's legacy, but without his charisma and energy, the new system faltered.

Corruption surged back with full force, democratization slowed, and the gangs running guns, prostitution, drugs and illegal immigration into Western Europe flourished. Fast-forward to now and the president is Aleksandar Vučić. In the Milošević regime he was information minister. Even after the fall of Milošević, he remained a disciple of the 'Greater Serbia' ultra-nationalist ideology. He opposed naming a Belgrade avenue after Djindjić, instead arguing that it should be named in honour of Ratko Mladić, the Bosnian Serb general who oversaw the worst mass killings in Europe since the Nazis and who was convicted of genocide. In 2008 Vučić broke with the Serbian Radical Party, tacked towards the centre right, began arguing that Serbia should join the EU, and in 2017 became president.

During a large part of this time, most of the world looked away. Even the assassination of Djindjić was barely noticed. He was gunned down just seven days before the invasion of Iraq began. The news channels mentioned his death in passing, then moved on. Politicians outside the Balkans noted it – and then also moved on. There was already a war in Afghanistan, another was about to break out in Iraq, and that was followed by the 2008 financial crash, the Arab uprisings, the Libyan and Syrian civil wars and then Russia's annexation of Crimea.

The Balkan Wars were the past; they'd bookended the twentieth century, and in the first decade of the twenty-first century the outside world was busy. In 2000 the EU had discussed the possibility of rapidly expanding to include most of the Balkans countries simultaneously in order to maintain the new rela-tive stability. After 11 September 2001, that plan quickly faded as the EU's attention switched elsewhere. The top-tier dip-lomats moved on to discussing Afghanistan, Iraq and other 'hot button' topics. When they did glance at the Balkans it was to approve the lower-tier plans to encourage each indi-vidual country to quickly enact social, political and economic reforms. In 2004, ten Eastern European states had joined the EU following a coordinated reform programme, but things were different for the Balkans. The new idea, which became known as the 'Balkan regatta', was that whoever won the race – i.e. reformed the quickest – would win EU membership. Croatia came first; everyone else either failed to finish or went backwards. Unsurprisingly, the race between the Balkan states encouraged competition not cooperation.

The outside world is still busy elsewhere, but now, after the drawdown in Afghanistan, the retreat from Iraq, and a partial recovery from the financial crash, there is enough diplomatic 'bandwidth' for the Balkans to come back onto the radar. A glance at the screen shows how much work remains to be done but the intention is to try to eventually draw the six Balkan states into the EU.

At the heart of all this is Serbia – or more specifically Serbia and Kosovo. As we saw in the opening chapter, one of the new ideas is for a land swap between the two regions (see map of Kosovo, page xiii), which would lead to Serbia officially rec-ognizing Kosovo and so finally bring their dispute to a close. The Kosovo leader Hashim Thaçi refers to this as a 'border correction'.

On one side of the proposals are three municipalities in the south of Serbia which are dominated by about 60,000 ethnic

Albanians. They are Preševo, Bujanovac and Medvedja, all of which border Kosovo and would be given to Kosovo.

On the other side are several regions in the north of Kosovo dominated by Serbs: Leposavić, Zubin Potok and some other parts of the Mitrovica municipality. They border Serbia and would be given to Serbia. But what sounds simple immediately becomes complicated as soon as you get into the details.

As well as the Serbs in the north of Kosovo there are tens of thousands living in enclaves in the south close to Preševo, Bujanovac and Medvedja. The total population of Serbs in Kosovo is thought to be about 100,000, while the Kosovar Albanian population is 1.7 million. If Preševo, Bujanovac and Medvedja are transferred to Kosovo then the remaining Serbs will feel cut off as the Serbian border is pushed further away. Their effective status in Kosovo is already that of second-class citizens; some feel they are living under siege. It is possible they would follow the route already taken by hundreds of thousands of Serbs in 1999 and leave, bringing to an end a 1,000-year-long presence in what they regard as the cradle of Serb civilization. The track record so far of the destruction of abandoned Serbian Orthodox churches, frescoes, graveyards and icons suggests that the last vestiges of Serb civilization in Kosovo would be wiped out.

On the economic side, Serbia has another problem. Its main north-to-south highway, the A1, runs through the Preševo Valley into Macedonia and on to Greece. If the three municipalities are transferred to Kosovo, then it would control landlocked Serbia's southern access to the sea. Many foreign investors in Serbia, such as China, would be anxious about one of the major trade routes running through a country with which Serbia can be expected to have difficult relations for the foreseeable future.

Kosovo has its own issues. Transferring its Serb-dominated northern municipalities to Serbia would mean transferring most of the Trepča mine complex. It may be in a poor state but it includes Europe's largest lead-zinc and silver ore mine, smelting factories and zinc refineries. It lies just 50 miles north of the Kosovan capital Priština.

Resolving the dispute through a land swap, and thus overcoming a major hurdle to joining the EU, has the potential to unlock the door to a brighter future for both Serbia and Kosovo. The 2017 EU Commission White Paper on the Balkans states clearly: 'The EU is adamant that all regional disputes and bilateral issues with neighboring states must be solved before accession. The recent strategy states that "The EU cannot and will not import bilateral disputes."'

Nevertheless, the land swap is also fraught with difficulty and with danger. As depicted in the opening chapter, a different door might open – one that leads back to war.

Another complicating factor is a resurgent Russia in a region it still regards as its backyard. In January 2019 President Putin showed up in Serbia for his third visit in eight years. A crowd of 100,000 greeted him in Belgrade. One placard implored him to 'Save the Serbian people' – from what was not spelt out, but the underlying sentiment was that Serbia and Russia are Slavic brothers who should unite against the West.

The Russian leader agrees. The two countries have a defence agreement and Moscow supplies Belgrade with its military hardware. Russia supports Serbia's position on Kosovo while Serbia backs Russia's position on Ukraine. President Putin has also met the Bosnian Serb leader Milorad Dodik on numerous occasions. Putin is not normally known for spending time with foreign politicians who are relatively junior. But despite

Mr Dodik leading a population of just 1.3 million, Mr Putin has met him at least eight times and took a keen interest when he became president of Bosnia in 2019.

A brief look at Bosnia's politics explains why. The presidency of the country rotates to reflect the three main groups: Croat, Bosniak and Serb. The Croat and Bosniak presidents both support joining the EU and NATO. Dodik is flat against this and on record as wanting to merge the Bosnian Serb territory with Serbia and align policies with Russia. As he said during his inauguration ceremony: 'I am a Serb – Bosnia is only my place of employment.'

For Putin, Dodik and the Bosnian Serbs are a vehicle to prevent another Balkan country siding with the West. In 2017 Montenegro joined NATO, but only after what was widely thought to be a Russian-backed coup d'état attempt had been foiled the year before.

The Putin/Dodik love-in, the state visits to Serbia, the alleged intervention in Montenegro, and a concerted effort via soft power to influence all of the Slavic regions are all part of the same strategy. Moscow seeks to plant itself more firmly in this geopolitical crossroads, just as it has in the Middle East and Central Asia. After the fall of the Soviet Union, Russia saw its power rolled back. It has spent this century pushing back out, via military means, cyber warfare, media strategies and with soft power – supporting Slavic culture in Macedonia, for example, and sponsoring a new Orthodox church in the Bosnian Serb territory.

On the hard-power front, in addition to the arms agreement with Serbia, an interesting relationship has grown between the Russian and Bosnian Serb security forces. Under the Dayton Agreement, the Bosnian army must be fully integrated with the different factions represented under the control of the joint presidency. Each faction cannot have its own army, but there are regional police forces. It is not a surprise that the Bosnian Serb police force is partly trained by Russian specialists, or that its 'special units' are sent to Russia for training. Sections of this 'police force' increasingly resemble military units.

Despite all of this, Russian domination of the Balkans remains unlikely. The EU is by far a bigger and richer market, and militarily NATO has troops on the ground. But Moscow knows that at the very least it can be a destabilizing factor in the effort to integrate this part of Europe into the Western sphere.

Hard-line nationalists in Serbia still want to 'freeze' the Kosovo question in the hope that eventually the EU will fall apart, NATO will disband and Russia will ride to their rescue and help rebuild their shattered dream of 'Greater Serbia'. Meanwhile liberal Serbia fights against what it sees as a slide back towards authoritarianism. All the while generations of students who are unprepared to wait another twenty years to join the EU simply move there. Polls suggest one in three young people in Belgrade would migrate if they could. As the liberal legal expert Savo Manojlović told the Balkan Insight website: 'Serbia has become a place where parents communicate with their children over Skype.'

Down in Kosovo many younger people also want to move. The economy is in a terrible state and, with the local mafia controlling so much of what happens, Kosovo remains a big black hole in the centre of south eastern Europe. Relations between the remaining Serbs and the majority population remain dire and the ongoing tensions between Serbia and Kosovo are never more than an 'incident' away from escalating.

The sorry picture painted above does not mean we are on the road to another outbreak of fighting between the Serbs and

Kosovars, or indeed between other actors on this blood-soaked stage. War does not seem likely, but the danger is there. After all, it seemed impossible before, until it happened.

WHERE ARE THEY NOW?

Slobodan Milošević was handed over to the Hague Tribunal by Prime Minister Djindjić in 2001 and went on trial in 2002. With the case ongoing, he died in his cell in 2006 aged sixty-four.

Mira Marković (Milošević's wife) fled to Russia in 2003 to escape charges of corruption. She was granted the status of a political refugee. She died in Moscow in April 2019.

Vojislav Šešelj surrendered himself to The Hague in 2003. In 2018, following a retrial, he was sentenced to twenty-two years in prison but was freed due to time served in jail. He is a politician in Serbia.

General Nebojša Pavković, the former chief of staff, was sent to The Hague in 2005 charged with war crimes. In 2009 he was sentenced to twenty-two years in prison.

Milorad Ulemek – 'the Legionnaire' – is serving a forty-year prison sentence for organizing the assassination of Prime Minister Djindjić.

Vuk Drašković went on to become Serbia's foreign minister but now is leader of the Serbian Renewal Movement party.

Goran Matić is a businessman based in Serbia.

Aleksandar Vučić became president of Serbia in 2017.

Madeleine Albright, former US Secretary of State, left office along with the Clinton administration in 2001. She then formed the Albright Group, a consultancy firm.

Richard Holbrooke, US diplomat, died in 2010 aged sixty-nine.

Mark Kirk, a US pilot during the NATO bombing campaign, served in the House of Representatives 2000–10 and as Senator for Illinois 2010–17.

'Captain Ken Dwelle', the pilot of the downed US stealth bomber, was later found to be Lt. Col. Darrell Zelko. He was wrongly identified because the name Ken Dwelle was painted on the plane's canopy. He retired from the USAF in 2011 and has developed a friendship with Zoltan Dani, the commanding officer of the unit that shot him down.

William Walker, head of the Kosovo Verification Mission, is retired. In 2017 he attended a ceremony unveiling a statue of him in Račak, Kosovo.

General Wesley Clark, NATO Commander, retired from the military in 2002. In 2004 he stood for the US presidency as a Democratic Party candidate but quickly dropped out.

General Mike Jackson went on to become Chief of the General Staff of the British military. He retired in 2006.

Fedja Grulović is Reuters' TV Bureau Chief in Belgrade.

Veljko Djurović retired and now spends as much time as possible at the seaside in Montenegro.

Milan Antić is a cameraman at Tanjug TV.

. . . and Jakša? Jakša is retired, lives in Belgrade and is a grandfather.

ACKNOWLEDGEMENTS

Acknowledgements and thanks to:

Tim Ripley, Zoran Kusovac, Paul Beaver, Jakša Šćekić, Mark Kirk, Miloš Vasić, Charles Crawford, Alexsander Vaska, Steve Erlanger, Aleksandar Vučić, Sir Ivor Roberts, Juliana Mojsilović, Duncan Bullivant, Maja Marsenić, Brian Donnelly, Branka Prpa, Professor Robert Hayden, Zoran Djindjić, Rollie Keith, Sonja Licht, Nick Pollard, Milan Antić, Simon Cole, Veljko Djurović, Margaret McDonald, all the people at the Foreign Office and the Ministry of Defence in London and their Yugoslav and American counterparts who, for obvious reasons, cannot be named. Thanks most of all to my wife for her help and support.

BIBLIOGRAPHY

Select bibliography

Balkan Insight, www.balkaninsight.com

Bujosević, Dragan and Radovanović, Ivan, *October 5: A 24-hour Coup* (Media Center, 2000)

Fighting with Ghosts, Sky News TV Documentary, 2000

Foreign Affairs Select Committee Report on Kosovo, House of Commons, June 2000

Joffe, Josef, 'A Peacenik Goes to War', *New York Times*, 30 May 1999

'Linking the Kosovo-Serbia Dialogue to the EU enlargement strategy – which accession prospects are at stake', Group for Legal and Political Studies, Policy Report no. 3/2018, July 2018

Marković, Mira, *Night and Day: A Diary* (Minerva Press, 1996)

Walker, Tom and Laverty, Aidan, 'CIA Aided Kosovo Guerrilla Army All Along', *Sunday Times*, 12 March 2000

INDEX

ABOUT THE AUTHOR

Tim Marshall is a leading authority on foreign affairs with more than thirty years of reporting experience. He was diplomatic editor at Sky News, and before that was working for the BBC and LBC/IRN radio. He has reported from forty countries and covered conflicts in Libya, Croatia, Bosnia, Macedonia, Kosovo, Afghanistan, Iraq, Lebanon, Syria and Israel. He is the author of the *Sunday Times* bestsellers *Divided: Why We're Living in an Age of Walls* and *Prisoners of Geography: Ten Maps that Tell You Everything You Need to Know About Global Politics*, as well as *Worth Dying For: The Power and Politics of Flags* and *"Dirty Northern B*st*rds!" and Other Tales from the Terraces: The Story of Britain's Football Chants*. He has written for *The Times*, *Sunday Times*, *Guardian*, *Independent* and *Daily Telegraph*, and his blog Foreign Matters was shortlisted for the Orwell Prize 2010. He is founder and editor of the current affairs site TheWhatandtheWhy.com.